Exploring Ethi

CW00428464

by the same author

Exploring Philosophy
(second edition of *The Philosophical Quest*)

Introducing Applied Ethics (editor)

Exploring Ethics

A Traveller's Tale

Brenda Almond

First published 1998

2 4 6 8 10 9 7 5 3 1

Blackwell Publishers Ltd
108 Cowley Road
Oxford OX4 1JF
UK

Blackwell Publishers Inc.
350 Main Street
Malden, Massachusetts 02148
USA

British Library Cataloguing in Publication Data

A CIP catalogue record for this book is available from the British Library.

Library of Congress Cataloging-in-Publication Data

Almond, Brenda.
  Exploring ethics : a traveller's tale / Brenda Almond.
        p.   cm.
  Includes bibliographical references and index.
  ISBN 0-631-19952-7 (hardcover : alk. paper). — ISBN 0-631-19953-5
(pbk. : alk. paper)
  1. Ethics.   I. Title.
BJ1012.A46   1998
170—dc21   97-37182
                                                              CIP

Typeset in 10½ on 12 pt Bembo by Ace Filmsetting Ltd, Frome
Printed in Great Britain by MPG Books, Bodmin, Cornwall

This book is printed on acid-free paper.

For Joe and friends

Contents

Preface

The background to this book is a widening gulf between theoretical and practical or applied ethics, and the increasing use in both cases of a technical vocabulary and mode of presentation that puts the ordinary non-specialist reader at a disadvantage and at a distance from important ethical reflection and argument. At the same time, many books on ethics convey a message that is in fact the reverse of ethical – either a detached relativism or an assumption that ethical problems are in the end to be resolved by an empirical assessment of costs and benefits.

I have tried, in contrast, to offer a text which follows through a single process of thought and argument, showing the relationship between theory and application, and also sketching out the links between the various applied areas themselves.

I hope, too, that there is an essentially ethical 'message', although one that respects the reader's own judgement. In this connection, it may surprise some readers that religion plays no overt role here. This, however, is deliberate, for part of the intention of the book is to stress the commonality of ethics, even across cultural diversity. This does not mean, though, that it is antithetical or unsympathetic to religion, and indeed the main religions of the world share the broad ethical perspective sketched out here in the imaginary setting that provides the background to the text.

Finally, a note on use. The book is designed, first of all, to be read for pleasure and interest; secondly, to inform and stimulate thinking about ethics and, thirdly, through the reading guides and bibliographies, to open up the different areas for those who want to pursue any of them in more depth. Finally, it is designed to be usable as a teaching text for either a single semester or a two-semester course. The latter makes possible a more leisurely and more realistic learning pace, but I am conscious of the fact that the former may be all that many students will experience of ethics in their course of studies. But, however it is used, the author's intention will have been realized if the reader gains a rounded rather than a fragmented view of the rich field of ethics in theory and in practice.

Acknowledgements

I am grateful to the University of Hull for granting me a period of study leave to complete the final stages of this project, and grateful, too, as on a previous occasion, to the Philosophy Department of the Faculty of Arts at the Australian National University for generously providing me with all the facilities I needed to accomplish this in a peaceful and friendly setting.

Preamble: The Traveller's Story

There are few unexplored parts of the globe, few areas that are considered genuinely impenetrable. It was as unexpected, then, as it was unlikely, that, pursuing some investigations for a charity involved with environmental questions, I found myself amongst a group of human beings who had developed over centuries their own society and way of living, cut off from contact with the world we tend to describe broadly as 'civilization'.

To begin with, I should perhaps explain briefly how this happened. I had been travelling alone – something I prefer to do, despite the obvious risk that involves in remote places. And on this occasion, the worst did indeed happen. I became ill with some unusual virus that was invulnerable to the whole panoply of remedies that modern medicine – at least in the portable form I had to hand – was able to offer. Perhaps I should simply have stayed where I was and hoped to improve, but instead I decided to try to find a quick way back. Having wandered way off my planned route, I found my progress checked by a great ravine, which, as far as I know, features on no map or chart. Its sides were near-vertical, and I would certainly have turned back and not have attempted to enter it. But in my confused state, I stepped on some treacherous undergrowth which turned out to be concealing the gaping void of the ravine. Catching at roots and vines as I fell, and passing waterfalls as well as trees on my way, I somehow found myself astonishingly still alive when I struck the marshy ground at the bottom.

After a while, I tried to continue my exploration until, exhausted, I collapsed. I lay for several days and nights passing between delirium and unconsciousness, with just occasional brief periods of clarity and awareness. Certainly the outcome would have been fatal had I not been discovered by a small group of strangers. Their clothing was odd and unfamiliar, and their language incomprehensible, but their behaviour seemed recognizably purposeful and considered. They were clearly intrigued by me rather than – I sensed – compassionate, but, for whatever reason, the outcome was certainly to my advantage. They arranged a makeshift stretcher, placed me on it carefully, and then began a long journey in which I was aware of days alternating with nights. I was dimly conscious of a long and difficult ascent up the other side of the ravine. At the same time, unfamiliar remedies were applied, so that by the end of the journey, my slow process of recovery was beginning.

I later discovered that I had been found by an adventurous group of scouts who had been exploring far beyond the usual limits of their territory – something that was in fact strictly forbidden to them – and I constituted for them a 'find' or trophy that might justify their rash behaviour to their superiors. And so in fact it turned out, although I had to endure nearly three years of being treated as a scientific specimen and being held a prisoner, at most times despairing of ever returning to the world I knew.

What follows is an account of the conversations I had in this unusual situation with this unique group of people, whose attitudes, customs and behaviour appeared to me so different from those of my own community. I present it here as an exploration of ethics, for indeed, what I learned most from my experiences is that assumptions about right and wrong, about good and bad, and about virtue and vice, are fundamental to almost every aspect of social, economic and political life. They are, I came to see, what constitute a community – not merely its cement, as people often say, but even its building blocks. And yet, as I also discovered, it cannot be assumed that everyone sees these things in the same way, or shares the same fundamental ethical attitudes.

This is perhaps to look too far ahead. My first task, of course, was to learn to exchange conversation and ideas with my captors – or protectors, as I suppose I should concede that they were, despite the fact that my protection was not, as I later discovered, their real goal. In this, however, I was greatly helped by the fact that they were as keen as I was to establish communication. Fortunately, as I also discovered, the Alloi – for this was the name I gave to them – were no mere primitive community; in their own way they were scientists and scholars, and well able to grasp the structures of languages other than their own. Thus we soon reached an understanding of how to talk about day-to-day matters. It was only when we attempted to move on to more abstract matters that I became aware of difficulties which at first I thought were problems of translation, but gradually came to realize were indeed fundamental differences of attitude and belief.

In what follows I have recorded some of the conversations I had with the Alloi. I became convinced that in many ways they were mistaken in some of their ethical beliefs and assumptions, and I tried to convince them sometimes of my own point of view. This was, of course, deeply influenced by some of the writers from my own tradition – philosophers I had studied in the course of my education – and I sometimes chose to draw their attention to those authors rather than to rely entirely on my own view of matters. This, I found, was indeed of considerable interest to them, for here the usual anthropological role was reversed. I was in no position to study *them* in any systematic way. They, on the other hand, clearly had a keen curiosity of their own, and were ever eager to investigate something new or unusual, and I was, for them, a scientific specimen of intense interest. Hence they allowed me scope to explain and discuss ideas at leisure, and they appeared to listen to me carefully. I will, I suppose, never know if my presence among them had any lasting impact, or whether my stay with them will continue in their records as no more than a peculiar blip in history – a visit from a time-traveller, or some such fanciful speculation. But here, for what it is worth, is the record of our encounter.

1

Free to Choose

The earliest conversations I had with the Alloi were more of an interroga-tion than an exchange of information. They regarded me as their prisoner – a realistic view, I have to admit – and their first concern was to be able to account for my presence amongst them. Their questions, however, revealed some assumptions about the form explanation can take where human actions are concerned. Ananke was the first of my interrogators – a spare, thin man with a concentrated gaze, he remained sceptical throughout about the truth of my story.

First conversation

Ananke: How did you come to be in the deep forest – the forbidden territory?

Traveller: I lost my way in traversing the great plain to the north. And then, without really intending it, I entered the great ravine where you found me. Because of the way I entered – dropping down, catching hold of roots or vines – it was impossible to retrace my steps even if I had been fit enough to try. The rest you know.

Ananke: Well, yes, of course. I know you were brought here, but what I want to know is how you came to be in this place at all.

Traveller: Well, I was gathering data for my organization –

Ananke: You mean, you were sent by someone else?

Traveller: Well, yes, as part of a project – a research trip.

Ananke: I see. Then I expect that if you had not come, you would have been punished in some way by your own people.

Traveller: No, no. I *wanted* to come. I *believe* in the organization that sent me. It has many excellent aims which I support. It is what we call a charity. People give money to help good causes – often these are other people, sometimes animals, or, in this case, the protection of the environment. I was fact-finding for this purpose. So, you see, it was entirely my own choice that brought me on this trip.

Ananke: A strange notion. We understand 'choosing' as a way of talking. But we don't take it seriously as an explanation of anything, any more than when someone speaks poetically of a plant choosing to face the sun. After all, you are a biological organism. Whatever you do must be the result of forces acting upon you from outside. In our society, we look for explanations of behaviour in terms that make some solid sense. From what you say, it seems you are some kind of scientist. Well, we have scientists here, too, you know – I am one myself.

Traveller: Scientists? That's a broad term. What sort of scientists do you mean?

Ananke: Well, we are interested in the stars, of course, and the changing skies. But we are mostly skilled in horticulture and crop husbandry – we know the ways of plants – and we spend a good deal of time observing the behaviour of animals. Our scientists do not see humans as different, except perhaps in degree of complexity, from the rest of nature. So the kind of explanation of your presence here that you have offered does not strike me as very convincing. Somebody or something *caused* you to be in our forest, and this talk of 'choice' sounds distinctly empty of content. What do you mean by it? Are you trying to tell me you could just as well have been somewhere else, doing something completely different? That could only appear to be true, I think, if we failed to take into account the whole network of causation – although, admittedly, that network does contain some facts about *you*. I would not want to deny that even the simplest animal organisms have their idiosyncrasies!

How could I explain that I really had acted as a free agent in coming to their country? And how could I convince them, too, of the benevolent motives of those for whom I worked? Well, I produced a variety of arguments over many weeks in conversational exchange, but I will try to sum up in what follows, as briefly and clearly as possible, the case I made to Ananke.

Humans as Subjects for Science

The question of whether human beings are subjects for science has often been posed in precisely those terms. Those who believe that individual behaviour is predictable and explainable find it easy to accept an analogy between studies that have human behaviour as their object and studies that are concerned with what the British philosopher John Locke (1632–1704), no doubt prematurely, labelled 'stupid, inert, unthinking, matter'.

But while humans have no problem in seeing themselves as *influenced* by a multitude of potential causes, they have a deep psychological reluctance to accept that they are *compelled* to respond to any of these. They tend, in fact, to explain their own behaviour by talking about motives rather than causes, and to explain their actions in terms of choice. This is in striking contrast to the view they take of the rest of nature, where the concept of choice is accorded a lesser or even non-existent role, and apparent choices are often explained away in terms of external causes. Animal behaviour, including apparent choosing-behaviour, which cannot be causally explained is likely to be described as random, pointless or arbitrary, while most of the change and activity we see in the rest of nature tends to be seen as either externally caused or purely the result of chance. Several consequences follow from this way of dividing up the world.

First, it seems to be necessary to look into the future, or at least the anticipated future, to explain the behaviour of human beings. That is to say, motives or intentions are crucial to understanding what human beings do, and these, of course, are essentially forward-looking, unlike causal explanations, which involve a reference to the past and knowledge of things that have already happened.

They are also essentially subjective, so that explanations of human behaviour are often to be sought by looking inwards – at what might be called *inner* causes – rather than outwards at preceding events or surrounding circumstances, the objective features of situations, the part that is open to observation by other people. In the case of humans, these are considered only *part* of the explanation of an action, whereas in the case of the rest of nature, they often seem to be sufficient, and it is not necessary to look for some inner 'controller' for an explanation.

Then again, if explaining human behaviour requires reference to what a human being hopes to achieve, it seems that it is in principle unpredictable by any third party. For how is anyone else to know what another human intends to bring about? How can someone else fully grasp that other person's perspective, their view of the situation? A modest example of the difficulties is given in a passage by the British philosopher A. J. Ayer (1910–89):

> Consider, for example, the simple action of drinking a glass of wine. As performed by different people in different circumstances, this may be an act of self-indulgence, an expression of politeness, a proof of alcoholism, a manifestation of loyalty, a gesture of despair, an attempt at suicide, the performance of a social rite, a religious communication, an attempt to summon up one's courage, an attempt to seduce or corrupt another person, the sealing of a bargain, a display of professional expertise, a piece of inadvertence, an act of expiation, the response to a challenge and many other things besides.[1]

In contrast, events in the non-human world raise no such problems of interpretation and consequently seem wholly predictable, at least in principle – although, admittedly, limitations in our present knowledge mean that nature will continue to surprise us from time to time. So for those aspects of the universe that are beyond the influence of human beings, while we may not in fact be able to make perfect predictions, we do think that perfect predictions might be possible, given complete knowledge; where human possibilities are concerned, on the other hand, we have a much more limited view of what science might achieve.

There is one other interesting and striking feature of human decision-making – one kind of motive that appears to stand outside any type of causal explanation, providing a quite different sort of reason for action even from these others. To appreciate this, it is worth reflecting upon the story of Socrates (469–399 BC), who was tried and eventually put to death by his Athenian compatriots. Why did he not try to escape from prison when his friends came to visit him offering a full plan of escape?[2] The only truly convincing explanation is that he thought it would be *wrong* . This is just one instance of a *moral* motive – a sense of duty, of having a moral obligation to do something despite an immediate inclination to do the opposite. It is, after all, only this that makes it possible to see humans as morally responsible beings for whose actions it makes sense to award praise, blame, punishment and reward – a contrast to our attitude to the behaviour of other living creatures. Indeed, the German philosopher, Immanuel Kant (1724–1804) argued that there is a closed circle here: the fact that free will is necessary for morality is itself a proof of the possibility of morality, while the possibility of morality proves that there is free will.[3]

Fatalistic Assumptions: What Will Be Will Be

There is, then, a popular assumption of freedom. But justifying the libertarian claim – the claim that humans have something called 'free will' – has long been an intractable philosophical problem. Although first recognized by pre-Christian Greek philosophers, it poses a particular problem for Christian theology. For if we say that the behaviour of individual human beings is in principle unpredictable, this seems to run counter to the Christian view that God has complete knowledge of past, present and future events. It also seems to run counter to the idea of God as all-powerful – a view that gives rise to belief in the doctrine of predestination which features in some forms of the Christian religion. Not all Christians believe in predestination – that God has mapped out for everyone in advance their path to salvation or damnation – since that would seem to make individual effort pointless and ineffectual. And yet, even the lesser idea that God, being all-powerful, *allows* whatever happens, including whatever any human being does, implies that it is God rather than humans who is to blame for any human action, and thus that it is God rather than humans who should be judged morally as deserving of praise or blame. Some try to overcome this difficulty by arguing that the spirit, if not the letter, of Christian teaching implies that God has deliberately handed over some of his power to human beings. If this is accepted, it means that even if God knows what choices humans will make, this knowledge does not affect their freedom. Alternatively, it could be argued that God does *not* know – that God has deliberately limited his knowledge in the same way as his power.[4.]

But these problems are not confined to the Christian religion. Indeed, they are generated by any kind of religious determinism, especially the form of fatalism associated with some of the religions of the East, summed up in the phrase, 'What will be will be'. For many people would see this, too, as nullifying effort, making it pointless to go on struggling in the face of adversity. It resembles in many ways the kind of belief in the powers of the Greek gods, and in particular in the fates, that is expressed in much of the literature of ancient Greece – a belief that seems to mean that the only appropriate way for people to respond to their problems is to accept their fate, not to attempt to resist it. This idea of the inexorability of fate comes out most strongly in the story of Oedipus, who helped to bring about his own tragic but predicted destiny. An oracle had warned that he would kill his father and marry his mother. Orders were given to kill him in infancy, but instead he was spirited away and brought up without knowledge of his origins or his parenthood. The irony of that story is, of course, that the very steps that he and others took to avoid his fate were what eventually helped to bring it about.[5]

Fatalism is easy to understand, then. But what sort of 'necessity' does it involve? Against the starkest form of fatalism, there is a simple argument that to pass from the indisputable but truistic proposition that what will be will be, to the quite different but highly disputable claim that what will be *must* be, is to confuse logical with causal necessity. At the root of this confusion lies a logical puzzle first noticed by Aristotle: if something is going to happen tomorrow – for example, if there is to be a military coup in some South American country – then it is true even today that there will be a coup there.[6] But if it is true today, could anyone intervene to prevent it? How could anyone make what is true not true? This tricky problem has led some to suggest that the mistake lies in believing that propositions can only be true or false. Instead, they say, we should think in terms of three rather than two possibilities: that propositions may be true, false or undetermined. In the case of this particular problem, then, it can then be said that statements about the future, including the statement about the military coup, remain in a kind of limbo as far as truth is concerned until the event actually takes place.[7]

There are, however, alternatives to sophisticated logical manoeuvres of this sort; one alternative is simply to recognize that the fatalist argument belongs to the world of logic and abstract concepts, while the world we live in is a world of concrete physical events. To think otherwise could be said to be like a young unmarried man reasoning that because a bachelor is by definition an unmarried man and he is a bachelor, he cannot ever get married. It seems to be a similar sort of mistake to suppose that the idea of timelessly true propositions affects our freedom to make choices and influence events in the physical world – the world of time and space. For factual truths, unlike logical ones, carry no guarantees of universality. Although this is not always understood by those who adopt a fatalistic perspective, fatalistic forms of determinism are in fact truistically harmless; they do not threaten our image of ourselves as agents, nor our conception of human existence as involving the possibility of choices which can be right or wrong, good or bad. However, this is not true of those forms of determinism that *do* deal in physical events, and these therefore pose a different kind of challenge.

Is Scientific Explanation Compatible with Human Freedom?

Increasingly, science seems able to explain apparently unforeseeable events in all the areas open to human observation. But how convincing is the general thesis – the dogma of scientific determinism? Its credentials are in many ways impressive: it is, after all, the underlying assumption on which the rapid technological progress of the twentieth century was based. Its most obvious successes have been achieved in the world of inanimate objects and physical phenomena, but even where the scientist's experimental material is closest to human beings – animals rather than inanimate materials – certain kinds of practical success have resulted from treating these for experimental purposes, rightly or wrongly, simply as units of physiological response.

Scientific determinism, then, must be understood as seeking explanations of human behaviour, in the first instance at least, which are not different in kind from this. And while explanation may begin in terms of sciences such as biology and physiology, if these sciences can themselves be reduced to more fundamental ones, it is easy to see why advocates of this point of view claim that explanation may ultimately be possible in terms of the more abstract sciences of chemistry and physics. But to accept this radical reductivism is to accept a thoroughgoing form of materialism which can draw no line between humans and the rest of nature. Even within the more limited domain of living creatures, it is to hold that, while humans, and perhaps, too, some of the higher mammals, appear to have some distinctive characteristics that separate them from simpler organisms – consciousness, self-awareness and the capacity to plan – this is only a superficial contrast: the line from the amoeba to the human being is essentially unbroken.

But it is not hard to see that a scientific determinism which suggests this degree of sameness is too crude a tool to provide a convincing and complete account of experience – our own or that of other creatures. To begin with, to talk about a continuum – the line from amoeba to human – is tacitly to assume that there can be no important differences at different points on a continuum. But science itself continually demonstrates that this is not so: in nature, barely perceptible changes often result in dramatic and striking transformations. The acorn becomes the oak, the egg the hen, the human embryo an infant: and even differences in degree, when they are marked enough, can amount to differences in kind.

There is another consideration, too, that confirms the dubious nature of reductivist arguments. This is simply that the very fact of being able to pose questions like these makes human beings unique. In other words, the continuity that is claimed breaks down precisely at the point that questions about it are raised. The reflective rationality of human beings, articulated in language, marks them out as unique occupants of the physical world – creatures of space and time with no real parallel in the known universe. This uniqueness, or novelty, offers, then, some justification for the psychological conviction of freedom of choice – which includes the freedom to be guided by rationality and even conscience. Nevertheless, there is still a problem about squaring this belief with the equally strong conviction, itself the product of rationality, of a network of causation within which human beings are themselves inextricably located.

One solution that has appealed to philosophers from the time of the ancient Greeks right up to the present day is to link freedom to the *source* of causation. This is a matter of recognizing, first of all, that few events have a single cause, and certainly that no single cause is sufficient to explain a human action. And it is to recognize, too, that of the various causes that may be needed to explain an action, many are external to the person concerned. These could include, for example, outside pressures, environmental factors, or other forms of coercion beyond the individual's control. External causes like these may all seem to limit freedom. But, according to this theory, it is only necessary for there to be one factor which is both an internal aspect of a person and at the same time also essential to a complete explanation of that person's behaviour, to refute any thesis of thoroughgoing determinism.[8]

Take, for example, the unexpected resignation of an important political leader and the questions that may be asked about what lay behind the resignation. For example, there may have been a threat to expose some scandalous secret, or a promise of some coveted honour. Or the person in question may have been physically bullied in private by an aggressive partner or browbeaten by a domineering colleague. If any of these are sufficient to explain the decision – if the resignation has resulted entirely from outside pressures – it is not a free action. But if the causal explanation is incomplete without reference to something that the person involved wanted to achieve, some personal perspective on the situation, then it can be counted as free. Both ordinary language and the way in which cases are defended in courts of law provide some support for this way of escaping the dilemma. For instance, the law commonly distinguishes between a situation in which someone has been hypnotized, threatened, or physically compelled, and one in which none of these things applies; between a case of kleptomania and a case of stealing; more generally, it distinguishes between an action that is constrained and an action that is merely caused;

and between cases in which people could not have done otherwise even if they had chosen to, and cases in which they could or would have done otherwise if they had chosen. In all such cases, the first half of the contrast is what ordinary language would ordinarily characterize as unfree or determined, the second what it would characterize as free choice. There is, in other words, a common conception of free will, illustrated by the way people ordinarily talk, that is compatible with taking for granted some basic assumption that everything has a cause.[9]

Some would dismiss this solution to the problem as an appeal to 'folk psychology'. And, indeed, there is the difficulty that, if it were accepted, it would seem to justify too *much* of the baggage of popular belief. In the Middle Ages, for example, it could have provided a justification for believing in witchcraft. Consorting with a black cat, failing to drown immediately on being submerged in water, being unable to recite the Lord's Prayer backwards without stumbling, were all commonly accepted as evidence that someone was a witch. And so, appeal *then* to what people would ordinarily say would apparently have established the possibility of witchcraft. So, it might be argued, the fact that people *talk* about free will does not actually show that it exists in any way that undermines scientific determinism. People found the language of 'witchcraft' useful in the past; they may find the language of 'free will' convenient in the present.

The appeal to language, custom and law, then, could be seen as a two-edged weapon as far as an attack on scientific determinism is concerned. But there is an argument from within the domain of science itself which at first sight looks rather more substantial. This has as its basis the theory that nature itself is fundamentally undetermined: the thesis known as as the Principle of Indeterminacy, which is associated with the physicist Werner Heisenberg (1901–76). According to this theory, the ultimate particles of matter move unpredictably, and are not subject to any general causal laws. If this were so, it would no doubt constitute an important refutation of the notion of a scientifically determined universe. Even in these terms, however, it is disputed. But if what is at issue is human freedom and the possibility of morality, there is no point in even beginning to assess the scientific claims for the ultimate indeterminacy of matter. For the kind of freedom of action or choice necessary for morality to be possible is not the kind of random behaviour of particles that the physical Principle of Indeterminacy could support. Where human beings are concerned, randomness means madness and lack of responsibility. It removes any possible justification for praise or blame, punishment or reward.

There is a striking illustration of this point in André Gide's novel *Les Caves du Vatican*. One of Gide's characters is philosophically interested in the issue of human freedom of action, and so he tries to break out of the chain of causation with an *acte gratuit* – an act he conceives of as genuinely free in the sense that it has no causal background at all. Gide's hero, Lafcadio, who is on an express train heading for Rome, pushes a complete stranger to his death from the train. But does this episode really reveal what a genuinely free act would be? It seems not. Indeed, the story only tends to show the confusion in the notion of an *acte gratuit*. There is, after all, a perfectly good, if unusual, causal explanation of what Lafcadio does: he wants to prove a philosophical point and he mistakenly believes that this is a way to do it. So after all, it is not a causally inexplicable action. But even if this were *not* so – even if there had genuinely been no causal explanation available – his action would not in fact have been hailed as the action of a free agent; on the contrary, it would almost certainly have been taken as a sign of lunacy, for the term 'homicidal maniac' precisely sums up the notion of a person who kills for no obvious reason.

Freedom, in the causally detached sense in which Gide's hero conceives it, is a recurring theme in many existentialist writers. It is expressed by another French writer, the existentialist philosopher Jean-Paul Sartre (1905–80) in the aphorism that man's existence precedes his essence. Sartre writes of the 'anguish' of choice, which is an ever-present reality for any human being. It is in choice that we display authenticity, that we become ourselves.[10] But this is not a goal that can be satisfied by random actions, for these are not the key to freedom in the sense in which freedom is of value to human beings. So the existentialist notion of authenticity is not, after all, the idea of the random. It requires a conception of choice as flowing from the will and intention of the individual person. Even an existentialist view of freedom, then, must place choice, in some way or other, in a framework of causation.

But reductivism – the wish to reduce everything to a single form of explanation – is not the way to do this. As the English philosopher Mary Midgley has pointed out, classical science aimed for clarity and parsimony. It was based on the belief that the world was fundamentally simple. So while it is true, as she remarks, that: 'The idea of a single, ruling scheme, underlying all others, answering all questions and transcending all differ-ence of viewpoint, has fascinated thinkers since the dawn of philosophy', it is also true, as she points out, that modern physics has long abandoned this goal.[11] Midgley describes the idea of a single underlying explanation as the core reductive mistake, adding that 'by evicting, not just the gods, but human and animal consciousness from the real world, it [reductivism] abandons that profound respect for life and for the experience of others which has always lain at the root of morality.'[12] .

Conscious and Unconscious Motivation

But if explanation in terms of the hard sciences fails in the end to convince, the social and human sciences tell a more plausible story. These are the sciences which are specially concerned with the *origins* of patterns of behaviour and the forces that shape character and disposition. Psychology, as the particular science of human behaviour, offers two special forms of the general thesis of determinism, which can be distinguished from the broader scientific claim. On the one hand, experimental psychology seeks to build correlations based on the notions of stimulus and response into causal laws; on the other, the psychoanalytic tradition posits a whole area of subconscious control and unacknowledged motivation, explaining a person's present choices and actions in terms of forgotten influences and experiences in childhood. It deals with what is least amenable to observation: the unconscious wish, the repressed motivation, the forgotten and suppressed early influence, the memory which can be recalled only under hypnosis – something which is not present to the conscious mind, but is no less influential for that reason.

The behaviourist's case is perhaps the most radical, for this reduces apparently distinctive types of motivation, including morality, creativity and originality, to the status of physical reactions of the organism to stimuli in its environment. Everything is to be explained in terms of drive-reduction and the desire to maximize satisfaction and avoid pain. The American behavioural psychologist, B. F. Skinner (1904–90) defended these deterministic consequences explicitly in a sustained attack on the notions of freedom and dignity. 'As we learn more about the effects of the environment,' he wrote 'we have less reason to attribute any part of human behaviour to an autonomous controlling agent.'[13] The kind of causes, or causal laws, that the behavioural psychologist looks for, then, are mechanistic rather than mentalistic. They are material, observable by others, and external to the agent or doer. Indeed, the very structure of the behavioural psychologist's experiments is based on treating creatures under investigation as objects rather than as organisms possessing what it would be natural to call a mind.

But what does 'mind' mean in this context? There is no need to understand this as suggesting something abstract and indefinable. The reference to a mind implies the existence of something which has the capacity to originate, to be creative, to make decisions, and so to respond to stimuli in more than a purely mechanical way. Purely mechanistic forms of explanation are inadequate even in the case of laboratory animals, and the science of experimental psychology itself has produced undeniable evidence of curiosity as a motive carrying with it the desire to learn, to understand the environment and to have new experiences. Beyond this, in the case of human beings, motives like love, self-sacrifice, duty, spite, revenge and the impulse to creativity all lie outside the narrow range implied by the notion of drive-reduction.

But those who want to narrow our understanding of human behaviour, as Skinner does, must cope with the sheer complexity of the human material involved; they are also likely to be hampered by the vast range of uncontrollable variables that operate when behaviour is looked at outside the narrow confines of the laboratory; indeed, they may discover that the very terms they use have undergone a shift in meaning when removed from the laboratory and applied to organisms in the world outside. As the American philosopher Noam Chomsky has pointed out, terms like stimulus, response and reinforcement can be given specific meaning only within the laboratory.[14] In an experimental setting, for example, a flashing light can be clearly identified as a stimulus because it is the only thing that changes in the laboratory animal's environment. For the same reason, any subsequent change in the animal's behaviour can be identified as a response to this change. But in the world outside the laboratory, an animal's or a human's surroundings are continually changing in a vast number of different ways. Some of these changes will be noticed and responded to, but not others. So how is any one thing to be identified as a stimulus? And similarly, all kinds of different patterns of behaviour can be identified as happening after a stimulus. How is one particular pattern to be identified as the response? There is much less tidiness and much more variety in the world than behavioural psychology recognizes. And so the 'truths' it has discovered, once transferred to the outside world, no longer apply universally. If they do seem to apply, this is only because their truth is safeguarded by the unnoticed ambiguities of quasi-scientific usage.

If there are problems, then, for those who dismiss choice in terms of observable mechanical causes, what of those who dismiss it in terms of unobservable and deeply internal causes? In many ways, they are con-fronted by an exactly opposite set of problems. In this case, it is the *absence* of an experimental scientific base that invalidates the approach or, at least – since it has to be admitted that there are many ways in which Freudian psychology is illuminating – provides reason to accept it only with important qualifications. The Freudian explains human behaviour by reference to factors that are beyond observation and experiment and, while the possibility of finding refuting evidence is the hallmark of a genuinely scientific theory, it seems that any evidence can be assimilated into a psychoanalytic theory. This is not simply a theoretical defect: it becomes practically crucial, for example, in relation to an issue like 'false memory' syndrome. Here the problem is to determine whether 'memories' of child-abuse emerging from psychotherapy are genuinely recollections of actual events or false memories implanted by the process of therapy itself. The same 'evidence' may appear to support either claim.

Apart from these challenges to the scientific standing of psychoanalytic accounts, it is also important to notice that they are every bit as damaging as those of behavioural psychology as far as moral responsibility is concerned. Psychoanalytic theory is another way of explaining away what people do in terms that take the burden of responsibility away from them and place it elsewhere – this time in the long-forgotten actions and attitudes of a parent or relation. Presumably, though, parents are not really responsible for *their* actions to their children either, since their behaviour, too, could be traced back to their own early treatment by *their* parents. So where behavioural psychology finds the explanation of behaviour in immediate externals, psychoanalytic accounts implicitly dissipate responsibility for action down the generations. But this kind of explanation can never be more than partial. As far as psychoanalysis is concerned, it is in any case only the more bizarre forms of human behaviour on the whole that are taken to psychoanalysts for resolution. No particular explanation is required for the vast amount of human activity which, however disputably, lies within the 'normal' range. But even if a disabling fear or phobia can be traced back with therapeutic effect to an incident in early childhood, this only shows that there are indeed *some* powerful influences upon human beings of a hidden and unrecognized kind.[15] The fact that psychoanalytic techniques can expose some of these causes, and that those who have been affected by them are then able to overcome them, far from casting doubt on the idea of humans as ultimately and essentially in charge of their own lives, actually lends support to this belief.

Social Science as a Subject for Humans?

There are those who argue that, while explaining and predicting *individual* behaviour may remain a problem, the same does not apply to *collective* behaviour: the differences between people may be insignificant when it comes to examining their behaviour in groups. If this is so, the social sciences may be able to offer insights into human action and choice without claiming that individual human beings are inflexible and identical bundles of physiological response. All they need assume is that the differences between people will be cancelled out if group behaviour is studied on a wide enough scale. If so, then whatever may be the case where *individuals* are concerned, the behaviour of people in groups will provide material for study not intrinsically different from that of other areas studied by conventional scientific methods. The French sociologist Emile Durkheim (1858–1917) put the point in these terms:

> Since the law of causality has been verified in the other realms of nature, and since it has progressively extended its authority from the physico-chemical world to the biological, and from the latter to the psychological, we are justified in claiming that it is equally true of the social world.[16]

It is in this strong sense, then, that, from its inception, sociology has aimed to be scientific. At its heart lies the deterministic hypothesis: humans are not governed by reason; they do not reach decisions, as they sometimes imagine, only by detached reflection on the evidence supplied by experience, or else by reasoning logically from first principles. Still less are they guided by the promptings of conscience or similar motives. Instead, the human person is seen as the product of environmental – in particular social, economic and cultural – influences. This thesis was famously expressed by Karl Marx (1818–83) in the words: 'It is not the consciousness of men that determines their being, but, on the contrary, their social being that determines their consciousness.'[17]

The broader picture, too, is deterministic. Sociology assumes the essential plasticity of human beings – that there is no fixed 'human nature'. So it replaces the search for an account of human nature in universal terms by attention to particulars – to factual data amassed by laborious enquiry. Because it is social context that shapes individuals rather than vice versa, the influence of individual human beings must be regarded as insignificant. So instead of assuming that individuals affect the course of history – for example, that if it had not been for Hitler, there would have been no Second World War, or that but for Henry VIII no Protestant Church would have emerged in England, some sociological theorists would explain events in terms of impersonal – ultimately economic – structures. Even major creative discoveries that have changed the course of history may be explained in a way that sets them in a network of causality: for example, instead of attributing the theory of relativity to the genius of Albert Einstein, according to this account, at a particular time in the twentieth century the theory of relativity was waiting to be formulated, whether by Einstein or someone else.

But can this degree of determinism be justified? Many significant discoveries are genuinely accidental, depending on the right person being in the right place at the right time – or in the case of adverse events, such as a war, the *wrong* person . . . What is more, while there are undoubtedly statistical truths about people, the fact remains that a statistical generalization says nothing about what any *individual* will do. Supposing it is true that the French have a particular talent for cooking, this is no guarantee that every young French person will head enthusiastically for the kitchen. This is recognized by some schools of thought. The German sociologist Max Weber (1864–1920), for example, wrote: 'If I am now a sociologist . . . I am so essentially in order to put an end to the use of collective concepts, a use which still haunts us. In other words: even sociology can only start from the action of one or a few, or many individuals, i.e. pursue a strictly "individualistic" method.'[18]

So although social science most typically looks at the individual person in the context of institutions and structures, or perhaps as an organic part of a system, there is an alternative view even within social science that starts from individual people and the way things look to them, including the reasons they would give for what they did. There is indeed a strong argument for preserving a reference to individual intentions and attitudes in explaining people's behaviour, for it is a peculiar feature of human beings that they are capable of responding *un*predictably to predictions about their behaviour, once they become aware of them. To begin with, they can act *against* a predicted trend; even an intelligently predicted trend can be falsified by many individual deviations from what is expected. The Austrian philosopher Karl Popper (1902–94) pointed to the truth of this on an individual level.[19] Elections provide a striking example of it on a wider scale. Opinion polls tend on the whole to be reliable in predicting how people will vote in political elections – if they were not, they would be neither so popular, nor so interesting – but they can also prove dramatically wrong, and this is not necessarily because the pollsters have made a mistake. Instead, it may be that people do not like the trend the pollsters have identified.

But people are not only able to decide to falsify a prediction; they can also respond by joining what they judge to be a bandwagon and working to bring about the predicted result. This is widely recognized as a problem for Marxist theory. Since Marxism presents the victory of the proletariat as a scientific prediction and assigns people inevitable roles in the class struggle, it is difficult to explain the position of middle-class people, like Marx and Engels themselves, who identify with the working class against their own interest and class membership. It is difficult, too, to understand the point of urging people to take part in the political struggle, since victory is guaranteed. However, Marxism has never been dispassionate in this way;

it has always been a movement, a cause and an ideology, not merely a theory of history. The orthodox way of resolving this tension is to argue that political activity is intelligible behaviour aimed at 'shortening and lessening the birth pangs' of the transition to a new social order. All the same, it runs counter to Marxism's own deterministic assumptions, demonstrating that even a strong historical analysis has somehow to recognize the contribution of individual behaviour.

The problem of accounting for the personal role played by Marx and Engels in promulgating communism is an instance of a more general problem for social science: the investigator or commentator comes from a particular social context or form of life. Some would say that, as a result, they cannot really detach themselves from their own way of construing the world; they can only operate within their own prior conceptual framework. In its most recent phases, this sensitivity to the possibility of distortion has led to a pervasive relativism: the postmodernist rejection of the very idea of truth. This is a challenge rooted in one particular aspect of sociology, the form of explanation known as the sociology of knowledge. According to this sociological perspective, the basic epistemological question is not, 'Is this true?' but, 'Who says it?', 'What power-group is behind this idea?' or, as Alasdair MacIntyre puts it in the title of his book '*Whose* justice? *Which* rationality?'[20] Such broader questions extend beyond the question of freedom, but they are embedded in the more sophisticated varieties of determinism current today. Of these, perhaps the most radical and most sophisticated is the form of social explanation which adds a genetic component to the deterministic brew.

Genetic Determinism and Sociobiology

While sociology looks predominantly for explanations in terms of 'nurture' or environment, it comes into conflict with the increasing recognition of the importance of 'nature' or genetic endowment. There has long been a popular view that musical and mathematical ability is an inherited trait. But while a genetic link with musical or mathematical ability would be relatively uncontroversial in its implications, new discoveries in genetics keep extending the frontiers of this type of explanation in more problematic ways. As discoveries of genes for homosexuality, criminality or aggressive behaviour are claimed, these give rise to new ethical dilemmas and an even tighter form of determinism, which leaves little or no scope for ethics or the development of character. In looking to biology, this form of determinism constitutes a turn to inner rather than outer explanations;

it does not, however, seek to reinstate the notion of self-determination. This is particularly clear when genetic factors are advanced as excuses for criminal or deviant behaviour. But while it is common for those who look for environmental explanations to regard an unhappy childhood and brutal upbringing as mitigating factors in the case of crime, people are reluctant to accept as an excuse that someone was simply 'born' a criminal – particularly if that person has had every advantage in life and has nevertheless chosen to kill in cold blood. In the case of a brutal upbringing, people are inclined to see these factors as having made the person other than he or she would otherwise have been. But in the second case, if it is said that something was not a person's own fault, it is not clear what 'person' means here, nor who the 'own' belongs to. For people are identified with their character and personality in a way that they are not identified with what merely happens to them.

One way to avoid these problems is to substitute a more limited question – not to seek a general understanding of human nature, but simply to ask whether some particular kind of behaviour can be influenced or changed by praise, blame, reward or punishment, including imprisonment and other kinds of threats. After all, these factors must play *some* part, for 'internal' explanation is seldom sufficient on its own. Everyone can be influenced in some way or other by what is external to them as well as by their own instinctive wishes or impulses. There is a parallel in the case of language-acquisition: everyone has a disposition to learn a language, but *which* language they learn depends on where they and what language they hear. Both genetic endowment and environment, then, must play a part.

Nevertheless, the hypothesis that nature and context might jointly account for everything a person does might well be called the 'worst-case scenario'. But even the worst-case scenario is not necessarily incompatible with freedom. The reason this is so also lies in genetic knowledge. But this time it is the evidence it provides of the enormous variability of human nature that is relevant. This extreme variability means that no two individuals are the same – each individual person is said to be the product of 6 billion pieces of genetic information. It was once remarked of Napoleon that nature, having made him, broke the mould. But this is no less true of any ordinary individual. There are no human moulds. It follows that the kind of general laws which are to be found in science simply cannot be established in the case of human beings. The discovery of causal laws depends on the possibility of assembling the evidence of a number of events – certainly not one only. What is more, these laws require the absolute repeatability of experiments. Any variation in the variables involved, and certainly any significant variation in the subject of the experiment, will produce variation in results and invalidate the experiment.

The sheer individuality of the human organism, then, means that any general rules, patterns or laws can be applied only on a single-instance basis, and therefore that they are not rules, patterns or laws in any sense that is damaging to the notion of individual freedom of choice or action. It is true that increased knowledge of genetics may lead to a deterministic view. But the threat people perceive in determinism is that of finding themselves to belong to a category of entities to which broad and inflexible causal laws apply. 'Laws' that affect just one person are hardly laws at all. One might say that the very individuality of the individual refutes determinism. As for predictability, since each genotype is unique, it would never be possible to predict what any particular individual would do in any specified set of circumstances. People think of genes as something separate from themselves, pushing them along – a mini-person inside a person. But who is the person to be pushed? We are only physical entities – what we are is what we are. No *other* person is pushing *this* person along. Statistical patterns are interesting and may be informative, but they do not entail that any particular person is bound to react to a situation in just one predictable way. Individuals may either form part of a trend or they may become the exception. The choice is theirs, and where the choice is a moral choice, the responsibility is theirs.

There is one other consideration that weakens the deterministic case: these theories, which each claim to explain human nature, all present themselves as offering a *complete* account of human nature and human behaviour. But, while each claims to offer the whole truth, their various programmes or agendas are essentially incompatible with each other. They cannot *all* be true, and this in itself is sufficient to cast doubt on the claims of any one of them.

Still, the dogma of determinism may not have been finally laid to rest. When every environmental and genetic factor has been taken into account – when both 'nature' and 'nurture' are accounted for – then, the dogma's defenders may argue, choice must be recognized as illusory, then at least there is no room left for personal free choice. This is true, but only because there is no room left for a person at all. Setting aside basic character and make-up is an important step in the determinist's position, but this very step is essentially incoherent. Particularly where morality is concerned, we have to take account of people as they are. The only freedom necessary for morality is the freedom for innate character to express itself.

The *ethical* problem is more likely to be solved by looking instead at the kind of freedom that is needed for moral choice to be a possibility. Once it is recognized that it is not required, and indeed would be counter-productive, for human-beings to be seen as somehow having escaped entirely from the causal nexus, it becomes clear that these two important features of human beings – individual uniqueness, and the need to refer to innate aspects of character and personality in explaining the behaviour of any particular individual – supply all that is necessary to counter the damaging aspects of most forms of determinism. There is infinite variety in the way in which human beings respond to situations, in their dispositions and character, in their grasp of problems and in their strength of purpose in reacting to situations – a conclusion that leaves ordinary scientific explanations of the behaviour of individual persons, including the explanations of both psychology and psychoanalysis, doomed to remain fundamentally and eternally inadequate.

Ethical and Social Implications of the Debate about Free Will

Behind these issues of freedom, choice and predictability lie complex questions about mind, matter and metaphysics. The contemporary philosopher Ilham Dilman summed up the argument for attributing distinctive features, including free will, to human beings in these terms: 'If . . . *we* are a "part of nature", it should not be forgotten that we also have powers or capacities which set us apart from nature, indeed which enable us on certain occasions to overcome those inclinations in us which make us "a part of nature". Unlike animals we can speak, think, form intentions, are conscious of and can reflect on our own inclinations and motives and endorse or repudiate them. We act with knowledge of what we are about and have conceptions of good and evil which make a difference to what we do.'[21]

But this is not only a metaphysical debate. For convincing oneself of the truth of determinism is in itself a way to lose control of one's life, to believe in one's own powerlessness to affect events. This means that the implications of the argument about free will and determinism are ethical and political as well as philosophical. The present-day political theorist Michael Novak has put the point like this:

> Human beings are the only creatures on earth that do not blindly obey the laws of their nature by instinct, but are free to choose to obey them with a loving will. Only humans enjoy the liberty to do what we ought to do – or alas, not to do it . . . It is this second kind of liberty – critical adult liberty – that lies at the living core of the free society. It is the liberty of self-

command, a tolerable mastery over one's own passions, bigotry, ignorance, and self-deceit. It is the liberty of self-government in one's own personal life.[22]

This is why it is not possible even to think about ethics until the bogey of determinism has been exorcized. Freedom matters, because individual freedom is a prior assumption of ethical reasoning.

Interlude

> I could see that Ananke remained unconvinced by my arguments. I had laid out for him the theories within my own philosophical traditions that supported the kind of belief he obviously held that all human beings find themselves trapped within a causal nexus that leaves no place for the concepts of freedom, choice, or individuality. I had also explained, even if briefly, the reasons that existed for rejecting this deterministic thesis in its many changing forms. But I was beginning to feel that determinism is a hydra-headed monster — extinguish one version and another springs up to take its place. For Ananke, one way or another, everything that happens, happens of necessity. Of course, there are philosophers — the ancient Stoics, for example, and the great metaphysician, Baruch Spinoza (1632–77) — who have not only been convinced of this, but have also concluded that freedom consists, paradoxically, in accepting this necessity — that freedom consists in not struggling against what has to be. No doubt Ananke would have had more respect for their views had I been able to expound them to him, but he became, I am sorry to say, rather impatient at the way our discussions had gone and left me to continue the argument with a companion of his, Egoge. A young, lively woman, with a colourful style of dressing, she was a little more sympathetic to my view, because she was prepared to allow some meaning to the notion of choice. However, this, it turned out, was from my point of view a somewhat worthless concession, since Egoge believed that the only choices human beings make are ones they believe to be in their own interest.

Notes to Chapter 1

1   Ayer, 'Man as a subject for science', p. 223.
2   For the arguments that Socrates himself brought forward, see Plato's dialogue, the *Crito*, in Plato's *The Last Days of Socrates* – a record of the conversations Socrates had with his friends while he was in prison awaiting the carrying out

of the death sentence imposed on him by the Athenian courts.

3   For Kant on free will, see chapter 3 of *Groundwork of the Metaphysic of Morals*.

4   In an early controversy on the subject, Pelagius (c. 360–431) argued that man could achieve salvation by his own efforts, and that freedom means being free to choose between good and evil. Augustine (354–430) responded that God's grace is necessary and provides the framework within which freedom of the will may be exercised. Pelagius was ultimately condemned as a heretic.

5   The story is told in Sophocles' play *Oedipus Rex*.

6   For discussion of Aristotle and the sea-battle, see Gale, *The Philosophy of Time*.

7   Dummett, 'Bringing about the past' in Gale, ibid. See also, Ayer, 'Can an effect precede its cause?'

8   This solution goes back to Chrysippus. For an account of its origins, see Berlin, 'From hope and fear set free'.

9   The standard 'compatibilist' solution. See, for example, Ayer, 'Freedom and necessity', pp. 271–84.

10 Sartre, J.-P. *L'Être et le néant: essai d'ontologie phénoménologique*, 1943, translated as *Being and Nothingness*.

11 Midgley, *The Ethical Primate*, p. 69.

12 Ibid., p. 31.

13 Skinner, *Beyond Freedom and Dignity*, p. 101. Skinner continued the work in behavioural psychology originated in America by J. B. Watson (1878–1958). Both owed a debt to Pavlov, the Russian psychologist whose experiments with animals established the theory of the conditioned response. Behaviourists presumed that the human organism was potentially fully controllable by external influences. They saw human behaviour as caused by environmental factors and counted the contribution of the individual as negligible or non-existent.

14 See Chomsky, 'A review of B. F. Skinner's "Verbal Behavior"'.

15 Freud in his later work divided basic instincts into Life (Eros) and Death (Thanatos). The former included the instincts of sex and self-preservation (e.g. hunger); the latter sadism, aggression and self-destruction. The mind was constituted of Id, Ego and Super-ego, the latter exercizing moral judgement and control. For a full discussion of Freud's theories and those of his successors, see Brown's *Freud and the Post-Freudians*.

16 Durkheim, *The Rules of Sociological Method*, p. 141.

17 Marx, *The German Ideology*.

18 Weber, Letter to Mommsen, note 117, quoted in Frisby, *The Positivist Dispute in German Sociology*, p. xliii.

19 In *The Poverty of Historicism*, Popper criticized the deterministic assumptions of both Marx and Freud.

20 MacIntyre, *Whose Justice? Which Rationality?*

21 Dilham, *Mind, Brain and Behaviour*, p. 135.

22 Novak, *Awakening from Nihilism*.

2

Born Selfish?

Second Conversation

Egoge: You may think that I share Ananke's view, but that is not so. I am not a scientist, and I don't claim any special expertise in the study of the human mind. So the general question of causation is of no concern to me. Since it seems so important to you, I don't mind conceding that humans have at least a degree of freedom of choice. But I do insist that when they exercise that freedom, it is always for what they consider to be their own good.

Traveller: What do you mean by that phrase, 'their own good'?

Egoge: Well, crudely put, I would say that they want to seek pleasure and avoid pain; less crudely, perhaps, that they want to maximize their own happiness and that they do not do things simply for the sake of other people.

Traveller: You mean, they do not put themselves to trouble in order to help other people? They never act altruistically?

Egoge: Well, they do, of course, sometimes go to help others, but if they do, this is always for their own self-interested reasons.

Traveller: So the kindness you and your people have shown me . . .

Egoge: . . . was, of course, in pursuit of our own ends. Not least now because you have become a subject of considerable interest to our academics and intellectuals. And one thing that intrigues us particularly is this extraordinary belief you appear to have in totally disinterested kindness, altruism and so on. Of course, there are people here with some such ideas, but as far as I myself am concerned, not only do I believe that people *can* only behave selfishly; I would say that people *ought* to act in a way that promotes their own interest. After all, trying to pursue the good of others leaves so much scope for error and misunderstanding that it is probably to be condemned on grounds of inefficiency alone!

Egoge's remarks gave me scope for thought. Her second claim seemed to deserve consideration in its own right, and so in offering her my considered comments on her position, I found it necessary to separate the two claims – that people can only act selfishly, and that they should act selfishly – and indeed, in doing so, I realized that Egoge's opinions, coherently and vigorously though she expressed them, were actually rather confused.

Forms of Egoism

Choice may be more than psychological illusion or self-deception, but how worthwhile is this concession if it turns out that the grounds for choice are exceedingly narrow? Supposing, indeed, that they shrink to just one: the motive of self-interest? There is a variety of related theories clustering round the notion of self-interest, variously described as hedonism or egoism; the claims they make may be different, but one central distinction is between those that offer an ethical judgement and those that make a claim about the facts of human nature. Some focus on the notion of pleasure: the hedonist recommends the pursuit of pleasure in general; the so-called 'psychological hedonist' insists that human nature is such that people *can* only pursue pleasure and that, faced with a choice between two courses of action, they will always choose the one they believe will provide the greater balance of pleasure over pain. While views can be labelled by different people in different ways, it can be useful to take psychological egoism as the rather wider view that, while people do indeed act only in order to promote some interest of their own, this self-interest need not be a matter of physical pleasure – it could be happiness in some wider sense, or even an ideal like self-perfection. Finally, there is *ethical* egoism, which *recommends* self-interest, whether in the narrow or the broader, more enlightened sense, as a moral policy.

All these positions are perhaps better recognized, though, by what they exclude: the possibility of altruism. They therefore reject any claim that altruism is an essential condition for a satisfying form of human life. This is not a new controversy; the general line of debate was mapped out in ancient times. In the *Republic*, Plato's dialogue about the nature of justice, Socrates defends the view that justice or morality is an asset or advantage in life, and that in the end it brings happiness. His interlocutors challenge him to answer two very difficult questions. The first is why someone who is reliably able to escape any unpleasant consequences for his actions, someone who can literally get away with murder, should not in fact do so. The story told in the dialogue to illustrate this point concerns a shepherd called Gyges who finds a magic ring with which he is able to become invisible at will. He uses this power to embark on a career of seduction, pillage and murder, pursuing his own pleasure whatever the cost to others. Socrates is asked to say why he should not do this – indeed, why anyone in such a situation should not behave like this. He is also asked to accept that anyone who had the chance *would* do this – that it is human nature.[1]

The second question develops the point further, and it is perhaps even more difficult to answer in a way that satisfies anyone who believes that there are alternatives to the pursuit of self-interest. In this case, Socrates is asked to imagine *two* people. One of the two is honest, upright and just. But he has exactly the opposite reputation, and because people think so badly of him, he ultimately dies in pain, poverty and disgrace. The other has a reputation for being a pillar of the community, but is in fact everything that is despicable – he is corrupt, dishonest and indeed criminal. But because he is so well regarded by everybody, he manages to survive to old age, rich, powerful and respected. He is even able to leave a considerable sum to pay for religious observances on his behalf after his death! Socrates is faced with the challenge of showing why it is better to be the first person in this fable rather than the second.

His answer in the end is that morality or justice fits and harmonizes with the nature of man; it is not something artificial or externally imposed. Vice, on the other hand, is alien and discordant – a disease of the soul analogous to disease in the body. In drawing this analogy between mental or spiritual health and the health of the body, Socrates hopes to show that the nature of morality is such that no one could ever be placed in the position of having to choose between moral virtue and personal happiness.[2] Plato had heard Socrates, in his own speech of defence at his trial (recounted in the *Apology*) express his confident belief that 'no evil can befall the good man, nor will the gods forsake him.'[3] The irony of this was, however, that Socrates made that statement just as he was about to be wrongly condemned and put to death. Plato undoubtedly had this in mind when he argued that, whatever material suffering may be involved, the link between virtue and happiness will hold; and that, whatever the material gains, vice is simply incompatible with a person's true happiness. But despite these ancient arguments about the link between virtue and personal happiness, which were later power-fully reinforced with the advent of Christianity, a cynical recommendation to make looking after one's own interests a first priority serves many people as a guide for life, while, at the same time, there is a widespread and pervasive belief that people are, in any case, inevitably selfish.

Ethical Egoism?

There are very few people who would hold the ethical view that promotes the pursuit of self-interest if they were not subconsciously assuming the psychological claim. In other words, it is usually because they believe people *do* act selfishly that they are inclined to build selfish action into a guiding principle. However, assuming for the moment that there *are* other possibilities, why should anybody *want* a situation in which all pursue their own selfish interest? Why, in any case, should anyone urge this policy on anyone else? At the very least, anyone who recommended it would be foolish or ill-advised, since if people followed the recommendation, then they would be bound to trample on their adviser's interests when these came into conflict with their own. This is as much a logical difficulty as a practical one. Ethical egoists, it must be assumed, place their own personal interests at the centre of the moral world. Therefore, they must believe that other people, too, should pursue these - their own personal – interests. But then, if ethical egoism is to be a generalizable theory, it can only be framed as the assertion that *each* individual should pursue his or her own interests.

This ambivalence clearly makes ethical egoists impossible people to consult for moral advice. If you ask them whether you should donate some money to a charity, or embark on divorce proceedings, or join a political demonstration, it will be difficult to say whether the answer you get is in terms of what will be good for you, or what will be good for them. It will not be any use asking them to clear up this problem, of course, because you can never be sure whether you are getting an honest answer – after all, this, too, will depend on whether they see honesty as being in their interest or not. If they settle for saying, 'Do what you think is best for *you*,' this is liable to raise yet more problems. 'Do what you think is best for *you*,' is, of course, sometimes good advice. But while it works well for the question, 'Should I look for a new place to live, or a new job?' it does not seem the best answer to the question, 'Shall I arrange to have my business colleague murdered in order to collect some jointly arranged life insurance?' It is for reasons like these that ethical egoism will not work as a generalizable ethical theory.

It is still possible, though, for individuals who are not interested in promoting a general theory to make the pursuit of self-interest their own guiding moral principle. The Italian philosopher, Nicolò Machiavelli

(1469–1527), for example, thought that rulers would do well to do this.[4] Even here, though, there are considerations that could be advanced against accepting such a policy. To begin with, there is what the English philosopher Henry Sidgwick (1838–1900) called the Paradox of Hedonism – that the impulse towards pleasure, if too predominant, defeats its own aim.[5] Study, business enterprises, sport, the arts – all these need to be directly absorbing, objects of enthusiasm in their own right, if they are to generate pleasure. Engage in them only *for the sake of* enjoyment and it is likely to elude you. It could be pointed out, too, that there are other ideals with at least an equal claim for consideration – kindness, respect for the rights of others and self-denial, for example – and that the practical consequences of applying these ideals seem to fit much better with the morality of common sense than the practical consequences of egoism.

It is also possible to draw attention to the pressing claims of others who might be important to the egoist – the egoist's own family, for example, or friends. Of course, some might detect another concealed paradox here, or at least a misconception. Concern for these immediate 'others', they might suggest, is just another form of egoism. But this is not really so. The view that identifies a person's interests with those of family or dependants belongs to an earlier period of human thought, when wives and children were not regarded as having any separate identity. Once their separate status is acknowledged, concern for one's 'own', whether family, friends or country, must count as altruism, not as selfishness.

One reason sometimes offered for recommending the pursuit of self-interest is that it is a strong motivating consideration. If something is in my interest, that provides me with a good reason for doing it. However, what is in fact in my interest is not necessarily my immediate pleasure, narrowly conceived. Indeed, it may be something much closer to ordinary morality. So, paradoxically, even an egoist may have good reason not to behave selfishly but to adopt what is generally accepted as good moral behaviour. This form of rational egoism was defended by Joseph Butler (1692–1752), a Bishop of the Church of England, who also provided a refutation of the cruder theory of psychological egoism. He wrote: 'though virtue or moral rectitude does indeed consist in affection to and pursuit of what is right and good as such; yet, when we sit down in a cool hour, we can neither justify to ourselves this or any other pursuit till we are convinced that it will be for our happiness, or at least not contrary to it.'[6] Butler distinguished this 'cool' self-love from the impetuous variety and recommended it to those members of his congregation who were not attracted to virtue for its own sake.

However, this does not necessarily clear the way for a thoroughgoing policy of egoism. For the egoist must ask the question whether, if other people were to adopt this policy for action, this would produce worse effects all round than a more conventional moral stance. Indeed, it was the belief that this would be so that led the British philosopher Thomas Hobbes (1588–1679) to describe the natural state of man as a state of war in which 'every man is enemy to every man . . . and the life of man, solitary, poor, nasty, brutish and short.'[7] For Hobbes, then, it was sheer self-preservation rather than the quest for pleasure that necessitated a willingness to renounce the satisfaction of immediate impulses.

Behind Hobbes's argument lies the idea that if everyone acts selfishly they lose disproportionately more than if they succeed in establishing trust and co-operation. There is a contemporary problem which supports this claim in a more structured and formal way. Known as the Prisoner's Dilemma, it is presented in different forms, but in its best-known form, the story can be told like this:

> Two prisoners are detained in separate cells, unable to communicate with each other in any way. Their captors approach each of them separately and offer them a deal, making it clear that this deal is also being offered to the other. The deal they propose is this: 'Supply incriminating evidence so that your co-prisoner can be convicted of a major charge. If you do this, you will go free, as long as there isn't any evidence against you. But it will mean the death penalty for the other detainee. Keep silent and you will both stay in prison, but on a lesser charge and for a limited term. Of course, if you keep silent and your fellow-prisoner incriminates you, *you* will be the one to face the death penalty. On the other hand, if you both incriminate each other, you will both stay in prison for life, which after all, is no more than you would deserve.'

The situation can be set out in a table where A and B are the two prisoners and 10 represents the maximum gain and 0 the maximum loss.

Prisoner's dilemma

	A speaks	A keeps silent
B speaks	bad for both 2, 2	best for B 10 worst for A 0
B keeps silent	best for A 10 worst for B 0	second best for both 5, 5

The table makes it clear that the consequences of both people acting selfishly are bad. The most personally advantageous situation for an individual is to be selfish while everyone else is unselfish, but the best *joint* policy is co-operation and self-restraint. It is easy to see the wider applicability of this, for the fact is that in their personal lives, people do not act alone, or in a social vacuum, and yet the reliability of others can never be guaranteed. There are many less dramatic examples. If one nation dredges the ocean for fish, wantonly killing young fish, that nation will gain if other nations keep to more restrictive rules. But if they all secretly over-fish, fish-stocks could be depleted beyond recovery. Similarly, individuals can gain by surreptitiously watering their garden with a hosepipe during a time of drought, but they stand to lose considerably more – the complete breakdown of the water-supply – if a large number of people do the same. Of course, the preferred situation, and the only one likely to command assent, is the compromise in which all exercise self-restraint and keep the agreed rules. In non-artificial situations – the social life of most people – securing assent must take priority over maximizing individual gain, and being an individual egoist is a policy to which no one but the egoist himself or herself could be expected to assent. In general, then, what these examples show is that, for most of the things that they value, people are dependent as a group upon harmony and co-operation with others.[8]

Would Egoism Contribute to the Common Good?

Not everyone would accept this point, however. Economists, in particular, are likely to point out that egoism is, on the whole, efficient. For people are probably better at judging what *they* want than they are at judging what other people want. This practical, economic and political argument for egoism is usually attributed to the British theorist Adam Smith (1723–90), author of *The Wealth of Nations* (1776), who argued that if individuals pursue their own interest, in doing so they will produce the best interest of everybody through a natural mechanism or 'hidden hand'.

Smith's theory is often extended from its origins in classical liberal economics, where it featured as an argument against attempts by the state to manage and control the economic activities of individuals, to a wider defence of the operation of the market and therefore of capitalism, individualism and the modern consumer society in its present form. But this founder of a long line of apparently materialistic economic theorists in fact took care not to equate material success with happiness. On the contrary, he wrote that 'wealth and greatness are mere trinkets of frivolous utility' and that 'in ease of body and peace of mind, all the different ranks of life are nearly upon a level, and the beggar who suns himself by the side of the highway possesses that security which kings are fighting for.'[9]

Unlike his critics and followers, then, Adam Smith was able to distinguish between economics and ethics. In the world of business, firms can come and go. But economic free enterprise need not be linked to grasping plutocracy or indifference to the lives or well-being of other human beings.

Is Altruism Possible?

Ethical egoism is best seen, then, as a theory that recommends selfishness in the ordinary sense of the word. This recommendation implies, though, that there are alternatives to egoism, and this is precisely what the *psychological* theory denies. The psychological egoist has no choice but to be an ethical egoist. It is obvious that if I *can* only act in pursuit of my own good, there will be little point in anyone asking me to do otherwise. So the psychological version of egoism, if it is compatible with any ethical theory at all, entails ethical egoism, but ethical egoism, on the other hand, does not entail psychological egoism. However, psychological egoism scarcely needs a moral theory: if people *can* only act selfishly, then there is little point in telling them what they *ought* to do. 'Ought' comes into operation only where there are real alternatives. Or, as this point has traditionally been expressed, 'ought' implies 'can'. It is nevertheless a natural transition to make. As Sidgwick put it, 'no cogent inference is possible from the psychological generalisation to the ethical principle, but the mind has a natural tendency to pass from the one position to the other.'[10]

Psychological egoism is itself, however, a strong theory. It is frequently attacked by citing counter-examples, but it is difficult to produce a decisive refutation in this way. For example, both Albert Schweitzer and Mother Teresa, whose lives appear to epitomize unselfish and largely unrewarded labour for the welfare of others, have been the subjects of denunciatory works interpreting their activities as self-seeking and self-serving. But it is this very strength – this invulnerability to refutation – that is the theory's weakness. For in the end it becomes clear that psychological egoism makes altruism not only unlikely but logically impossible.

The reasons for this are complex. To begin with, it is clear that it is often based on a misunderstanding about language. Instead of acknowledging that people desire or want specific things – food, drink, sex, warmth, exercise, information, peace of mind, revenge or the happiness or misery of other people – the psychological egoist suggests that the only possible *object* of desire is some desire. Or, the only thing it is possible to *want* is a want (that is, desire, pleasure or satisfaction) of my own. But this is to overlook the fact that there is a whole range of possible objects of verbs like 'desire' and 'want'. The egoist is setting up an empty tautology as a barrier between desires and the objects of desire in the guise of making a psychological claim about people and their motivation.

This misunderstanding about language is often linked with a confusion about the facts. It is true that people can sometimes act in pursuit of pleasure. It is quite common to distinguish, for example, between the ordinary person who eats to live, and the gourmet who lives to eat; the first wants food, the second wants the pleasure of the table. The egoist who is not making a purely grammatical point may be claiming that the second case is the standard one. But as a factual claim, this looks decidedly unconvincing. Indeed, it is only because it is mixed up with the mistaken claim about language that anyone would *want* to assert it. For one thing, it seems to make it impossible ever actually to *attain* satisfaction. If the only thing people can aim at is a state of pleasure – if, that is, they are not able to gain direct satisfaction from, for instance, good food, listening to music or physical activity, then everyone is doomed to perpetual disappointment. For you can only get pleasure from listening to music if listening to music is an activity yielding satisfaction. Indeed, if it is not possible to find listening to music immediately pleasant, then there would be no reason to see the pleasure of listening to music as a possible immediate object of desire. It might only be possible to achieve it by way of the pleasure of the pleasure of listening to music and so on, and on, indefinitely – a classic example of an infinite regress.

Once these misunderstandings have been cleared out of the way, it becomes possible to approach the real issue that lies at the root of egoism. Psychological egoists are interested in the many instances of apparent human unselfishness or self-sacrifice, but only because they want to expose what they see as the root selfishness at their core. A woman makes a generous donation to charity. 'Ah well,' it is explained, 'there are tax advantages for her there, you know.' Someone confesses to a crime he has committed when he sees that an innocent person is about to go to prison for it. 'Well, he would have suffered painful remorse throughout that person's prison sentence and he would have found that worse than accepting the punishment himself.' A harder case still: Dickens' Sydney Carton takes somebody else's place on the scaffold. 'The misery of continuing to live with the knowledge of that person's death, and of the grief it caused for the woman they both loved, outweighed the pain of losing his life.'

The problem with these cases is that everyone knows that sometimes the cynic is right. Not all charitable donations are the result of pure altruism, and psychological hang-ups occasionally account for freakishly generous gestures. But psychological egoism and cynicism are two different things. The argument with the cynic is about how *often* people are unselfish, and this must in the end be a matter of personal judgement based on observation, and to some extent on introspection – though in this case introspection cannot be decisive, since introspective reports on these matters say more about the person making the judgement than about the people being judged. Indeed, it would be sensible to look quite closely at the 'generous' gestures of someone who claims to detect selfishness in other people's acts, while it would be safe to assume that people who attribute generosity to others are themselves rather more likely to act in the interests of others.

The psychological egoist, on the other hand, unlike the cynic, may be refuted by a single case of unselfish action. For many people, the free donation of blood or bone-marrow by public-spirited individuals would seem a sufficient refutation. It is worth noticing, too, that people often appear willing to sacrifice their self-interest for ideals – truth, freedom or religion, for example, as well as for more doubtful goods like fame or power. But perhaps a more telling point, made by Bishop Butler, is their willingness to sacrifice it for negative goals – revenge, spite, envy or anger. People often have too *little* self-love, not too much, he pointed out. 'Unselfishness', then, is not necessarily always an admirable trait, or even a useful one.

Supposing, however, that we accept that what is at issue here is not so much whether people are always guided by self-interest – these examples suggest that they are not – but whether they are ever capable of altruism in the sense in which that *is* an admirable and useful quality. If an example is to be found which can carry conviction, it will probably have to be a case in which self-sacrifice involves death, since it is hard to see how, apart from belief in an afterlife, immediate death can be a preferable option to anything else. By remaining alive a person has a chance to cope with even the biggest regret or disappointment. And yet people who do not necessarily believe in an after-life do sometimes choose to accept death. For example, from time to time, there will be a reliable report that a pilot whose plane was about to crash on a populated area has stayed with his plane, saving the threatened population at the cost of losing his own chance to save his life by ejecting safely. It is impossible to argue that a pilot who does this has no other choice, because incidents like this are balanced by others in which pilots in similar situations have indeed made the non-altruistic choice. Perhaps those who have done so do indeed regret it later – but there is, after all, psychotherapy, and the possibility of moving on to a new life in a new social sphere.

So a person who insists on interpreting even a case like that of the altruistic pilot as selfishness is not really arguing about the facts. Indeed, what the argument really amounts to may be something like this: 'The pilot wanted to do his duty more than he wanted to remain alive. Doing what you want is selfishness; so the pilot's action was really selfish.' This, though, is a harmless truism. It is a perverse use of the term 'selfish'. It also involves insisting on saying of everything that anyone does that he or she *wants* to do it. If the claim is that it is no longer possible simply to do things, but that each activity has to be prefaced by an actual phase or psychological experience of wanting, then again this is a factual claim, but one for which there is no evidence. However, it is very likely that the person who asserts it with such conviction does so only as a result of confusing the factual assertion with the truism. It is the mark of a truism, though, that it says nothing about any matter of fact, and certainly not about anything of such vital importance to ethics as human motivation.

Selfish Genes

There is one other theory of universal selfishness that may seem harder to refute than these, because it places the pursuit of self-interest at the level not of the human person but of the gene. This popular thesis of sociobiology has an advantage over older theories of universal selfishness since it appears to allow for the *fact* of human self-sacrifice – for family, friends or even total strangers. And yet this kind of sacrifice is still interpreted as selfishness because by a mixture of biological and *a priori* reasoning it is claimed that the human gene ensures its own survival, even at the expense of the individual. This is a difficult theory to refute because it is hard to identify a testable claim. And even where there does seem to be an identifiable claim, it appears to run counter to many known facts. Inconsistent facts are taken care of, though, by certain prior assumptions: that only successful genes survive (and here 'success' is defined as the ability to survive); and that strategies to promote survival are by definition selfish.

Other strands may be unravelled from the composite thesis. The actions of individual human beings are once again being explained deterministically. This time, however, the determining cause is found not within the person but in a part of the body which is not itself sentient or capable of knowledge – a minute part of each body cell which is responsible for the pre-programming of its host in evolutionarily stable strategies, just as the migration patterns of birds are inbuilt and pre-programmed in them. Nevertheless, it is held to be able to decide – or, rather programmed – to sacrifice its host in order to preserve another variant of itself in another member of the species.

But if this is the theory, something has obviously gone very wrong with the programming of humans, in view of the willingness of humans to engage in large-scale slaughter and murder of other members of their species – all gene-carriers to a man (or woman, or child). Indeed, this reflection suggests that the theory is in fact a biogenetic version of the story of the Garden of Eden, in which man alone of all species was given the freedom to choose, and used it to choose what was bad rather than what was good. The kind of instinctive control that guides the flight patterns of birds has a clear survival value for the species, but, in the case of humans, the instincts that result from genetic influences do not necessarily promote the interest of group or species. In the case of other species, too, nature does not leave them the option of accepting or rejecting genetic control. But the sociobiologist Richard Dawkins, in his book *The Selfish Gene,* holds that humans are not necessarily bound to follow the programme dictated by their genes. On the contrary, their natural programming can be influenced, he suggests, by culture and education. And so he urges 'Let us try to *teach* generosity and altruism, because we are born selfish. Let us understand what our own selfish genes are up to because we may then at least have the chance to upset their designs, something which no other species has ever aspired to . . . We have the power to defy the selfish genes of our birth.'[11]

But the facts of human behaviour, whatever they are, cannot reveal whether 'pre-programming' operates to preserve, at the expense of others, the host ('survival-machine') in which the gene finds itself temporarily housed, or to preserve other hosts or gene-carriers at its own expense. The second sounds like altruism, the first like selfishness. This lack of clarity about the kind of pattern of response that is supposed to be built in genetically is a fundamental weakness of this type of theory – the more so when the proviso is added that not all human behaviour *is* controlled by this involuntary survival mechanism.

But in what sense *can* genes be credited with moral qualities? The very attempt to do so seems to be based on a confusion of types or levels. *People* decide, assess, judge, make sacrifices, particularly self-sacrifices. Genes, just because they lack brains, nervous systems, sense organs and all the other necessary conditions of judgement and action must, important though they may be in other ways, be left out of discussions about selfishness and unselfishness.[12]

Gene selfishness, then, need not be added to the armoury of the egoist; the doubts remain, then, about both the ethical and the psychological forms of egoism. Neither as a matter of fact nor as a matter of principle is it necessary to reduce the range of options for human beings to the narrow confines of what individuals can gain for themselves. The variety and richness of human motivation remain for better or worse extensive enough to provide alternatives for ethical choice based on a much wider range of possibilities.

What egoism has stressed, though, is the motivating force of concepts like pleasure, satisfaction, personal fulfilment and happiness. Most people will certainly be influenced by the argument that something will make them happy, even if in the end they reject this as a decisive consideration. But one of the grounds on which they might well reject their *own* happiness as a decisive consideration is that they feel strongly influenced, too, by consideration for the happiness of other people.

Interlude

I hoped I had convinced Egoge. She always smiled and nodded in a pleasant and agreeable way when I produced my arguments, apparently appreciating my conviction and sincerity. But then I realized that that was just what she would do, given her principles, whatever she actually thought. For it was not in her interest to arouse my antagonism, even if, as I suspected, my friendship was of no particular importance to her. I imagine, too, that she liked reporting back on our conversations to her friends – perhaps, indeed, there was even some more formal arrangement by which she had to give an account of my arguments to the faceless officials I sensed played some behind-the-scene role in these interviews.

For whatever reason, however, the issues we had discussed remained unresolved. Egoge came back to talk to me from time to time, but almost invariably it turned out that she had come across some new example of someone who appeared to have performed a particularly self-denying action, but one which, on closer inspection, turned out to be self-interested. I was forced to concede that she was probably right about many of these examples, but they only revealed to me how far Egoge was from really understanding the thrust of the arguments I had put to her: that either altruism was a real possibility, in which case sooner or later there would, or at least could, be an example of it. Or it was an impossibility, but only on the basis of some verbal trumpery which could have no implications at all about people's behaviour or about human nature.

Egoge was anxious for me to know, however, that her own views were not necessarily the standard opinions of her group. Her twin sisters Nomia and Physia, for example, often discussed these matters with her, she said, and took a very different view. She promised to bring them to meet me later, but first, she said, she thought she should give me an opportunity to discuss matters with her father Panhedon, who had always been a great influence on her, even though she could not accept all his ideas.

Notes to Chapter 2

1   The story is told in *Republic* II 359d–362d

2   'But really, Socrates, it seems to me ridiculous to ask that question now that the nature of justice and injustice has been brought to light. People think that all the luxury and wealth and power in the world cannot make life worth living when the bodily consitution is going to rack and ruin; and are we to believe that, when the very principle whereby we live is deranged and corrupted, life will be worth living so long as a man can do as he will, and wills to do anything rather than to free himself from vice and wrongdoing and to win justice and virtue?' *Republic*, IV 444.

3   Plato, *Apology*.

4   Machiavelli, *The Prince*.

5   Sidgwick, *The Methods of Ethics*, p. 48.

6   Butler, *Fifteen Sermons*, sermon 11, para. 20.

7   Hobbes, *Leviathan*, part I, ch. 13, pp. 185–6.

8   The prisoner's dilemma, attributed to A. W. Tucker of the Rand Corporation, is discussed in Campbell and Sowden, *Paradoxes of Rationality*. Many papers on the subject are published in the *Journal of Conflict Resolution*.

9   Smith, *Moral Sentiments*, part iv. chap. i.

10 Sidgwick, *The Methods of Ethics*, p. 42.

11 Dawkins, *The Selfish Gene*, pp. 3, 215.

12 Midgley, 'Gene-juggling', pp. 439–58.

3

Pursuing Happiness

Third Conversation

Panhedon: My daughter tells me you are a very persuasive talker. But from what I hear, there is a flaw in what you say is the kernel of your argument – that if all pursue their own individual interest, there is no point in saying that they ought to do anything else. I say, on the contrary, let everyone pursue the *common* interest, the happiness of all.

Traveller: But then I take it that you do not agree with Egoge that everyone is self-interested?

Panhedon: On the contrary, I agree with her absolutely. Everyone is indeed out for their own interest. There is a way round this difficulty, though, which you appear to have missed.

Traveller: How can that be? The two things you are saying are just incompatible: one, it seems, is a general principle about people's motives – a psychological theory about what prompts them to action. The other is what I would call an *ethical* principle – a claim about what people *ought* to do – not what they do in fact do.

Panhedon: I am not disputing that.

Traveller: Then I can only repeat what I said to Egoge. It is no good saying people *ought* to do what they *cannot* do. Perhaps I ought to try to leave this place, for example, but I don't have the means . . .

Panhedon: Well, whether my two claims are compatible or not depends on how people choose to organize things. I was impressed by what you reported Adam Smith as saying – that when each person pursues his own good, this adds up to all pursuing the common good. But you mentioned a 'hidden hand'. That sounds too *magical* for me, if you'll forgive me putting it like that. No, I like to help things along.

Traveller: How? What do you mean?

Panhedon: Well, I think we have to bring in wider considerations. I'll confess that there are many things I don't like about Alloi society. And much of what is wrong could be put right by the right sort of laws. So, suppose someone is jealous of a neighbour who has something he would like to have. Because people do indeed pursue their own pleasure, the natural tendency would be for that person simply to take what he wants – by force or even murder if necessary. But if you can set up a system of laws, and enforce compliance with them by well-devised punishments and a real threat of detection, this changes the balance of choice for the potential criminal.

Traveller: I see. The balance of pleasure over pain shifts, so that what is in a person's selfish interest changes. It actually matches the public interest.

Panhedon: That's right.

I considered telling Panhedon that that his ideas came very close to those of the British philosopher and jurisprudentialist Jeremy Bentham (1748–1832), whom he also strikingly resembled in his physique. How could I know this? Well, I had seen not only portraits of Bentham, but even his auto-icon. In an eccentric gesture, Bentham arranged to have his body preserved and put on display in University College, London after his death. I could easily have imagined Panhedon doing something of the sort!

It would be wrong to describe Bentham as the inventor of utilitarianism. But he was the first to formulate it comprehensively and to make the principle 'the greatest happiness of the greatest number' into something of a popular slogan. He also differed from his predecessors in not wishing to assign any significant role to the motive of benevolence – the point that had so far been at issue between myself and Egoge and in which, as I gathered, Panhedon supported her. As utilitarianism has played and continues to play such a key role – in politics, ethics, economics and law – in my own country, I thought it reasonable to give Panhedon a fairly substantial outline of the theory, as well as some well-known objections to it.

Promoting Happiness

Is morality a matter of increasing the amount of happiness in the world? At first sight this may seem no bad objective. Indeed, if more of those with power and influence – leaders, politicians, planners – would take it as their guiding principle, this would be an improvement on the motley assortment of dishonest, corrupt or fanatical goals that are often the hidden guides to policy in many parts of the world. Utilitarianism is the theory that this is indeed the essence of morality – that to say that some action is right is to say that it is productive of happiness; and to say that something – some state of affairs – is good is to say that it yields happiness or satisfaction; while what people call *the* right action – that is, the action that someone *ought* to choose – is the one that, out of all the available alternatives, produces the greatest possible amount of happiness. Put like this, utilitarianism offers a description of what people *mean* by terms like 'good', 'bad', 'right' and 'wrong'. But the point of offering this description is usually to support utilitarianism as a normative theory – a theory about what *is* good, a recommendation about what people ought to do. Interpreted in this way, it expresses the view that the right action *is* the one that produces the best outcome in terms of happiness.

If happiness seems too loose a concept – after all, what *is* it to make someone happy? – it is not essential to the theory. Although it was the term favoured by some of the earlier utilitarians, contemporary utilitarians may prefer to speak of satisfying desires or preferences or of maximizing welfare. But there is something to be said for the original version, since preferences may be foolish, idiosyncratic or damaging, and utilitarianism does not seek to support those kind of choices. And so it may need to find a way of specifying an impersonal viewpoint, an 'ideal choice' situation. There is another objection, too, to the modern variants. Talk of preferences also loses the main virtue of utilitarianism as originally conceived in turning the attention back from objective or external features of situations to internal psychological ones. Speaking of welfare avoids this, but creates the different problem of identifying and agreeing the contentious question of what are the interests that constitute welfare.

In all its versions, however, utilitarianism seeks, in the social and political sphere, to offer a science of ethical decision-making, a means of resolving issues by testable practical methods which, at the extreme may be quantitative and statistical. Above all, it claims to be a rational theory: indeed, it takes the strategy of pursuing the best available option as the standard of rationality. It is this that makes it the ethical code most likely to appeal to law-makers and economists. Bentham, whom Leslie Stephen described as a 'codifying animal', devised a 'felicific calculus' with seven dimensions of pleasure and pain. These were intensity (how intense is the pleasure or pain?), duration (how long does it last?), certainty (what are the chances of that type of sensation resulting?), propinquity (how soon will it result?), fecundity (If pleasurable, is it likely to be followed by sensations of the same kind?), purity (is it likely to be followed by sensations of the *opposite* kind?) and extent (how *many* people will it affect?).[1] Someone contemplating taking up or giving up smoking, or offered a sample of a hard drug at a party, may realistically go through a process of calculation like this in asking the question, Is it worth it? Formalized in the public sphere, it becomes the economist's strategy of cost–benefit analysis.

Utility and Principle

But from the point of view of morality, there is one striking flaw involved in taking the unselfish goal of producing the general happiness as the standard of right and wrong. This is that, although it may be ethically superior to pure unadulterated selfishness, the pursuit of happiness still sometimes conflicts with intuitive moral judgements. In particular, it can easily find itself in opposition to the requirements of justice. For it is not difficult to think of situations in which the happiness of the majority can best be secured by a deliberate injustice to a few. This could be an individual scapegoat or it could be a group. Take, for example, a situation in which anger and civil unrest at a terrorist bombing campaign is in danger of boiling over. If this can only be contained by the arrest and conviction of someone who could plausibly be believed to have planted the latest bomb, the authorities might judge it better not to be too fussy about the evidence. Or again, if the majority in a society resent the presence of a small racial or religious minority, the balance of happiness, unlike the balance of justice, might be served by expelling them. Keeping a promise, too, can sometimes produce more grief than happiness, and this makes it hard for a utilitarian to justify keeping a promise in all circumstances. Yet if promises are to have any meaning at all, they must be given priority over considerations of expediency. A broken promise leaves a sense of betrayal and injustice in its wake, whatever the benefit to the majority.

So there is a great deal of difference between taking the end-product of an action as the test of whether it is right or wrong and taking the quality of the action itself as the standard. The first of these, since it deals in consequences, is usually described as a consequentialist or teleological ethic; the second is described as deontological – that is to say, an ethic according to which certain kinds of actions are right or wrong in themselves, independently of the consequences. It is the difference between thinking the good is something people *aim* for, and thinking that it is a quality of the way they try to *achieve* their ends, whatever they are.

It is also the difference between holding that an action is right or wrong because of what it achieves and holding that it is right or wrong because of the kind of action that it is.

Consider, for example, a situation in which a lie can produce some generally beneficial effects. One person may approach a situation like this with an unconditional presumption in favour of truth, regarding it as something that is not simply set aside according to circumstances. A utilitarian appears to be committed to looking at the way in which the choice between honesty and deceit will affect the happiness of everyone involved, and only then coming to a conclusion about what is the right thing to do. The question of who is involved need not be taken too narrowly; utilitarianism can allow the happiness of the particular people most directly concerned to take second place to more long-term and general considerations, as long as it is still only the practical consequences that are allowed to feature in the calculation. It seems that Bentham would not have disagreed with this account of the matter, since he gave short shrift to 'principles adverse to utility', saying of justice in particular that it was 'nothing more than an imaginary instrument, employed to forward on certain occasions, and by certain means, the purposes of benevolence.'[2]

Problems of Utilitarian Calculation

These are fundamental difficulties, then, for utilitarianism. But there are further problems of a more practical nature when it comes to the details of its implementation. If 'human happiness' is a truly global term then it presumably covers all human beings, past (admittedly, about whose happiness we can no longer do anything) but also present and future. Future generations, however, are likely to vastly outnumber us, and who is to say what their desires and preferences will be? Even the happiness of all human beings in the world at present is an impossible measure for anyone to use as a basis for calculation. But if some more limited reference group is taken, what should this be – family, friends, social class, nation or race? Depending on the answer to this question, the outcome of the calculation is likely to be very different.

Nevertheless, some people and some relationships, it seems, *ought* to count for more than others. The happiness of a spouse, a child or a parent *should*, it seems, count for vastly more than the happiness of an acquaintance, even if the needs of the acquaintance are more pressing and important than those of the close relative. Suppose, for example, that someone knows that an acquaintance has a distressing debt problem and that this could be solved by precisely the amount she is about to spend on a scarcely needed birthday present for her child. Few people would say that the need to maximize happiness, even in one's immediate circle, must be interpreted so as to give priority to dealing with the difficulties of people who are no more than acquaintances.

The consistent utilitarian may deny this, particularly when turning away from the immediate or local context to take account of famine, malnutrition, disease and early mortality in other parts of the world. Many utilitarians insist that people *ought* to consider the claims of others who are not in any way connected with them.[3] Their arguments, however, when extended like this, carry too *much* rather than too *little* weight, since consistency would not stop short of anything less than living at just above subsistence level, something which no one who pursues this argument is likely to be willing to do. This is not necessarily a bad thing, however, for, while some people would admire a person who chose to make this kind of sacrifice on an individual basis, they would almost certainly think her morally at fault if she imposed the same degree of sacrifice on her dependants. It seems, then, that it is impossible not to accept some degree of preference for those who are close to a person, or those for whom that person is specially responsible. It would also seem that, from a personal point of view, utilitarianism may be *too* demanding, not only of money but also of time, energy and commitment, in its insistence that the right thing to do is not simply one of a number of options; it is always the single *best* option that is available.[3]

These difficulties could perhaps be met by the adoption of a more general principle: that of restricting utilitarian calculation to something that can be meaningful in the situations someone has an interest in and is able to affect. In fact, in most practical contexts, utilitarian calculation usually *does* confine itself in this way to those most immediately and directly affected by the action. In a healthcare setting, for example, a utilitarian-based decision as to whether to switch off the life-support machine of a patient in irreversible coma would tend to focus on the interests of the patient and relatives. Similarly, decisions about fertility treatment and procedures in reproductive medicine are often guided by the needs and interests of those immediately and most directly involved, although that very situation brings into existence long-term 'others' – new people – whose interests stretch indefinitely into the future, and who might also be expected to count. A similarly specific approach might well be taken, too, in an education setting: for example, if the question is whether a child should be allowed to attend an over-subscribed school on the basis of parental preference.

But while narrowing down the utility considerations to the immediate participants may be an option for practitioners in some cases, the broad issues involved will have to be decided by governments and legislators on a much wider basis, which will ultimately have repercussions for the particular cases. The problem for utilitarian legislators could be described as that of summing utilities; the economist will describe it as the problem of aggregating individual utilities into a measure of social utility: in other words, how can the good of each be made to add up to the good of all? Bear in mind, too, that each person differs, so that you cannot assume that what suits one will suit another. Nor can you even assume that goods themselves are comparable or commensurable. How do you compare, for example, access to dialysis machines in the case of kidney failure, access to supermarkets by public transport, access to higher education, to good quality accommodation, to art galleries, operas or major football matches?

On the other hand, there are those who, following Bentham, prefer, rather than narrowing the focus of calculation, to *extend* the area of coverage not merely to all human beings, but to animals and perhaps to other non-animate aspects of the universe. But if the whole of humanity is an unmanageable reference group, how much more must this be true of the universe of sentient creatures and beyond? And then, even those utilitarians who wish to include animals in the scales of happiness calculation must in practice draw a line somewhere. Otherwise as much consideration must be given to the happiness of each of the cat's fleas as to the happiness of the cat. But line-drawing is precisely what cannot be achieved on the basis simply of utilitarianism itself. *Who* or *what* to include in or exclude from the moral universe – the list of those to be given ethical consideration and perhaps also regarded as having moral obligations – is itself a kind of moral judgement, but one that cannot itself be made on utilitarian grounds. This is not to say that the happiness of creatures other than humans is of no importance, only that this huge addition to the calculation of happiness and interests drags the initially clear lines of utilitarian theory into a realm of mathematical obscurity from which it can hardly be rescued.[4]

But what happens when happiness is used as a yardstick on the smaller, very restricted, scale previously suggested? Then we enter a world of calculation problems of a different sort. Actions do have consequences, both immediate and remote. Which should be singled out as decisive? Supposing someone offers to take a friend on a safari trip to see wildlife in some remote but reputedly safe location. This seems a good happiness-promoting project. But then suppose that a rogue animal attacks and injures the friend. Does this change the moral assessment of the original invitation?

Then again, what if, despite all the odds, the friend unexpectedly finds happiness *as a result of* the injury – perhaps reconciliation with a departed admirer who suddenly realizes the importance of that person to her own life? Does the assessment change again? All this illustrates the fact that an individual action is a stone cast into a pool with an indefinitely extending ripple effect. Deciding at what point to stop noticing the ripples is bound to be fairly arbitrary given the limitless nature of the pool of human interaction.

Consequences or Intended Consequences?

But then, is it *fair*, in any case, to judge an action by what it does as a matter of fact bring about, when what must strike any impartial observer as most relevant is what the person involved actually intended to achieve? If the animal attack was something the organizer of the trip had maliciously intended to happen or even if he was negligent in not guarding against the risk, it would be reasonable to blame him. But surely not otherwise – not for a simple unforeseeable misfortune.

It seems that two aspects have to be considered: both the intention of the organizer of the trip and what he could reasonably have expected to be its outcome. But utilitarianism cannot *afford* to take the question of motive seriously, because to do so would in a sense be destructive of the whole edifice of utilitarian doctrine. Utilitarianism looks to the future, while both motive and the question of expected outcome (reasonable expectations) involve looking back at the past, at the state of mind of the agent. Utilitarianism seeks objectivity. Motives and expectations belong to the world of subjectivity and inner experience.

One way out of this difficulty is for the utilitarian to distinguish between judging the action and judging the person – between judging an action to be wrong, and blaming the person concerned for doing it. In the case of the safari trip, the organizer, one might say, was not to blame for doing something that turned out to be, on an objective utilitarian assessment, the wrong thing. However, this involves accepting two odd things: first, the paradox that a person will sometimes have to be commended for doing wrong things and condemned for doing right things – or, if you like, it is sometimes good to do wrong and bad to do right; and, secondly, the fact that, unless some arbitrary cut-off point is set, this may have to be a fluctuating judgement.

There is also another odd feature of this whole discussion about praise and blame. The utilitarian must, in a sense, always put these words in inverted commas. For praise and blame can only be understood in terms of utilitarian theory as *devices* for encouraging or discouraging certain sorts of actions. If no utility is involved, then utilitarianism really has nothing to say.

Rules to Generate Happiness

However, there may be another, more radical, way to deal with some of these difficulties. Many tricky calculation problems are soluble if, instead of looking at individual cases, or individual actions, the happiness test is applied at a higher or more general level. As a result, certain general rules will emerge which will then be followed because, whatever may be the result in particular cases, following these rules on the whole makes for a happier society. This theory is usually known as rule utilitarianism, in contrast to the 'single occasion' form which is often described as act utilitarianism. It avoids the difficulties involved in having to judge each new case on its merits by allowing a limited number of broad principles to be taken as guides to action. The problem about duties to close dependants might be resolved, for example, by recognizing a rule according to which people are justified in failing to maximize happiness on a particular occasion if, on balance and in the long term, more happiness is generated by people taking special responsibility for members of their own family.

This idea can be extended so that most of the widely recognized principles of moral behaviour feature at least as rules of thumb, if not as absolute rules; it will support, too, a social policy of encouraging unreflective *habits* of following such rules as telling the truth, keeping promises, not stealing and so on. John Stuart Mill (1806–73), who followed Bentham in expounding and developing utilitarian doctrine, held that many moral rules, especially the principle of justice, could be justified in this way, and that : 'justice is a name for certain moral requirements, which, regarded collectively, stand higher in the scale of social utility, and are therefore of more paramount obligation, than any others.'[5] These, he says, have tended over the course of millennia to be found to promote human happiness by being taken as absolute principles – principles that allow of no exceptions. Apart from this, Mill regarded the conscious pursuit of happiness as being to some extent self-defeating, and believed that following well-established moral norms would probably, in the long run, and apart from certain extreme cases, be more conducive to happiness than setting bare utility as the goal of action.

However, it is precisely these extreme cases that are problematic. Should an innocent man be sacrificed, for example, to prevent a murderous mob going on the rampage and indiscriminately killing a large number of equally innocent people? Should an innocent man be tortured or judicially executed if this is the only way to prevent nuclear war? Should the Intelligence Agency of a liberal democracy arrange an assassination to prevent a political shift it sees as a threat to its very existence? These are the touchstone cases for utilitarians. But can the problem they pose be solved by substituting rule utilitarianism for the standard act utilitarianism? It would seem not, for someone who is not prepared under any circumstances at all to sacrifice the innocent, or to plan murder, is not a utilitarian at all. On the other hand, those who would accept the sacrifice of important principles such as justice and truth in these extreme cases are indeed utilitarians, but it is not clear that they have any need to invoke a special form of the theory. For what is involved in all such cases is, after all, a straightforward calculation of utility, and all that is in question is the time-scale and extent over which the calculation is to be made. The rule utilitarian merely takes a longer view.

Types of Happiness – Quantity or Quality?

Of course, in extreme cases like these, happiness tends to be equated with the indisputable good of saving lives. But the question of what exactly the goal of happiness involves is not in fact usually as clear-cut as this. Bentham interpreted the notion of pleasure in a practical, materialistic way; indeed, it was this that made the hedonic calculus possible. Mill, on the other hand, argued that human happiness was a matter of more complex and intellectual pleasures than this. So what *does* the recommendation to pursue happiness involve?

First, it may be easier to say what it does *not* involve. It is not simply a description of a psychological state unrelated to the actual world. If happiness were simply a psychological sense of well-being, there would, of course, be many short cuts to it. Drugs, medically prescribed or illicit, can change how people *feel* about their environment or situation while leaving the environment and situation unchanged. The equivalent of the soma-drug of Huxley's *Brave New World* has in various ways become part and parcel of everyday life since Huxley published his novel, and what chemistry cannot achieve, perhaps psychosurgery could. But most people can see a difference between *being* happy and *feeling* happy and, hard though it is to produce a rational justification for their preference, they would mostly opt for the first. Drugs tend in practice to be life shortening and life threatening, but even supposing that the science-fiction possibility of a lifetime of safely and convincingly hallucinating the achievement of all one's most longed-for goals were on offer, most people would refuse it in favour of actually achieving some of those goals.[6]

These goals might be quite complex and sophisticated. One person hopes to be an opera singer, another to grow large vegetable marrows. But on the purely material level, there are certain concrete goods – including health and an adequate standard of living – that people would consider important for happiness, though they would probably agree that it is possible to achieve happiness in their absence. This materialistic conception of happiness in terms of the possession of certain basic goods may not be a very elevated one, but in politics and social policy in general, intelligible and limited goals of this kind may well be preferable to the pursuit of ideological utopias. These goals may well be appropriate, then, for utilitarianism as a social and political theory. But if utilitarianism as a *moral* theory is in question, then it seems to be necessary to look for an interpretation of happiness with less prosaic, richer and more distinctively human features – in other words, a theory that recognizes the special potentialities of human beings for happiness as conceived of by both Mill and Moore.

Intellectual Pleasures

Mill's view of happiness emerges in his rejection of a criticism made of the Greek philosopher, Epicurus – that his philosophy is only fit for swine. Mill argues that the accusation supposes that human beings are only *capable* of the same sort of pleasures as swine. This claim that there are different kinds of pleasure – Mill speaks of higher and lower pleasures – and that human beings would, on the whole, prefer intellectual pleasures to those of the senses, marks the point at which Mill's theory departs from that of Bentham, who had written: 'Quantity of pleasure being equal, pushpin is as good as poetry'.

Mill has been criticized for the position that he held on the grounds that it inconsistently invokes a different standard from that of pleasure – one which goes beyond pure utility. But Mill's position is not in fact inconsistent; it simply expresses a particular and enriched conception of human nature and of what is necessary for happiness. Mill believed that human beings need to satisfy their intellectual as well as their physical hunger. He also believed that choice and individuality, together with the political and social freedom needed to practice choice and to display individuality, were essential ingredients in a full conception of happiness.

Ideal Utilitarianism

Writing fifty years later, at the end of the Victorian era, G. E. Moore (1873–1958) offered an idealized form of utilitarianism which reiterated the view that human satisfaction is wider and more spiritual than the early utilitarians has assumed. For Moore, the ingredients of happiness were 'certain states of consciousness which may be roughly described as the pleasure of human intercourse and the enjoyment of beautiful objects'.[7]

Moore's emphasis on personal affection, love and aesthetic appreciation provided a very different account of happiness from that of Mill. If Mill's was more intellectual and cerebral, Moore's was sufficiently suggestive of a full and even sensuous life-style as to become the inspiration – the philosophical underpinning – of the Bloomsbury group, variously inspiring such diverse figures as Virginia and Leonard Woolf, Rupert Brooke, Lytton Strachey and John Maynard Keynes. They looked to Moore as an iconoclast of Victorian morality, as one who rejected conventional rules in favour of these other, mainly aesthetic goods – a surprising outcome, given his quiet and domestic personal life-style, and the deliberately pedestrian flavour of the rest of his philosophical work.[8]

Enriched Happiness or Plural Values?

There is some scope, then, for amending the utilitarian position so that it avoids the crudest kind of interpretation and makes room for alternative conceptions of happiness. The question is, though, whether these should all be reduced to 'happiness' or whether it should not rather be recognized that there are other values in life than simply happiness. In other words, if freedom and individuality, or intellectual engagement, or the pursuit of truth and love, beauty and friendship are all valuable, why not simply assert that this is so – that there are many goods rather than one?

But if there are other values, then there is no reason why these should not include, in addition to this list, values of a more distinctively moral kind such as entitlement, justice and fairness. For example, it seems to matter morally not just how *much* happiness, however interpreted, is generated by a particular action, but how it is distributed. It does not seem fair, in distributing goods, that all should go to one and none to others, even if, in some quantitative sense, the amount of happiness shared remains the same. Questions of fairness also come in when it is asked whether people's own behaviour – effort, work, honesty – should make any difference to their level of happiness. Certain things, too, seem not to be available for distribution, since they belong to particular individuals who are *entitled* to enjoy them, even if others might enjoy them more. Take, for example, the attitude people take to their own bodies. It might be a good thing for me to leave my body to a hospital for purposes of research, but there is a strong tendency to feel that the hospital should not simply *take* it – useful though it might be – because I suffer a fainting fit on its doorstep. It is, after all, my body.

Means and Ends

Justice, fairness and entitlement, then, are amongst the competing goods that challenge the idea of happiness as a priority pursuit. The key question seems to be, after all, *how* happiness or good things in general are achieved and bad things averted. Are *any* means justified to obtain a desirable-enough end? A morality that answers this question in the affirmative is a dubious candidate for the term and yet it is a defining feature of a consequentialist justification that the end must often be taken to justify the means. This means that, for the consequentialist, it is an open question whether lying, murder, deceit or betrayal may not sometimes be morally justified, and indeed morally obligatory.

The notion that necessity may sometimes demand the otherwise morally unthinkable has now become such a commonplace assumption that it is even subtly incorporated in major public statements of ethical policy – statements whose *intention* or *purpose* is to set moral boundaries to what people may do. For instance, the Hague Convention, which was intended to ban especially horrendous forms of warfare, prohibited 'arms, projectiles, or material calculated to cause unnecessary suffering'.[9] It might seem that this clause is sufficient to outlaw the use of poison gas, napalm and chemical weapons, and that it would apply, too, to nuclear weapons with their long-term radiation effects. However, since most use of weapons in war will be defended as being necessary to achieve military objectives, the subtle and unremarkable inclusion of the word 'unnecessary' is sufficient to justify the use of any of these weapons in appropriate cicumstances.

Again, the rules of conduct of Great Britain's Council of Engineering Institutions use the word 'needlessly' with rather similar effect. The rules specify that the engineer 'shall not do anything, or permit anything under his authority to be done . . . [to] needlessly pollute the environment'. While it may not be the case that British engineers are in fact deliberately polluting the environment, the introduction of the word 'needlessly' is striking in these rules because of the implication that the actual pollution of the environment – on the face of it something much more serious than risks to individuals or property – may be justified as the necessary means to some practical end.

The utilitarian position, then, is a position that enthrones necessity in place of principle. But any reference to necessity essentially involves appeal to the facts, whether facts about what particular courses of action are likely to achieve or psychological facts about human attitudes to those effects. But facts do not finally determine values, although it may be important to take account of them in formulating moral judgements. It is always possible to respond morally in a different way to what is the case or to what will be the case if a certain course of action is chosen. The more generously the principle of maximizing happiness is interpreted, the easier it becomes to deny the obligation to aim for it. Perhaps, in the face of arguments about utility, I simply obstinately insist that I have promised to do something else or that what is proposed would not be fair. Or perhaps I prefer my own personal happiness to the promotion of the best outcome for all concerned. Even a description of a world in which poverty and disease have been abolished and nations live in harmony with their neighbours is no more than this – a mere description. Something else is needed to create an argument from which it follows that I should do something to bring it about.

The Worm-eaten Ladders of Expediency

Why should such a flawed theory – a theory to which there are so many practical and logical objections – have so many advocates? For utilitarianism is perhaps the most influential of all contemporary theories, widely presupposed in philosophy, politics, law and economics. It is tacitly assumed by many to be incontrovertible as a theory of social and international morality – and is currently often taken for granted in relation to issues of public choice and social policy. Despite its defects, it is the favoured child of many Western philosophers, particularly those working in such applied areas as medical ethics, educational theory or the environment.[10]

The explanation for this widespread appeal can only be a dismissive impatience, a collective tiredness with morality – and perhaps, too, a generalized reluctance to take it seriously. And yet this repudiation of the moral is surprising in view of recent history. It shows the inadequacies of the collective human memory, which still seems unable to learn from even the most searing experiences. One of the most eloquent and compelling statements of this point of view was put forward just after the end of the Second World War by the novelist Arthur Koestler. Koestler's talk took as its focus Captain Scott's decision in the 1912 Antarctic expedition to try to save Petty Officer Evans, who had become ill and so a burden to the party – a decision which eventually contributed to the tragic outcome. Koestler presented Scott's choice as a choice between two roads: the road of expediency, in which Evans is thrown to the wolves in the hope of saving the remaining four members of the party, and the road of respect for the individual and the rejection of violence. Drawing a parallel with events in the dark period through which the world had just lived – the politics of appeasement, the Nazi atrocities and finally the atomic bombing of Hiroshima and Nagasaki – Koestler wrote that 'the logic of expediency leads to the atomic disintegration of morality – a kind of radioactive decay of all values'. He ended his talk with these words: 'I am not sure whether what the philosophers call "ethical absolutes" exist, but I am sure we have to act as if they existed. Ethics must be freed from its utilitarian chains; words and deeds must again be judged by their own merits, and not as mere makeshifts to serve distant and nebulous aims. These worm-eaten ladders lead to no paradise.'[11]

Interlude

There was a pause when I finished. Panhedon looked slightly embarrassed at the note of emotion that had come into my voice towards the end of my account of utilitarian theory as it prevails in the part of the world from which I had come, and he was clearly not inclined to be won over by any of the arguments I had advanced. In fact, many of the points that I had presented as problems he continued to see as virtues of a point of view he recognized as being virtually identical to his own. I do not think he would have hesitated long over the fate of Evans, nor yet over my hypothetical coma patient. And the idea that the state could not rightly just help itself to useful parts of dead bodies was, frankly, simply puzzling to him.

Instead of taking issue with me directly, though, he looked at me fairly dispassionately – in a way, indeed, as if I were a laboratory specimen – and said, 'That is just your opinion, and I can find you as many opinions as you have arguments. But let me introduce you to my friend Polydox. He has made a special study of the varieties of ethical opinion in our society and amongst the inhabitants of some settlements bordering our territory. You may be surprised to know that even here we have deviant individuals, subcultures and nonconforming groups. Polydox makes no attempt to pass judgement on any of them because he believes that everyone's opinion on right and wrong, good and bad, is as valuable as anyone else's. Naturally, I don't go along with that, since I believe that problems of ethics can be resolved by just the kind of theory we have been discussing, and I have no time for the half-baked ideas of the ignorant. But, by all means, hear what Polydox has to say. You may find it interesting.'

Notes to Chapter 3

1   Bentham, *Introduction to the Principles of Morals and Legislation*.

2   Ibid., ch. 10. sec. XL, n. 2.

3   See, for example, Singer, *Practical Ethics*. For full discussion of obligations of this kind, see chapter 12, pp. 213–16.

4   See chapter 12, pp. 219–22, for discussion of ethical issues concerning animals.

5   Mill, *Utilitarianism*, p. 59.

6   Nozick, describes an imaginary 'experience machine' for realizing this possibility in *Anarchy, State and Utopia*, pp. 42–5.

7   Moore, *Principia Ethica*. See in particular ch. 6, 'The ideal'.

8   For general background to this period and the influence of Moore, see Rosenbaum, *The Bloomsbury Reader*.

9   Article 23(e) of the Hague Convention No. IV (1907).

10   Anscombe, 'Modern moral philosophy'.

11   Koestler, 'The dilemma of our times'.

4

Relativist Mutations

Fourth Conversation

Polydox: I find it quite puzzling that anyone should think there is just one answer to ethical questions. In my experience, opinions about right and wrong, about good and bad, differ. And since they differ, I do not think, like my friend Panhedon, that there is just one good to be pursued, or one right action to be done in any particular situation. On the contrary, there are as many right actions as there are people who think them right.

Traveller: I do understand what you are saying, Polydox. For there is a very well-known story in the part of the world I come from that goes back to ancient times. It is an account by the historian Herodotus of an occasion when some Greek visitors were summoned to the court of King Darius of Persia. It seems that he asked them what he would have to give them to persuade them to eat the dead bodies of their fathers. They said that no money in the world could persuade them to do that. He then brought in the members of a tribe called the Callatians whose custom was in fact to eat their parents' dead bodies, and he asked them how much he would have to give them to persuade them to burn them. They were horrified and asked Darius not even to talk about anything so dreadful.

Polydox: I must make a note of that story. It certainly fits with my observations. So if you ask me about *duty* or obligation, I would simply say that everyone ought to do what they think they ought to do. I might add that I'm a firm believer in toleration. I'm against dogmatism in any form, and so I believe in accepting, indeed supporting, the choices other people make.

Traveller: I'm afraid I don't find that very clear.

Polydox: What do you mean?

Traveller: Well, your first point underlies what we in our society would call pluralism. You are pointing out that ideals of right and wrong, good and bad, vary from place to place and even from person to person.

Polydox: Yes. That's so.

Traveller: Well, many people would describe that as a kind of cultural or descriptive relativism – although, admittedly, calling it relativism could add to the confusion – pluralism is really a less ambiguous term. But who could deny that, up to a point, people's opinions do in fact differ? If I were in any doubt, my own position here in your society would be enough to convince me of the opposite!

Polydox: I'm glad you take such a reasonable view.

Traveller: Yes, but then I see that you go on to infer what some of our philosophers have called *normative* relativism – it is this for which I would reserve the simple term 'relativism'. But whatever name it goes under, it amounts to the claim that these different ideals and norms are all equally valid – and thus that individuals ought in fact to follow the practice of their group.

Polydox: Well, that is indeed my opinion.

Traveller: But that is not quite what you said to me a moment ago. What about someone who does *not* share the opinion of his group? You seemed to be suggesting that he should follow his *own* opinion.

Polydox: I suppose that *is* what I meant to say. That *is* what I meant by saying, 'everyone ought to do what they think they ought to do.'

Traveller: Well, it seems to me there is quite a difference between saying *that* and saying that people should do what the group they belong to thinks is right – between a relativism of individual opinion and a relativism of groups or cultures.

Polydox: That's an interesting point. I suppose, if pressed, I would have to opt for the first of those, after all.

Traveller: I am not sure it's quite as easy as that to avoid the difficulty. But there's another thing – a difficulty of a different sort. I can't help noticing that when you talk about your obligation to be tolerant, you seem to imply a rather more direct and substantial kind of obligation than your own theory allows – that is to say, an obligation that does not depend entirely on your state of mind at a particular time. I don't say that's necessarily a bad thing, but it's certainly worth noticing that on certain matters you don't seem to *mind* being a dogmatist.

Polydox: Well . . .

Traveller: But let's leave that for a moment, for I think I can see a third
claim behind what you are saying – it seems to be yet another kind
of relativism. Indeed, I believe I have heard it called 'meta-ethical'
relativism. It means that you think no one *theory* of ethics is better
than any other, and so that there can be no general rules for sound
reasoning in morals. You are a moral sceptic!

Polydox: I don't know if you think that a rude term – but anyway, yes.
I am happy to go along with it.

Traveller: I see. But in that case, can we look more closely at the way you
get to that position?

Moral Relativism

It is indisputable that people debate matters of right and wrong and of good
and bad. It is also indisputable that views may sometimes be 'localized'.
That is, in some places at some times, and amongst some groups but not
others, an opinion will be settled or 'firmed up'. It may pass beyond
discussion and become a settled constant of that group or society. There are
societies, for example, where it is believed that honour must be vindicated
by the pursuit of the vendetta – killing uninvolved third parties to avenge
a wrong. In Britain, too, in the nineteenth century, as in some parts of the
world at the present day, public executions were thought the right and
appropriate way to deal with people who broke the law. And while sexual
behaviour has seldom been free from regulation in any human community,
some societies will accept polygamy and others insist on monogamy. The
ancient Spartans, it seems, admired the successful thief, despising only
cowardice, weakness, or lack of nerve – an attitude that is to be found today,
as well, in some urban subcultures, and is tacitly conveyed in some media
products – novels, films and plays.

The notion of pluralism, then, draws attention to the multiplicity of
beliefs and ideas. Because they recognize that opinions differ, many people
accept the moral relativist's view that there is no external or objective
measure of right and wrong. There is moral opinion, but it is always the
opinion *of* someone, or of some group or society. This makes for a problem,
of course, when people try to think of their *own* attitude to some difficult
issue – or when someone needs to make an ethical choice between one
course of action and another. For what is it they are wondering *about*? They
may *think* they are wondering what is the right thing to do, but according
to their own account, they can only be wondering about their own state

of mind – indeed, the useful but empty phrase 'exploring your own values' might have been invented just in order to cover this confusion.

It is hardly surprising, then, that people who hold such views go on to draw some conflicting conclusions. First of all, when thinking about *other* people's moral opinions, they seem to have a high respect for conscience, even if they do not use that term; for, however they describe it, they do believe that following conscience is always right. But then, secondly, as far as they themselves are concerned, they seem to draw the conclusion that they are only justified in holding their *own* opinions very weakly or tentatively. And because they see their own moral opinion as just one of a multiplicity of possible options, they are reluctant to attempt to give advice, or to express a view about other people's actions, even if they happen to be directly asked for an opinion.

But these ambivalent attitudes are hard to justify. In one sense, the advice to follow conscience cannot be faulted – that is, from the point of view of the individual concerned and from the point of view of attributing praise or blame to that individual. But whether it is in fact *right* to follow your conscience must, after all, depend on what your conscience tells you to do. Indeed, there is a kind of paradox here. Take the statement which most typically sums up the view that following conscience is always right:

'Everyone ought to do what they think they ought to do'

or, more briefly,

'Do what you think is right'.

People usually make the mistake of testing this principle only against other moral principles they are not too concerned about, or even regard as trivial. For example, many people think that lying is not necessarily or always wrong. So they will regard a principle like, 'Do not lie' as subsidiary to, 'Do what you think is right'. But if they were to take another principle as their test – for example, 'Do not commit genocide', or even 'Do not be judgmental' – they would be unlikely to judge *that* as taking second place to, 'Do what you think is right'. The paradox here is that if they continue to try to hold *that* principle as pre-eminent whilst holding to their strong belief that genocide or judgementalism is wrong, they will end up endorsing two contradictory statements: that, via the principle, 'Everyone ought to do what they think they ought to do', genocide is right, but that, taken independently of that principle, it is not.[1]

The situation is no better if it is a matter not of an individual judgement, but of the opinion of a group – perhaps, even, a cultural or religious minority. Suppose, for example, that there is a sect that believes in the ritual torture and killing of animals. The moral relativist may say that, while torturing animals is in general wrong, it is right, 'for the members of that sect.' Or if a cultural group favours female infanticide, the relativist may say, 'For the members of that culture female infanticide is right.' But the addition of the 'for *x*' in cases like these is strictly meaningless. 'Right for *x*' comes close to being a contradiction, or at least to what has been called an 'epistemological absurdity'.[2] For 'right' opens up a judgement to the world, while 'for *x*' immediately restricts its scope. In some contexts this makes sense – it may be obligatory, for example, for Roman Catholic nuns in a closed order to remain unmarried, but, if so, this is a special duty for a limited group of people, and the nature of the group explains the duty. It is not a matter of the accidents of time and place. On the contrary, it is actually a universal duty applying to anyone who chooses to become a member of that group.

This differs from the moral relativism that makes 'right' an internal matter for any arbitrarily defined group. For this kind of group relativism comes very close to the discredited view that right is whatever the majority thinks is right – discredited because saying that '*x* is right' means '*x* is what the majority approve', like other forms of ethical subjectivism, changes the nature of an ethical dispute from a matter of moral judgement to a judgement of fact. It also makes *moral* disagreement impossible, since the facts in question in every dispute turn out to be facts about people's attitudes. Indeed, the cultural or group relativist *must*, in a sense, embrace the view that right is what the majority thinks is right, because if, as a member of a cultural group, I think that what is right is what the group believes is right, I can find out what that is only by counting heads. There is no room for private dissent or deviance here.

A comparison with matters of fact makes it clearer what is at issue. For it is easier to see that the existence of different opinions, some of them wrong, does not rule out objectivity in the case of empirical truth. The fact that people once believed – and some people perhaps do now believe – that the sun moved round the earth, does not mean that there is in fact any reasonable doubt about the matter. Someone may, of course, point out that belief in the geocentric hypothesis – that the earth is the centre of the universe – is a feature of culture and period. This is true. But nothing of scientific significance follows from it – certainly nothing at all that relates to the arrangement of the physical universe. So when the philosopher John Mackie (1917–81) argues for moral scepticism on the grounds that our moral judgements depend on cultural facts (actual ways of living), it can harmlessly be conceded that our moral opinions do in fact owe a lot to our environment and upbringing, including economic, cultural and religious influences.³ But the fact is that this is true of *all* our opinions, not just our moral opinions. All our beliefs are subject to these influences.

Moral Dilemmas

This progression from the possibility of moral disagreement, via ethical pluralism to relativism, is a common assumption. The problems are illustrated in some remarks of the Austrian philosopher Ludwig Wittgenstein (1889–1951), in conversation with his friend and colleague Rush Rhees. Rhees had asked Wittgenstein to comment on the moral dilemma of a husband who was obliged to choose between his marriage and a career in cancer research. Wittgenstein replied:

> 'Someone might ask whether the treatment of such a question in Christian ethics is *right* or not. I want to say that this question does not make sense. The man who asks it might say: 'Suppose I view his problem with a different ethics – perhaps Nietzsche's – and I say: "No, it is not clear that he must stick to her; on the contrary . . . and so forth." Surely one of the two answers must be the right one. It must be possible to decide which of them is right and which is wrong.'
>
> But we do not know what this decision would be like – how it would be determined, what sort of criteria would be used, and so on. Compare saying that it must be possible to decide which of two standards of accuracy is the right one. We do not even know what a person who asks this question is after.'⁴

But in reflecting on Wittgenstein's observation, it is important to notice that the *fact* of conflict, of difference of moral opinon, does not carry sceptical consequences. So, for example, the statement, 'Christianity classifies torture as wrong' is simply a statement of fact, capable of being settled by reference to authorities on the content of Christian ethics. It is important, too, to distinguish the level of conflict between *theories* of ethics from that of substantial conflict at the level of ethical *judgement*. Compare, for example,

'torture is wrong'

with

'the claim that torture is wrong is no more "valid" than the claim that it is not wrong'.

In making the first statement, I am actually committing myself to it, and conveying to the world my belief in its validity. If I immediately go on to question its validity, I am implicitly withdrawing my claim. To try to insist on maintaining it and at the same time asserting the statement about validity is to fall victim to another kind of epistemological absurdity. If I can make the second type of statement at all, it will be from the position of moral philosopher, or ethical anthropologist, not as a moral agent. Even so, to do that I would need to occupy a position it is in fact impossible for me to occupy – one outside the world of interacting human beings, beyond the community of moral agents. Wittgenstein is, after all, right on this point. It *is* like asking which of two standards of accuracy is the right one, and the question could only be answered by someone using a third overarching, more comprehensive standard of accuracy – something that would hardly be possible except for a god or superior being. It would have to be made, in other words, from what has more recently been called 'the view from nowhere' and we ourselves are inevitably 'somewhere'.[5]

A different analogy – a matter of factual dispute – makes it clearer what is at issue. It may be difficult to tell when a long way from a mountain-range whether two mountains are the same height. It may not be so easy even when nearby. Now suppose that geographers from two neighbouring countries disagree on the matter. Here it is clear that while the rival geographers no doubt deserve respect and courtesy as hard-working and conscientious individuals, there is no need to accord equal respect to the views that they hold, for one view is undoubtedly nearer to the truth than the other – there *is* a fact of the matter. The same is true in the case of many ethical disputes. But it is easier to isolate the steps that feature in the geographers' example, than in the parallel argument in ethics:

1 the recognition of the existence of rival *factions*, that is, actual people who do not agree with each other;
2 the recognition of the existence of rival *views*, that is, abstract positions that are incompatible with each other;
3 the positing of a right to respect owed to the *holders* of the various disputed positions on a personal basis, that is, the political and social principle of toleration;
4 the claim that the conflicting *views* that they hold have equal standing and an equal claim to be considered valid, and therefore deserve equal respect.

The fourth step is often mistakenly seen as a corollary of the third, but in fact there is no reason to treat with deference ideas or claims that are false or misleading. (This is simply to emphasize the first rather than the second part of the statement attributed to the French satirical writer Voltaire (1694–1778), 'I disapprove of what you say, but I will defend to the death your right to say it.') Nevertheless, it is this sequence of propositions that maps out the familiar progression via the principle of toleration from factual pluralism to an essentially incoherent relativism.

Ethical relativism has been defined as 'the assertion that two people or groups may hold contradictory views without either being mistaken.'[6] As such, it appears to make moral conflict impossible. Nevertheless, there are many *apparent* conflicts, for life frequently does present the kind of situation envisaged by Wittgenstein. People *are* sometimes faced by moral dilemmas; they do sometimes feel themselves subject to the pressure of two conflicting moral requirements. Two incompatible courses may seem to be equally morally binding on one person, or two different individuals may each believe they have a moral obligation in circumstances in which it is impossible that both actions could be performed. There is a conflict between the generally accepted principle that 'ought' implies 'can' and the supposition that someone may have a duty to do action A and a duty to do action B when it is not possible to do both. A classic case of this is where two children are in danger, but only one can be rescued. To choose to save one is to fail to save the other.[7] A further dimension is that very often both courses of action may be morally bad, and yet it seems that one or other *must* be chosen. For this reason, the problem is often described as the problem of Dirty Hands.[8] Whatever choice is made, it leaves behind a residue of guilt and regret.

It would be easy, then, to take the question of whether moral dilemmas occur as a factual dispute to be settled by producing examples, of which there are many. Perhaps the most famous moral dilemma in recent philosophical literature was that of the young man who, during the Second World War, came to consult the French Existentialist philosopher Jean-Paul Sartre as to whether he should leave his mother, who had lost both her husband and her other son, and leave the country in order to join the Free French Forces, or whether he should stay, doing what seemed to him might be his duty as a son, but ignoring his patriotic duty to participate in the war effort. Sartre used this example to support his own philosophical view that there are no right answers: that the young man could make one choice in this situation; someone else in the same circumstances could do the opposite and be no more and no less right or wrong. This is in contrast to the views of many philosophers, not least Aristotle and Kant, who hold that, in the words of one commentator, 'the best moral theory must show either that moral requirements never really conflict or that such conflicts are always resolvable by finding the one right action.'[9]

But must holding that moral judgement should be consistent across cases really mean there can be *no* moral dilemmas? To answer this question, it is necessary to distinguish the formal concept of a moral dilemma from the everyday concept of a difficult, possibly agonizing, choice. It is this second claim that is undeniable. People do find themselves sometimes at a testing moral crossroads. But difficult choices are not necessarily genuine moral dilemmas. That is to say, choosing between options which are not morally equal is not, strictly speaking, a *dilemma*; on the other hand, though it may be emotionally traumatizing, choosing between moral obligations that are indisputably of equal weight is not a *moral* problem, any more than choosing between two paths of equal length to a desired destination is a mathematical problem. If Buridan's ass had been capable of grasping this point, it might not have starved to death between two absolutely equal bales of hay. The moral challenge in such situations – and, indeed, the reason for the moral agony – is that of assessing whether the two choices are indeed of equal weight. If not, then necessarily one answer, or one solution, is the morally right course of action.

Emotivism, Postmodernism and Other Forms of Subjectivism

The view that there can be insoluble dilemmas is a natural consequence of holding some kind of subjectivist account of moral reasoning. Subjectivist accounts of moral reasoning have been influential in the contemporary period partly as a result of such diverse influences as Marxism and Existentialism, but also because of anti-metaphysical, science-oriented tendencies in analytic philosophy. In the earlier part of the the twentieth century, the ethical theory known as emotivism made each individual person the arbiter of right and wrong; at the century's close, various forms of postmodernism – sociological, literary, feminist, philosophical – identified 'standpoints' as collective perceptions by the 'others' in society. As Richard Rorty put it , there are 'an indefinite plurality of standpoints' in which 'truth is made rather than found'.[10] At the same time, the postmodernist tendency favours supplanting the dominance of the old ethnic and patriarchal 'standpoints' with new ones – a rainbow alliance of those who have until now been the 'others' in society.

But this kind of power analysis of morality is no new phenomenon. Indeed, a view of this sort is recorded as one of the first philosophical discussions of the Western tradition. In the *Republic*, Plato (428–348 BC) gives an account of a conversation between Socrates and Thrasymachus, a philosophical opponent who insists that right is what is in the interest of the strongest in society, or at least that it is what they *believe* to be in their interest and are able to enforce by law.[11] Some of the difficulties in Thrasymachus' position are a result of his claim that moral judgement reduces to factual claims of one sort or another. Straight subjectivism of this sort equates '*x* is right' with some person or group's attitude to *x*, and so is always vulnerable to this objection. Subjectivism may take various forms. It may define '*x* is right' as 'I approve of *x*', or as 'My society approves of *x*' or as 'The majority approves of *x*'. But these are all factual statements. The emotive theory of ethics avoids *this* difficulty by claiming that to say '*x* is right' is not to make a statement about someone's psychological state. Indeed, it is not to make a statement at all, but simply to *express* an attitude and also, perhaps, to try to evoke it in others.[12]

A. J. Ayer summed up the theory in a brief statement in his book *Language, Truth and Logic*: 'We shall set ourselves to show that in so far as statements of value are significant, they are ordinary "scientific" statements; and that in so far as they are not scientific, they are not in the literal sense significant, but are simply expressions of emotion which can be neither true nor false.'[13]

Ayer presented the theory as a deduction from logical positivism, which is a general philosophical position characterized by the fact that it limited meaningful statements to two categories:

1 analytic statements – statements which are true in virtue of the meaning of the terms involved and so, if true, are truisms;
2 empirical statements, which are defined by the fact that some sense-observation is relevant to establishing whether they are true or false.

This latter feature led to the underlying theory being described as verificationism ('the verification theory of meaning') since, more loosely, it was the theory that whether or not a statement was meaningful depended on the possibility of verifying it, or even that its meaning *was* the way in which it could be verified or 'cashed out'. If there was no conceivable way to verify it, a statement would be considered literally meaningless. But ethical statements are not analytic and cannot be empirically verified; this means that they, along with metaphysics, must be classed by the emotivist as meaningless. However, since ethical language clearly has a use, it was not suggested that it be abandoned altogether. Instead, Ayer explained:

'We begin by admitting that the fundamental ethical concepts are unanalysable . . . We say that the reason why they are unanalysable is that they are mere pseudo-concepts. The presence of an ethical symbol in a proposition adds nothing to its factual content. Thus if I say to someone, 'You acted wrongly in stealing that money,' I am not stating anything more than if I had simply said, 'You stole that money.' In adding that this action is wrong I am not making any further statement about it. I am simply evincing my moral disapproval of it . . . But in every case in which one would commonly be said to be making an ethical judgement, the function of the relevant ethical word is purely 'emotive.' It is used to express feeling about certain objects, but not to make any assertion about them.[14]

Ayer acknowledged the debt this theory owed to David Hume (1711–76).[15] Hume lived in an age when philosophers disputed the roles of sentiment and reason in morals, and in his own theory favoured the former. As he put it: "'Tis not contrary to reason to prefer the destruction of the whole world to the scratching of my little finger.'[16] Consistently with this, he argued that facts and values should be kept apart – it is not possible to derive an 'ought' from an 'is'. Similarly, for the contemporary emotivist, a moral judgement – a value judgement is the term preferred within the emotive theory – is not an addition to a description of some event, but rather a verdict on it. This means that two people could agree on all the facts and still disagree about the relevant ethical judgement. But while it is true that it adds nothing to the description of a brutal murder to add 'and it was wrong' – that judgement is a conclusion from the facts, not an extra fact – the theory is open to many objections.

To begin with, it is a fallacy to suppose there can be moral rules that apply only to oneself, but emotivism as an ethical theory seems to imply there can be duties that apply to just one person in one situation; it is a unique-instance morality, which, no less than the older forms of subjectivism, turns ethical disagreement into a dispute about taste. It seems to make moral conviction a fickle and changeable condition; nor does it require any consistency in the application of moral categories.

It also *exaggerates* the emotive function of moral language, failing to draw any clear line between that and mere propaganda. Moral judgement is often a matter of cool assessment rather than hasty reaction, but the term 'emotive' fails to give this element the weight it deserves. Indeed, moral judgement often has more to do with attitude than with emotion, and so it was a weakness of the emotive theory that it tried to replace the traditional subjectivist emphasis on attitudes, which are more secure and longer term than emotions, with an emphasis on emotive utterances.[17]

While its philosophical roots are different, contemporary postmodernism could be said to follow the original thrust of emotivism to its logical conclusion.[18] But postmodernism goes beyond this analysis to regard intellectual assent to a proposition as submission to the social power of its author. It portrays ideas, arguments and beliefs as pawns in the power-struggles of human beings. This is an idea that flourishes in many sophisticated forms. Sociologists, in particular, stress the flow and succession of ideas and theories. But a remark that the philosopher W. D. Ross (1877–1971) made in the 1930s is still relevant as far as this current controversy is concerned: 'There are not merely so many moral codes which can be described and whose vagaries can be traced to historical causes; there is a system of moral truth, as objective as all truth must be, which, and whose implications, we are interested in discovering; and from the point of view of this, the genuine ethical problem, the sociological enquiry is simply beside the mark.'[19]

The sociological stance, however, has widespread appeal, and feminists, too, have joined in rejecting overarching accounts of human history: of narratives like those of Hegel and Marx that claim to offer a comprehensive account of the unfolding of the course of human history. Stressing, again, the particular and the contingent, Nancy Hartsock writes that there is only what is 'ad hoc, contextual, plural and limited' while, according to another feminist writer, Susan Bordo, objectivity, foundations and neutral judgements are 'pretensions and illusions', now exposed by political (rather than philosophical) movements which emerged in the 1960s and 1970s 'not only to make a claim to the legitimacy of marginalized cultures, unheard voices, suppressed narratives, but also to expose the perspectivity and partiality of the official accounts.'[20]

Against this, two problems emerge. One is what might be called 'The Case of the Disappearing Subject'. Postmodernism provides no place from which to survey the world, no position from which the correspondence or otherwise of our ideas with reality may be judged. And yet, the knowledge–power analysis associated with Michel Foucault (1926–84), with Rorty or with feminism, is entirely dependent on being able to locate a source of judgement or a determiner of knowledge. In other words, the power analysis itself depends upon the ability to locate, define and recognize a knowing subject. Of course, the point of this analysis is to fractionalize, to suggest that there are only particular persons, located in particular times and places. But here a second problem appears, which might be called 'The Puzzle of the Preference for Particularity'. For the focus of the postmodernist attack is the individual as construed by liberal philosophy and politics. This 'individual' is held to be suspect because of its very universality – it is the individual abstracted from all the particularities of time and place, as well as from individuating features such as race, sex and physical and mental endowment. However, this attack is based on a very widespread misunderstanding. For the individual of liberal political theory is not a universal in the sense intended by these detractors – not a transparent, featureless entity – but on the contrary, the ultimate particular, always set in contrast to the state, the political totality or the source of power. Not to be defined by membership of any group, this 'individual' is in the end a list of names – not an infinite or endless list, but one which could only be exhausted by enumerating all the human inhabitants, past and present, of the world.

As far as feminism in particular is concerned, the postmodernist liberation was a false dawn, since if there is no universal man, there can be no universal woman, either. So the basic rationale of the (political) feminist movement drops away. If the only thing held in common is gender, this itself becomes submerged under differences of race, wealth, class, religion and education.

Tradition and Religion

But if radical subjectivism in its various mutating forms is to be rejected, what can provide a ground for the objectivist theory to which it must implicitly yield ground? Could some particular tradition provide a ground for morality? In defence of tradition, T. S. Eliot perspicuously wrote: 'When morals cease to be a matter of tradition and orthodoxy . . . and when each man is to elaborate his own, the *personality* becomes a thing of alarming importance.'[21] It is true that egotistical personality may seem a worse hazard than conformity to mere current practice. But must morality slavishly follow in the wake of whatever tradition is dominant in a particular place at a particular time, or are there some certainties or convictions that stand the test of time as well as the test of place and culture? If there are, then it should be possible to place differing traditions side by side, subjecting the traditions themselves to moral scrutiny – an approach that cannot itself, of course, provide a basis for morality in terms of tradition. To try to ground morality on an unappraisable tradition is once again to tread the borders of moral relativism.

So can religion provide a basis? The standard response of the modern secular philosopher to this question is that religion itself cannot provide the answer because it must itself, in the end, depend on an ultimate moral judgement – that of the goodness of God who is held to be the final authority for morality. If this argument is correct, it means that the attempt to found morality on religion is essentially circular. But it is significant that the major contemporary religions are closely associated with systems of morality, suggesting that this may be a spurious logic based on a misunderstanding of the nature of religious commitment. Religion is as much a matter of 'following' as 'believing' and its ethical code is at least as important an aspect of a religion as intellectual assent to the details of a creed.

Nevertheless, we live in a divided world and in societies divided by cultural and religious differences, which are a major source of conflict and alienation. So if answers to moral questions can be found which do not *depend* upon a particular religious perspective, but are capable of cutting across cultural and religious divisions, these will be more effective both socially and politically in inspiring moral commitment. They are also likely to be ultimately more personally rewarding for the individual, who will have used his or her own reasoning capacity to arrive at solutions to moral problems, rather than taking the short-cut of mere acceptance of extraneous authority. Ockham's Razor applies here, too – interpretable in this case as the principle of not pointlessly increasing the number of claims that need to be accepted before moral life is possible.[22] So if a basis for morality can be found which does not require belief in metaphysical entities and difficult and complex doctrines outside its direct concern, this is to be preferred to seeking a basis in religious doctrine – even though, as a matter of fact, most of the world's main faiths lead to common ethical norms and even though it is true that, for those whose religious faith is strong, their ethical life, too, will be secure.

Toleration

Instead of leading down the route to relativism, the recognition of pluralism in its factual sense, the appreciation of cultural and ethical variation, can lead in the best case to the valuing of toleration of people, their ideas and ways of living, where these are compatible with the way of life of which the spirit of toleration is itself a manifestation. The ideal of a tolerant society – one involving respect for individuals, their wishes and their freedom – is deeply embedded in Western cultures and traditions. Whether expressed in ethical, social, or politico-legal terms, the principle of toleration recommends minimizing interference by one person or group with the beliefs, statements or conduct of another. It is especially associated with the idea of a private domain and with drawing a distinction between the public and the private spheres. This distinction was most famously expressed by J. S. Mill in his classic essay, *On Liberty*:

The only part of the conduct of anyone for which he is amenable to society, is that which concerns others . . . Over himself, over his own mind and body, the individual is sovereign.[23]

Mill's defence of an autonomous private sphere led to a long and continuing debate about the limits of tolerance.[24] The origins of the debate, however, lie in ancient Athens, when the statesman Pericles addressed the people of Athens about freedom of behaviour and conduct:

'There is no exclusiveness in our public life, and in our private intercourse. We are not suspicious of one another, nor angry with our neighbour if he does what he likes; we do not put on sour looks at him which, though harmless, are not pleasant.'[25] This freedom and diversity was, as it happens, exactly what made Plato a critic of Athenian democracy, although the terms of his criticism might strike many people as an attractive portrait of Athenian democracy. Slaves and women, he said, begin to take themselves too seriously, and even 'the very dogs behave as if the proverb "like mistress, like maid" applied to them; and the horses and donkey catch the habit of walking down the street with all the dignity of free men.'[26]

Almost two millennia passed before anything like this conception of liberty found philosophical expression again, and this was in the context of different preoccupations – the wars of religion and religious persecutions of sixteenth-century Europe. Certain arguments were formulated then which continue to have force: the argument that truth may emerge over time; the conviction that truth is bound to triumph in the end; the recognition that it can never, in any case, be imposed by force, and the belief that toleration should be extended to holders of views that are wrong as well as of those which turn out to be true.[27]

So toleration is itself an important moral principle. But this makes it even more important that it should not be confused with moral relativism. Where ideas are concerned, in tolerating, one may well condemn. For even a strong principle of toleration only means that one should not interfere; it does not mean judging the ideas or behaviour in question to be right. Indeed, the very use of the term 'toleration' tends to imply that the tolerator thinks that the behaviour or the view is wrong.

What do Humans have in Common?

But is the conception of difference on which moral relativism is based exaggerated? It has become fashionable to dismiss as 'essentialist' the idea that there is a core of universal values which transcend cultures and other differences – to denigrate the humanistic enlightenment tradition. But anthropologists have long been interested in seeking out common factors in the ethical beliefs of the many 'tribes' of humankind. The writer and anthropologist Clyde Kluckhohn, in an influential article in the 1950s, wrote that 'Human beings generalize as well as discriminate. The human parade has many floats, but when one strips off the cultural symbolism, the ethical standards are akin.'[28] Kluckhohn described this idea of common ethical standards as the idea of a pan-human morality. He wrote:

> While the specific manifestations of human nature vary between cultures and between individuals in the same culture, human nature is universal. All value systems have to make some of the same concessions to the natural world of which human nature is a part. Some needs and motives are so deep and so generic that they are beyond the reach of argument: pan-human morality expresses and supports them.[29]

As Kluckhohn pointed out, then, every culture has a concept of murder, distinguishing this from execution, killing in war, and other 'justifiable homicides', while notions of incest, the regulation of sexual behaviour, and mutual obligations between parents and children are universal. There are other features, too, to be found in virtually all societies: language, with underlying common elements of structure; art, music, dance; the concept and duties of kinship, and certain broad features of universal human experience including war, family relationships, and religious belief and observance. There are also what Kluckhohn called 'universal sentiments' such as love, jealousy, respect and the need for respect.

Philosophers, too, from Aristotle and the Stoics onward, have endorsed the idea of a common humanity. Hume expressed the view that human beings are much the same in all times and places. Jean-Jacques Rousseau (1712–78), too, took this as a basic premise in his political philosophy. But despite the similarities between societies – despite, too, the common *external* features of human experience, the shared global environment, and the constants of birth, illness, ageing and death, it would be a mistake to insist that rational consensus is inevitable. This would in any case be a factual claim, in part psychological and in part sociological. What does follow from the idea of a common humanity is that rational consensus is *possible*. From a philosophical perspective, confidence in this possibility is simply a belief that people as independent individual thinkers and agents *could* reach shared conclusions on matters of morals; that they can in the meantime construct positions and argue for them in the face of opposition or conflicting opinions, secure in the conviction that some positions are better-grounded than others, some conclusions more suspect than others. This grounding must ultimately lie in a fuller understanding of human nature – an understanding, that is, that human potential is more likely to be fulfilled under some conditions, and subject to some rules, rather than others.

It is here that the link between facts and values is to be found – in the facts of human biology, psychology, history and of political and social organization, which provide a clue at least as to what interests humans might agree to share, and what restrictions and limitations of action they might be willing to accept. It is clear, for example, that those practices or principles will not commend themselves widely that limit human potential, first biologically – by imposing a threat to life and health – then culturally, spiritually and intellectually. The facts that are of most direct and immediate ethical relevance here are both simple and indisputable: humans are first and foremost biological entities; but their consequent need for food and shelter and for conditions in which they can reproduce and raise their offspring, means that the realm of the biological extends immediately into the realm of the economic, social and political.

Far from being a suggestion emanating only now from our contemporary culture, the perception of a common humanity as a fruitful starting-point for moral and political reflection was already present in the Stoic notion of natural law, which first related morality to the conception of a human being as such – neither citizen nor foreigner, male nor female, slave nor free. But the idea was forged in the fire of awareness of cultural variation in custom and convention. It carried with it two further important notions: first, the idea of moral values as transcendent – as by-passing the particularities of social and political arrangements and of temporal and geographical location; and secondly, the ideal of allotting primacy to the ethical in human affairs. Today, the successor of the notion of natural law is to be found in the notion of human rights, with which it shares these two important characteristics.

Interlude

❝ Polydox heard me out with polite attention. Indeed, it may well have been more than politeness, for I do believe he was rather keen on arguments and ideas, and I suspected that he would go away and try to take to pieces the arguments I had put to him, to see if he could preserve something from the wreckage of what he had obviously begun to recognize were rather uncoordinated and incoherent ideas.

Not, of course, that that would inhibit him from putting them forward to anyone who would listen. That is the strange thing about relativists. I reflected. They are always trying to convert other people to their point of view. But towards the end of our conversation, someone else had arrived, although so far she had not intervened to express an opinion. This was Physia, one of Egoge's twin sisters. A woman of calm yet imposing appearance, she expressed her views firmly, but listened with every appearance of interest to my own observations. I had already heard that she did not share her older sister's views, and indeed she was nodding her agreement at some of my last remarks.

Notes to Chapter 4

1   This argument is presented in more detail in 'An ethical paradox', ch. 9 of Almond, *Moral Concerns*.

2   The term 'epistemological absurdity' was used by A. D. Woozley in Phillips Griffiths, *Knowledge and Belief*, to describe a statement like '*x* is true but I don't believe it is.' Both claims are independent, and so, from the point of view of logic, they could both be true. But it would be absurd to assert both.

3   Mackie, *Ethics*, p. 49.

4   Rhees, 'Some developments in Wittgenstein's view of ethics', pp. 17–26.

5   See Nagel, *The View from Nowhere*.

6   Taylor, 'Social science and ethical relativism', p. 32.

7   Judith Wagner De Cew discusses the dilemma featured in the film *Sophie's Choice* in 'Moral conflicts and ethical relativitism'.

8   From the play by J.-P. Sartre, *Les Mains sales*, in which a political leader betrays his friends for the sake of their cause.

9   Sinnott-Armstrong, *Moral Dilemmas*.

10 Rorty, *Contingency, Irony and Solidarity*, p. 51.

11 Plato, *Republic*, Book 1.

12 Emotivism was associated in the United States with C. L. Stevenson, whose work took as its focus the analysis of 'good', and in Britain with A. J. Ayer who gave attention to the analysis of sentences containing the words 'right' and 'wrong'.

13 Ayer, *Language, Truth and Logic*, pp. 102–3.

14 Ibid. pp. 107, 108.

15 Hume drew attention to two fundamental distinctions at the root of empiricism: between matters of fact and matters of logic or reason, and between statements of fact and normative (moral) assertions.

16 Hume, *Treatise of Human Nature*, II iii 3.

17 R. M. Hare's universal prescriptivism was a development of emotivism in that it recognized the dynamism of moral terms. In *The Language of Morals* Hare

had pointed out that even imperatives have a logic, but in his insistence that all prescriptions have an imperative element, he was placing himself in the subjectivist, non-cognitivist camp. In his later book, *Freedom and Reason*, Hare retained the element of personal choice or decision, but placed more emphasis on the rational aspect of the moral 'ought.' In particular he emphasized two essential characteristics: universalizability and prescriptivity. These views were further developed in *Moral Thinking* (1981).

In 'Moral arguments', Philippa Foot attacked the view of Hume, Stevenson, Ayer and Hare that moral conclusions cannot ultimately be proved by argument, but depend ultimately on a personal decision. On the contrary, she insisted, to refute a moral conclusion, you need to disprove the evidence on which it is based, and it is not the case that *any* evidence will do.

18 The roots of postmodernism lie in French philosophy from the mid-twentieth century on, while emotivism stems from the logical positivism current in Vienna in the 1920s and 1930s.

19 Ross, *The Right and the Good*, pp. 14–15.

20 Bordo, 'Feminism, Postmodernism and Gender Scepticism', pp. 136–7.

21 Eliot, *After Strange Gods*.

22 Ockham's Razor is a principle of parsimony in reasoning. It states, 'Do not multiply entities needlessly' – which suggests that it is better always to prefer a simpler explanation to one which is more complex.

23 Mill, *On Liberty*, p. 73.

24 Devlin, *The Enforcement of Morals*, and Hart, *Law, Liberty and Morality*.

25 Quoted in Bury, *History of Greece*, p. 404.

26 Plato, *Republic*, VIII, 562.

27 For a history of toleration, see Kamen, *The Rise of Toleration*.

28 Kluckhohn, 'Ethical Relativity – sic or non?' cited in Ladd, *Ethical Relativism*, p. 89.

29 Ibid., p. 93.

5

The Resort to Rights

Fifth Conversation

Physia: The thoughts you have just expressed will strike my friends and companions as very strange. And yet it is exactly the notion you describe as 'rights' that I have been pressing in my conversations with my older sister and also with my father who, I'm sorry to say, dismissed the idea as 'rambling idiocy'.

Traveller: I'm delighted to find someone who agrees with something I have to say! The notion we both have in mind, I suspect, is what people call 'justice' – something that is closely bound up with the idea of rights. But you have my sympathy. There are obviously few people here who would have any sort of feeling for either of these ideas.

Physia: Yes, even my twin sister Nomia, who comes closest to me in what she believes, says that if she were to allow the idea of what you describe as a right, it could only be as something artificial and man-made – the result of a common agreement amongst people to yield up some freedom of action in exchange for parallel protection from the actions of others.

Traveller: What exactly do you mean by that? What kind of freedom would be sacrificed?

Physia: Well, for example, the freedom to take from others, if you are strong enough, what you want for yourself. Nomia really shares the views of the rest of the family about what motivates human beings – that, as rational agents, they try to maximize their own satisfaction by yielding to others only what is necessary to secure their own needs or comforts. But she is prepared to concede that they may well decide that living in a community where laws are enforced is the best way to achieve this.

Traveller: I see. Then perhaps you would like to hear something about
   how that point of view has featured in my tradition, if only to see
   how your own views differ from it.
Physia: That would be very useful.

Is Morality Based on a Social Contract?

Is morality based on some kind of implicit or tacit agreement with everyone
else to secure a framework for social living from which everyone will
benefit, at the cost of only some small sacrifice of their own freedom action?
The idea that this is so goes back to ancient times. It is to be found very
clearly sketched out in Book II of Plato's *Republic*, where Glaucon, one of
Socrates' interlocutors, paints a simple picture of people coming together
to fulfil specialist functions – the cobbler to exchange the products of his
trade with the farmer for food, and so on. But this is not presented just as
a primitive economic theory. It is also offered as an explanation of the
origins of justice – of morality as the agreed rules for the ordering of a simple
society. Right and wrong, justice and injustice, are explained as the
creation of people who have formed the intention to live together in this
way for their mutual advantage. And as far as the young are concerned,
according to Glaucon and his brother Adeimantus, if people bring up their
children to follow the social conventions, it is only because they want them
to become rich and successful – not because they value justice for its own
sake.

But while the rudiments of the idea of a social contract were sketched
out in this early discussion, it was really only fully developed in modern
times, from the seventeenth century on. The modern conception was not
so much of individuals coming together as equals to form a contract
amongst themselves, as of the people, on one side, forming a contract with
their ruler or rulers on the other. The modern theory was intended to
explain why anyone should obey the commands of a ruler or the laws of
a state. It represented a break with prevailing assumptions, too, in seeking
to answer this question without reference to either religion or secular
authority.

Thomas Hobbes (1588-1679) found the answer to the question of
political obligation in the idea of individuals surrendering, once and for all,
their political will to an absolute sovereign, subject only to one proviso: that,
since the basis of the contract was self-interest, there could be no obligation
to surrender the freedom to resist an order for one's own death. Hobbes
described existence without law or morality – which he called the 'state of

nature' – as a 'war of every man against every man'. He pointed out, too, that even the strongest were subject to ambush, attack and murder. Hence, even the strongest had an interest in an ordered society. For another British philosopher of the period, John Locke (1632–1704), the social contract was not a single event, but rather a tacit and continuing one, constantly confirmed and re-confirmed by a person's willingness to remain within the borders of a particular country and to be governed by its particular set of laws – if they did not suit you, then you could and should move on.

Approaching the issue from a different perspective, which included a more generous conception of human nature, the Swiss philosopher Jean-Jacques Rousseau (1712–78) argued that the social contract was represented by a *process* – the democratic system of majority voting – which generated what he called the General Will. Rousseau believed that the outcome of the majority vote, even if it turned out to be the opposite decision to the one you had voted for, would reveal what you *really* wanted, as opposed to what you may have *thought* you wanted.

The early social-contract theorists wrote as though they might be describing a state of affairs that actually existed in the distant past, although it is possible that they simply preferred this more colourful way of presenting the idea. But present-day versions of the theory are carefully hypothetical rather than historical. A number of contemporary writers have produced theories of this sort to explain ethical and political obligation, and the debate continues in economic and philosophical discussion of games theory.[1]

Probably the best known modern version of the theory is that put forward by the Harvard philosopher John Rawls who, in *A Theory of Justice* (1971), developed an account of justice based on the idea of an imaginary or hypothetical contract amongst free and equal individuals. Rawls's method was designed to arrive at basic principles of justice from an impartial perspective. This impartiality would be achieved by means of a thought experiment in which the potential members of a society work out behind a 'veil of ignorance' basic principles for organizing life in the community they are about to share. The people in this 'original position' are assumed to be, first, self-interested and non-partisan, and secondly, rational. In other words, they are, in economists' terms, 'rational contractors'. The 'veil of ignorance' protects them from knowledge of the particular social conditions in which they will live their own lives – the contingencies of life which make one person rich and another poor, one advantaged in terms of family and upbringing and another disadvantaged; some talented, intelligent or strong, others mentally or physically more limited in what they can achieve.

The immediate result of the condition of ignorance is to create a presumption in favour of equality, for if you do not know the position you will occupy, Rawls believes that you will want to make sure that you will not be arbitrarily treated worse than anybody else. The way to guarantee that this will not happen, he suggests, would be to adopt two basic principles. The first of these is a principle of absolute equality as far as basic liberties are concerned; the second is a principle which allows for some qualification to the presumption of equality: it sanctions inequalities in the distribution of goods in society so long as the opportunity to become better-off than others is open to everyone, and so long as any differences that are allowed actually benefit the least well-off. Specifically:

1 the *Principle of Equal Liberty* holds that each person is to have an equal right to the most extensive total system of equal basic liberties that it is possible to guarantee to everyone;
2 the *Difference Principle* holds that social and economic inequalities are to be arranged so they are (a) of benefit to the least well-off members of society and (b) attached to jobs and positions open to everyone on the basis of equality of opportunity.

The first part of the Difference Principle is known as 'maximin'. It is the rule for choice under conditions of uncertainty and it means that the rational course of action in such circumstances is to identify the worst possible outcome in the case of each choice that is available to you, and then to choose the policy that results in the best of these 'worst outcomes'. This is to protect your interests in case you are unlucky enough to find yourself at the bottom rung of the ladder. If equality would leave you poorer than a system allowing vast inequalities of wealth, then you would naturally accept inequality in order to be a little better off. Or, put the other way round, no rational person concerned to maximize their own self-interest would insist on equality if that made them poorer than they otherwise need be. It is a distinctive feature of Rawls's system that the basic principles are not left to compete with each other for priority in particular situations; instead, it is agreed that the first principle takes priority over the second, but that the second half of the difference principle takes priority over the first. That is to say, Rawls believes that a rational person would first insist on personal liberty, and only then turn to questions of economic and social justice.

The primary goods which people in the original position are concerned to distribute fairly are not only income and wealth, but also rights and self-respect. This means that, while the social and political aspects of the two principles are important, so, too, are their ethical implications. Rawls writes:

> for one who understands and accepts the contract doctrine, the sentiment of justice is not a different desire from that to act on principles that rational individuals would consent to in an initial situation which gives everyone equal representation as a moral person. Nor is it different from wanting to act in accordance with principles that express men's nature as free and equal rational beings. The principles of justice answer to these descriptions and this fact allows us to give an acceptable interpretation to the sense of justice. In the light of the theory of justice we understand how the moral sentiments can be regulative in our life and have the role attributed to them by the formal conditions on moral principles. Being governed by these principles means that we want to live with others on terms that everyone would recognise as fair from a perspective that all would accept as reasonable. The ideal of persons cooperating on this basis exercises a natural attraction upon our affections.[2]

So Rawls sees familiar moral principles – principles in the ordinary sense – as following from the conception of justice which forms his starting-point. They are the principles of justice which 'free and rational persons concerned to further their own interests would accept in an initial position of equality.'[3] And these principles are given an extra justification in the fact that they fit harmoniously with human nature. They must also cohere with each other and with the two principles of justice. On the whole, Rawls believes that straightforward utilitarian calculation will be in conflict with this requirement; nor is it needed, for the contract argument itself is intended to provide a rational ground for morality and social justice, and one on which people will tend to agree. He writes: 'Thus our object should be to formulate a conception of justice which, however much it may call upon intuition, ethical or prudential, tends to make our considered judgements of justice converge.'[4] The outcome of such a process of reflection is called by Rawls 'reflective equilibrium' and he says that this state is reached after individuals have weighed various conceptions and have, as a result, either revised their judgement or decided to stick to their original convictions.

But can a hypothetical contract create actual obligations? Of course, the thought experiment is valuable in suggesting what the ideal moral rules might be. The question is only whether it can also justify adopting them. Rawls's own answer is modestly disclaiming: 'I do not hold that the conception of the original position is itself without moral force, or that the family of concepts it draws upon is ethically neutral. This question I simply leave aside.' He adds that his object was not to provide any self-evident conditions as a foundation for moral reasoning, only to show that 'the theory matches the fixed points of our considered convictions better than other familiar doctrines.'[5]

It seems, however, that if the idea of a contract is to succeed in providing a meeting-point between self-interest and moral obligation, this can only be on the basis of some assumptions that are less matters of fact than of intuitive conviction: the natural sociability of human beings and their instinctive sense of justice. And indeed, in his later work *Political Liberalism*, Rawls abandons the claim that the liberal theory of justice has universal appeal, and is prepared instead to confine its application to those societies that accept its basic suppositions, and in particular its prioritizing of liberty.[6]

Rather different psychological assumptions form the starting-point for a theory proposed by another contemporary American philosopher, R. B. Brandt, who, like Rawls, seeks to found morality on rational deliberation, but takes a less abstract, more 'embodied' and particularistic view of motivation.[7] For where Rawls sees as the test of his system how far the moral judgements it results in would fit with the 'fixed points of our considered convictions' Brandt believes that it is best to start by *dismissing* our prior moral conceptions just because they are rooted in culture and upbringing and vary with time and place. And where Rawls's rational contractors are depersonalized and stripped of knowledge of their own desires, Brandt's 'fully rational persons' take their own personal wants and desires as their starting-point for reflection.

Brandt uses the term 'rational' to refer to desires, actions or moral systems which survive criticism and correction by facts and by logic – a process he describes as 'cognitive psychotherapy'. It is an evolutionary – that is, Darwinian – notion, for a rational desire is interpreted in survival terms, or as a desire that survives the complex process of deliberation. This creates a problem for the justification of altruism and benevolence in Brandt's system, as well as for the idea of acting from a purely moral motive. To some extent, Brandt is prepared to allow early conditioning simply to feature as a given – as something that affects the outcome of cognitive psychotherapy and therefore a person's view of what it is rational to accept. For him, the question, 'Why should we be rational?' is a practical question about motivation. The answer is that this is the way to satisfy the maximum number of our desires.

So for Brandt, as for Rawls, the ethical question is what kind of social moral code a fully rational person would support for a society in which he or she intended to live. Like Rawls, he believes that pure egoism can be ruled out as a policy, since on practical grounds even rational egoists would choose a system that could be accepted by a large number of others, not just by themselves as individuals. Although Brandt believes that some kind of rule utilitarianism would best meet this requirement, his account resembles the contract theory in seeking a basis for morality in considerations that are ultimately *a priori* and theoretical.[8]

It is this feature, together with the importance it attaches to consent, that marks out the essential nature of the contract theory; and since the need for consent arises out of a presumption in favour of individual freedom or autonomy, the contract theory is inextricably associated with the political and moral ideals of freedom, rights and justice.

Unfortunately, these aspects of contractarianism as a moral theory seem doomed to remain in permanent tension with each other. For, because it depends upon an ultimately egotistical account of what it is to be a rational person, the contract theory cannot supply the universality or stringency of moral claims that, at least in some versions, it appears to be seeking. The idea of rights and justice as moral absolutes, not grounded in individual desires – the Platonic vision which provided a contrast even to the earliest version of the theory – is bound to elude those who ground obligation on nothing more than social convention.

What is more, the idea of a convention, with its overtones of honesty, trust and keeping promises, if taken seriously, seems to presuppose the very moral notions it is trying to justify. It is only an *alternative* to the idea of basic moral concepts, including rights and justice, when it confines itself to emphasizing the artificiality of the contract and the dominance of self-interest. When it tries to avoid doing this, it builds on a deep underlying sense – an intuited conviction – of the priority of rights and justice, in a sense which is absolute rather than artificial.

Rights and Justice

If justice is regarded simply as social convention, then, its scope is ultimately restricted and local: the rights people enjoy can apply only within a particular society and under a particular system of law. But is it possible to take a wider, indeed universal, view? Is it possible to say that those who torture, rape or rob are violating other people's rights and dealing with them unjustly, whatever the local laws may say? The idea that there can be a higher court of appeal, a stronger notion of justice, was eloquently expressed by Antigone in Sophocles' play of that name.

Antigone decided she had a duty, at whatever cost, to disobey the command of the ruler, her uncle, to leave her brother's body unburied, and the words she speaks in the play are often quoted as a poetic expression of the important ethical conception of natural law:

> Nor did I deem
> Your ordinance of so much binding force
> As that a mortal man could overbear
> The unchangeable unwritten code of Heaven;
> This is not of today and yesterday,
> But lives forever having origin
> Whence no man knows.[9]

This claim that ethical considerations are overriding – that they can in certain circumstances take precedence over human laws and conventions – was set out, too, in rather more formal terms by Aristotle:

> There are two sorts of political justice, one natural and the other legal. The natural is that which has the same validity everywhere and does not depend upon acceptance; the legal is that which in the first place can take one form or another indifferently, but which, once laid down, is decisive.[10]

This idea of a natural or universal law that can be contrasted with the actual (positive) laws of states was not the result of any inability on the part of the Greeks of that period to appreciate the fact of diversity. On the contrary, as a result of their own experiences of trade, travel and war, they were acutely conscious of the variety of cultural and ethical differences amongst different nations and groups. But while some, like the sophist Protagoras, concluded from this that there were no universal moral claims, others drew a distinction between the laws that could rightly be regarded as varying from place to place, which they called laws of *convention*, and a universal law – a law of *nature* – which was not variable or relative in this way. As Antigone put it in poetic terms, this was a law which anyone could have access to through conscience, and it represents a higher court of appeal, according to which the actual laws of states or rulers may be found wanting.

While the further step of moving from the idea of a natural law to that of rights was not taken at the time, the conception of a right is implicit in that idea. Antigone's duty to bury her brother would be more likely in modern times to be expressed in terms of a right of her brother to burial, but both the modern claim and Antigone's conception of a natural law point to the same higher and wider notion of duty and obligation. But if its origins lie in the reflections of ancient Greek philosophy, two other threads must be added to the weaving of the modern notion of rights: one is the Roman concept of a 'law of nations' which is above purely local customs; the other the Christian belief that the individual is answerable morally directly to God. That the individual ruler, too, is equally answerable to God gave a political, and indeed a subversive, edge to a primarily ethical notion, particularly as appeal to God in these cases would not be appeal to revelation or to authority, but once again simply to individual conscience.

Mediated, then, by the influence of Roman law and the Christian religious tradition, the idea of natural law and justice in the form of rights has played a role in the foundations of modern political thought, and particularly the liberal tradition. Linked, as it was, with the contract theories of the seventeenth and eighteenth centuries, the concept of rights became a practical political force in the eighteenth century, when rights became the rallying cry of revolutionaries in Europe and America. They were embodied in two key political statements: the American Declaration of Independence (in 1776) and the French Declaration of the Rights of Man and of the Citizen (in 1789). Thus, in the words of D'Entrèves: 'The old notion which lawyers, philosophers and political writers had used down the ages had become . . . a liberating principle, ready to hand for modern man in his challenge to institutions.' He continues: 'Rationalism, individualism and radicalism combined to give the old word an entirely new meaning. The notion which had been invoked to construct a universal system of law and to provide a rational foundation for ethics, inspired the formulation of a theory of rights which will not easily be cancelled from the heart of Western man and which bears witness to his generosity and idealism.'[11]

But opposition from the new philosophy of utilitarianism appeared simultaneously with the flowering of the new notion. Ironically, Bentham, whose support for the French Revolutionaries had led them to make him an honorary citizen, dismissed the idea of rights as nonsense, and absolute rights as 'nonsense upon stilts'. Having rejected rights, Bentham also rejected the notion of justice: 'justice, in the only sense in which it has a meaning, is an imaginary personage, feigned for the convenience of discourse, whose dictates are the dictates of utility, applied to certain particular cases. Justice, then, is nothing more than an imaginary instrument, employed to forward on certain occasions, and by certain means, the purposes of benevolence.'[12]

It was no doubt partly as a result of this utilitarian opposition to the notion that the idea of rights waned in influence in the nineteenth century, and they only regained their position as an important moral and political concept in the twentieth century, a century riven by wars of such horrific dimensions and destructiveness that countries combined in their aftermath to seek declarations, agreements and sanctions to provide some kind of guarantee against the worst violations of the rights of man by man. The United Nations Declaration of Human Rights (in 1948) and the European Convention for the Protection of Human Rights and Fundamental Freedoms (in 1950) were important practical outcomes of this aim.

In the process of securing agreement, however, the concept of rights itself suffered a shift of meaning from a moral concept that ruled out certain things, to one that made demands – from proclaiming a liberty to making a claim. And indeed, it was only by agreeing to add a new concept of rights – positive rather than negative – that these agreements were ultimately finalized. Where the older negative rights had set limits to government, protecting citizens from interference by their rulers and also by each other, the new species of positive rights had the effect of expanding the role of government to provide various kinds of welfare goods. On the whole, negative rights belong to the area of formal justice – the notion of justice as reciprocity that forms the basis of legal systems with their apparatus of law-enforcement, policing and punishment. According to this view, justice is blind – it must be consistently applied, not arbitrary. The notion of positive rights, on the other hand, is concerned with allocating goods and benefits and so belongs to the area of social or distributive justice.[13]

In contemporary discussion, the opposition between the positive and negative conception of rights is reflected in a contrast between rights as protecting choice, and rights as providing benefits. The first is the idea of rights as grounded in autonomy and guaranteeing freedom to choose; the second is the idea of rights as protected interests which are grounded in needs and a person's good – a concept that generates entitlements to goods of various sorts. In the end, then, the positive and negative conceptions of rights – the profligate versus the parsimonious interpretation – are in tension with each other, providing a focus of political and ethical conflict.[14] So what indeed are rights? Can a better understanding of the notion resolve the problems of their function and extent?

What are Rights?

While many rights have been embodied in law, this does not mean that there are no rights independent of law. There is indeed a view, common amongst British jurists in particular, and known as legal positivism, that a right is only something that is laid down within a legal system. But while it may be necessary and proper for judges and lawyers to confine their attention to rights of this sort, there is no reason to reject the idea that there are in fact, whether generally recognized or not, three categories of rights: specific legal rights; specific moral rights; and universal human rights, which are claimed as moral rights but are not always recognized as legal rights under all jurisdictions.[15]

Rights have been described (by Ronald Dworkin) as trumps, by analogy with card games in which a low-value card of the highest suit outranks even a high-value card of any other suit, and (by Robert Nozick) as side-constraints which limit what you may take as a possible option for action, whatever it is you want to achieve.[16] But what a right is may be better understood if two other questions can be answered.

First of all, it is important to ask, who or what can be the *subject* of a right, and, secondly, what can be the *object* of a right? It would be natural to answer the first question by saying, only human beings. But this leaves problem cases in some areas of medical ethics, where the conclusion has practical significance. Do fetuses, embryos and the irreversibly comatose have rights? Judging that they do affects the way in which it will be appropriate to treat them. So some prefer to identify possible subjects of rights by a capacity or characteristic that they can have or lack. So the capacity to suffer, for example, which is often put forward as one such characteristic, includes animals but excludes comatose and, possibly, early-stage human beings.

A broader criterion still, having interests, includes some but not all of these and could possibly include aspects of the natural world, too, such as trees and plants; while a narrower criterion, possessing reason and the capacity for choice, may include some animals and exclude young and brain-damaged or comatose humans. On the other hand, having the *potential* for acquiring a capacity for choice and an ability to reason is often discounted, particularly by those considering questions about the earliest stages of life. Sometimes an attempt is made to encapsulate the key characteristics in the all-embracing criterion of being a person.[17]

A mere listing of these different possibilities is enough to suggest that there may be a strong case for confining rights to the area of relationships between human beings. For the notion is inevitably weakened by its extension to the world at large, while restriction to the world of human beings does not prevent the inclusion of the so-called 'marginal cases' – the mentally handicapped, the comatose and early or potential human beings. The argument that they would be excluded depends on pointing to their inability to share in the essential rationality of human beings. However, they *can* still be included, but on the basis of generosity rather than logic, out of respect for their future or past human status. The same generosity can extend to higher mammals which share many relevant characteristics with human beings.

This suggests, too, at least part of an answer to the second question: What can be the *object* of a right? What kind of things can there be a right to? For there can be a right to something only if the behaviour of other people is relevant to securing that right – for example, there can be a right to pure water only if this is something within the power of particular human beings to provide.

As for the question of the parsimonious versus the profligate conception of rights, the problem with approaches based on positive rather than negative rights is practical and political, as well as philosophical: inevitably, they generate a need for heavy taxation to support not only the provision of goods and services, but also the enormous army of bureaucrats needed to administer the system and arrange distribution. This is, as the economist F. A. Hayek points out, a threat to the liberty that it is the function of rights to protect. He writes: 'It is sheer illusion to think that when certain needs of the citizen have become the exclusive concern of a single bureaucratic machine, democratic control of that machine can then effectively guard the liberty of the citizen.'[18]

But if these considerations make it clearer what people who talk about rights mean, there remains the question of how rights are to be justified. Do they in fact *need* a separate justification? The contract justification, it seems, can only justify rights artificially as social convention. Utilitarianism, too, appears to leave no room for them. But later utilitarians, unlike Bentham, *have* been prepared to accept a justification of rights in terms of utility – talking about rights is acceptable, they say, if, as they concede to be the case, it is useful or productive of happiness. So, for example, while Bentham preferred to base law and punishment directly on utilitarian considerations, Mill, Bentham's successor, sought to integrate the idea of justice within utilitarian theory, with a form of utilitarianism which places major ethical principles like justice beyond the scope of day-to-day calculation. In the fifth chapter of *Utilitarianism*, he wrote: 'Justice is a name for certain classes of moral rules, which concern the essentials of human well-being more nearly, and are therefore of more absolute obligation than any other rules for the guidance of life.'[19]

An alternative to appealing in this way to human interests and welfare is to rest the case instead on the requirements of human freedom, a step which the American philosopher Alan Gewirth takes in arguing that rights are *necessary* if humans are to function as moral agents, displaying autonomy in the exercise of choice.[20]

But is it really necessary to find a further moral ground for rights? Why not consider at least the possibility that the idea of rights is *self*-justifying? After all, a right is no more suspect as a moral concept than other moral notions such as duties or obligations, or promises. Critics of rights theory too often make the mistake of dismissing them simply because they are an abstract notion. Of course, it is true that a right is not the kind of thing that is visible to the naked eye; it cannot be touched, felt, or observed by any of the senses; but a large part of human activity is concerned with what are in the end non-empirical concepts. Why should it be supposed that anything of a sceptical nature follows in the particular case of rights from this?

But if intuitive conviction fails, it is possible to fall back on a purely pragmatic justification of rights. To begin with, they have the advantage of giving status to the wronged person, where other moral notions centre on *other* people's duties or obligations, thus putting potential victims of their wrongdoing into a demeaning 'object' category. Even more important is the fact, too, that the idea of rights and their violation is widely understood under different political regimes and different religious authorities, so that there is a very broad consensus in support of them and against their violation. Rights are in fact an accepted currency of international debate in important arenas. If lawyers and philosophers find them problematic, it seems that people and politicians do not. In sum, their main virtue is that they represent a decision to give priority to the ethical over the purely expedient.

This is not to deny that rights can sometimes conflict. For example, in the case of the debate about Salman Rushdie's book, *The Satanic Verses*, it seems there was a practically irresolvable conflict between the right to freedom of speech and publication and the right to practise a religion in the way its adherents wished it to be practised, including a right to prevent the publication of writings deemed to be blasphemous and to punish an offending author by death. And if economic and social rights are acknowledged, many of these may be unattainable for the world population as a whole, with the rights of residents of some countries in conflict with those of others, and the rights of present people in conflict with those of future generations. This raises the question of whether at least *some* rights – mainly negative rights – might not be absolute. Prime candidates would be the rights to life and to liberty, and a right not to be subjected to torture. Others might be freedom of speech, freedom of association, freedom of publication and freedom from arbitrary arrest and imprisonment.

Rights are ultimately based on what human beings have in common, their common needs and capacities, as opposed to their purely selfish interests, and it is this feature that enables them to transcend social and economic contexts. While it is always possible to think of circumstances in which rights may be put in question in extraordinary circumstances, there is no doubt that to recognize any 'conditionalizing' of rights is to weaken the notion. Perhaps the degree of flexibility that might be required is in any case supplied by a simple recognition that, while rights are an important element in a universal morality, they cannot stand alone; they need the support of other equally potent moral notions – duty, obligation, responsibility and care and consideration for others.

The moral force of the concept of rights has not prevented them being attacked from a variety of sources – by Marxists (although they make use of them in some liberation movements) and by cultural relativists, as well as by utilitarians like Bentham. In the world of practical politics, they may be unpopular with right-wing governments of an authoritarian colour, since they set limits to a government's arbitrary powers; they may also be seen by some nations as just another form of Western liberal cultural imperialism. There are critics, too, in the Western liberal democracies themselves, who see the rights-claiming individual of Western liberalism as rootless and anarchic, and who seek to replace individualism with the concept of the individual-in-community.[21]

Some of these criticisms can be dismissed as depending on a deterministic view of human beings, others on the ground that rights are not incompatible with social responsibility – social responsibility is in fact assumed in the very act of demanding recognition of the rights of others. Ultimately, however, rights may have to be justified not by the fact that they *are* universally accepted – they are not – but rather by the fact that they could be: they have the *potential* for securing agreement and acceptance. As Margaret Macdonald put it: 'Assertions about natural rights, then, are assertions of what ought to be as the result of human choice . . . To assert that "Freedom is better than slavery" or "All men are of equal worth" is not to state a fact but to choose a side. It announces *This is where I stand*.'[22]

Both justice and rights, then, are strong moral notions which demand more than intellectual assent – as in the Platonic account, desire and emotion may need to be enlisted in support. But the term 'rights', because of its legal and political history and connotations, is an effective reminder that the moral life of the individual can only be pursued in a social and legal context. The associated powerful notion of justice, which is historically connected with idea of balance and harmony, also has the function of regulating relations between individuals in society, and, on a larger stage, amongst nations. There is scope, too, for the idea of justice as governing the relations between present and future human beings and between humans and the rest of the natural world.

Interlude

> Nomia had arrived in the green arbour where this discussion was taking place and had quietly joined us soon after the beginning of my account. She appeared pleased with the way in which I presented the contract theory, particularly as she recognized that the contract theorists I had mentioned were weighty and important thinkers in my own cultural setting, and she evidently saw this as evidence that her own ideas deserved to be taken more seriously by her colleagues and friends.
>
> But she seemed less pleased as I went on to show that my own sympathies lay with a view more like that of her sister Physia, which she had always regarded as indefensible, if not downright absurd. For Nomia, abstract notions such as justice and rights were unacceptable. Like her father Panhedon and the majority of the Alloi, she liked what she called 'the firm ground of empirical certainty' – concepts that can be 'cashed out' in terms of things or events that can be seen, heard or otherwise experienced by the senses.
>
> Physia, on the other hand, was clearly moved by what I was able to tell her about the way the idea of a stronger and more absolute notion of rights, freedom and justice had featured in the world I came from, though I knew she could feel only sadness that it was unlikely such ideas ever taking root amongst her own people. In spite of these doubts, she offered to introduce another thinker on these matters, a sombre individual named Deon whom she regarded as an ally or supporter for her point of view. Deon appealed to no contract and no convention, but he was an ally in the sense that he, too, supported the idea of a moral conception that had universal application.

Notes to Chapter 5

1 See chapter 2 for an account of the Prisoner's Dilemma. There is a helpful contemporary discussion of the problem in Hollis, *The Cunning of Reason*. The broader field of games theory was originated by Von Neumann and Morgenstern in their book *Theory of Games and Economic Behavior*. See also Braithwaite, *Theory of Games as a Tool for the Moral Philosopher*.
2 Rawls, *A Theory of Justice*.
3 Ibid. p. 11.
4 Ibid. p. 45.
5 Ibid. pp. 579–80.
6 Rawls, *Political Liberalism*

7   Brandt, *A Theory of the Good and the Right.*
8   See also the discussion of rule utilitarianism in chapter 3.
9   Sophocles, *Antigone*, 452–60 (trans. George Young).
10 Aristotle, *Ethics*, p. 189.
11 D'Entrèves, *Natural Law*, pp. 60, 62.
12 Bentham, *Introduction to Principles of Morals and Legislation*, ch.10, sec. XL, n. 2.
13 The contrast between formal and distributive justice is discussed in chapter 10.
14 For history and discussion of this conflict, see Cranston, *What are Human Rights?*
15 The American jurist Wesley N. Hohfeld distinguished four categories of rights: as claims, powers, liberties and immunities. These can roughly be explained as rights to do or not to do certain things to others and rights to have or not to have things done to oneself. See Hohfeld, *Fundamental Legal Conceptions.*
16 See Dworkin, *Taking Rights Seriously* and Nozick, *Anarchy, State and Utopia.*
17 For fuller discussion of 'personhood' see chapter 9, pp. 151–2.
18 Hayek, *Constitution of Liberty*, p. 261.
19 Mill, *Utilitarianism*, p. 55.
20 Gewirth, *Human Rights.*
21 See, for example, MacIntyre, *After Virtue* and *Whose Justice? Which Rationality?*
22 Macdonald, in Waldron, *Theories of Rights*, pp. 34–5.

6

Principles and Intuitions

Sixth Conversation

Deon: I agree with what you have said about justice: that there should be no discrimination between people on irrelevant grounds, and that each and every person deserves equal respect – at least until they have forfeited that respect by their own actions. I agree, too, that it is only too easy for those who obtain power over others to deny them rights to freedom of speech, and to arrest and imprison or even kill those who disagree with them. But while I don't object to the language of rights, I prefer to speak in terms of duties or obligations on the part of the people who may be considering *doing* any of these things.

Traveller: Well, this need not create any difficulty between us. After all, these two things may amount to the same thing in practice. For example, where I come from, there are political liberation movements and campaigns for various minority causes which are often promoted in terms of rights, but which can just as easily be supported in other moral terms.

Deon: I see. Well, that is an important practical point. But perhaps we share a more theoretical point of view, as well. For you, I understand, were critical of what might be called the ethics of expediency – and I have always opposed that myself. So I wonder if you would agree that those who adopt a position like that are making the mistake of putting forward an invalid argument?

Traveller: What exactly do you mean by that? What sort of argument do you have in mind?

Deon: I mean that they try to reason from what *is* the case to what *ought* to be the case. They start with facts and hope to end up with what are not facts at all – or at least not facts of the same sort. In other words, they begin with *factual* premises and end with *moral* conclusions.

Traveller: You mean that they argue like this: 'Such-and-such an action will produce such-and-such results. Therefore, this is the right action; this is what I ought to do.'

Deon: Exactly.

Traveller: It is striking that you should say that, for what you say reminds me of a statement made by the philosopher David Hume (1711–76). Admittedly, the kind of appeal to facts that he had in mind was an appeal to past facts, while you are talking about making appeal to future or prospective ones. But you can judge for yourself because, as it happens, I once had to memorize the passage in question, so I can tell you exactly what it was that he said on this subject:

> In every system of morality, which I have hitherto met with, I have always remark'd, that the author proceeds for some time in the ordinary way of reasoning, and establishes the being of a God, or makes observations concerning human affairs; when of a sudden I am surpriz'd to find, that instead of the usual copulations of propositions, *is* and *is not*, I meet with no proposition that is not connected with an *ought*, or an *ought not*. This change is imperceptible but is, however, of the last consequence. For as this *ought* and *ought not*, expresses some new relation or affirmation, 'tis necessary that it should be observ'd and explain'd; and at the same time that a reason should be given, for what seems altogether inconceivable, how this new relation can be a deduction from others, which are entirely different from it. But as authors do not commonly use this precaution, I shall presume to recommend it to the readers; and am persuaded, that this small attention wou'd subvert all the vulgar systems of morality, and let us see, that the distinction of vice and virtue is not founded merely on the relations of objects, nor is perceiv'd by reason.[1]

But I think I should add, Deon, that Hume cannot really be cited as a supporter of your own position, for in that last observation, he makes it clear that he thought morality could not be based upon reason at all, and I gather that that is precisely what you do believe.

Deon: You are quite right. But does Hume have anything more to say on that matter?

Traveller: Well, he says quite explicitly that 'Reason can never of itself be any motive to the will'. I should perhaps admit, too, that Hume, because he saw utility – that is, being useful or agreeable to human beings – as the key to justice, is often regarded as a forerunner of utilitarianism – and obviously that is not something you would support.

Deon: You are right on both points. In my opinion, utility is not relevant to the question of whether an act is right or wrong – the act itself, or at least the motive from which it is done, is what matters. And I certainly do *not* think that it is impossible to ground morality on reason. Are there no thinkers in your own tradition who have held views like this?

Traveller: Well, indeed, the German philosopher, Immanuel Kant (1724–1804) reacted sharply against Hume's empiricism, and argued that in morality there must be an *a priori* element, something, that is, that can be known by reason, not by sense observation. The same, he thought, was true where our knowledge of the physical world is concerned. This is why he thought it a great mistake to confuse morality with something purely empirical like happiness.

But I think it would be best if I were to tell you in more detail about Kant's views and about some more recent philosophers who take the idea of principles seriously, or who at least believe that there is such a thing as distinctively *moral* knowledge.

Deon: That seems a useful suggestion.

Kant's Categorical Imperative

Unlike many other moral philosophers, Kant did not believe that morality should be based on observation of the facts of psychology or anthropology. On the contrary, he insisted that the supreme principle of morality could be discovered by reason alone. As he put it: 'a law has to carry with it absolute necessity if it is to be valid morally – valid, that is, as a ground of obligation . . . the ground of obligation must be looked for, not in the nature of man nor in the circumstances of the world in which he is placed, but solely *a priori* in the concepts of pure reason.'[2]

In the *Groundwork of the Metaphysic of Morals*, which he presented only as a preliminary to a more substantial theory of ethics, but which in fact sets out the essentials of his moral theory very clearly, Kant takes as a starting-point the proposition that the only thing that is good without any qualification at all is a good will. For example, while strength of purpose and determination are usually good things, they may be the reverse when someone puts them to a corrupt or evil purpose, and this is true of many other apparent goods. In contrast, having a good will – that is, wanting simply to do what is right – is a good which had no need of qualification. For human beings, then, the appropriate aim is not a material goal such as happiness, but the motive of duty – to want to follow the moral law simply because it *is* the moral law.

Sometimes, of course, duty and happiness coincide, and then it is hard to separate out motives. Kant's observations on this have led many to conclude that he believed that actually liking doing something which was your duty would detract from its moral worth. A contemporary of Kant's mocked him with a poem based on this assumption:

Gladly I serve my friends, but alas I do it with pleasure.
Hence I am plagued with doubt that I am not a virtuous person.
Sure, your only resource is to try to despise them entirely,
And then with aversion to do what your duty enjoins you.[3]

However, Kant's point was not that it is better to hate whatever is your duty – that duty is something that must always be done reluctantly – but rather that the moral motive cannot be seen in action when what you ought to do is what you *want* to do anyway. For example, it is hard to see whether two people have a moral commitment to a relationship as long as it is mutually satisfying. It is only when the going gets harder that the difference between a moral commitment and an arrangement of convenience really emerges. The example Kant himself provided was that of an honest shopkeeper. From a practical point of view, it hardly matters whether the shopkeeper's honesty is based on the judgement that this will bring more custom in the long run, or whether it is a matter of principle. But if the shop-keeper is acting on the adage that 'good ethics is good business' or that 'customer trust brings customer loyalty', the fact that his conduct is honest, while practically important, of course, is morally irrelevant.

Kant's belief that duty is a matter of acting out of reverence for the moral law was expressed in a principle described as the Categorical Imperative. It is an imperative because it says what must be done; and it is categorical in that it asserts that something must be done unconditionally – subject to no conditions at all. In contrast to this, a purely hypothetical imperative, on the other hand, says that something must be done, *if* some desired end is to be achieved. Kant insisted that there was only one Categorical Imperative, although it could be presented in different ways. He offers a number of formulations of which the best known is this:

> *Act only on that maxim through which you can at the same time will that it should become a universal law.*[4]

Some of the alternative formulations closely resemble this, with the exception of one, which emphasizes respect for persons rather than universality – the Formula of the End in Itself:

> *Act in such a way that you always treat humanity, whether in your own person or in the person of any other, never simply as a means, but, always at the same time as an end.*[5]

The Categorical Imperative, then, is a universal imperative which allows no scope for arbitrary exemptions, and it is purely formal – it describes the *form* that moral obligation must take rather than its *content*. Kant held, however, that substantial moral rules can be worked out from the formal principle, by asking in the case of any particular action, 'What is the maxim I am following here? Is it one on which I simply and arbitrarily *choose* to act, or is it one that can be regarded as valid for any rational agent?' It is only in the latter case that it can be accepted as a formal maxim, and thus as a consequence of the Categorical Imperative.

Kant illustrates the way in which the Categorical Imperative works with some examples. He follows two divisions customary at the time between perfect and imperfect duties and between duties to self and duties to others. This results in four distinct categories of duties: perfect self-regarding duties, perfect duties to other people, imperfect self-regarding duties and imperfect duties to others. The example Kant gives of the first of these – a perfect self-regarding duty – is that of someone contemplating suicide. A person who is tempted to commit suicide because life is miserable would be acting, he suggests, on the maxim: 'From self-love I will shorten my life if it is causing me more misery than pleasure.' But Kant argues that once this maxim is universalized, it is easy to see that a law of nature which allowed this would contradict itself, since self-love is directed towards maintaining life, not to ending it. In other words, the survival instinct cannot be turned on itself.

The second example is concerned with promise-keeping. Someone considers borrowing money on the basis of promising to pay it back, although in fact he has no intention of doing so. His maxim, says Kant, is: 'Whenever I am short of money, I will borrow money and promise to pay it back, although I know this will never be done.' But a maxim of this type, Kant argues, would nullify the very purpose of promising, and make it impossible for the form of words 'I promise' ever to be taken seriously. In fact it would destroy the *institution* of promising, which is the only thing that makes promise-*breaking* possible at all.

Because it is impossible to conceive of applying these maxims or principles of action universally – the very idea is self-contradictory – they stand as examples of perfect duties, the first a self-regarding duty, the second a duty owed to others. The two examples of imperfect duties supplied by Kant are different. In their case it *is* possible to conceive of their maxims being universalized, or even becoming universal laws of nature. The point in their case is simply that it is not possible for someone to *want* this to be the case.

The example Kant gives of a self-regarding duty is that of cultivating a natural talent. While there is no direct contradiction in the idea of universalizing a maxim of neglecting natural gifts, Kant holds that rational beings cannot will that that should become a universal law of nature since, *as* rational beings, they necessarily will that all their own capacities should be developed, for the sake of the many useful functions these serve.

Similarly, in the final example, which concerns a duty to others, there would be no inherent contradiction in a state of affairs in which people always adopted a maxim of not helping others, but again Kant suggests that it is impossible to will that such a principle should hold universally, since people can expect to find themselves at some time or other in a position in which they will want help or sympathy from others, and in these circumstances their own will would be in conflict with the maxim they have adopted.

These examples are intended to show what a Categorical Imperative must be like. Through the application of the universalizability test, they demonstrate that when people break a moral rule, they are in effect making an exception of themselves. Kant goes on to show that when the Categorical Imperative is formulated, as it may be, in terms of respect for persons – *act in such a way that you always treat humanity, whether in your own person or in the person of any other, never simply as a means, but always at the same time as an end* – the outcome is the same as far as the four examples are concerned. In this case, the question to be asked is, 'Is the action proposed compatible with the idea of persons as ends in themselves?' Making false promises, failing to help others, neglecting one's talents or gifts, even deciding to commit suicide, all fail this test.

Not everyone agrees with this restriction on using people merely as means, and the opposition can be based on considerations that are themselves ethical. For example, despite Kant's rejection of the idea, it would seem that sometimes it *is* morally permissible to use *oneself* as a means to other people's ends – many acts of self-sacrifice would seem to fit this description. So, for example, there is all the difference in the world, morally speaking, between the case of someone who gives blood voluntarily for medical purposes and someone whose blood is taken from them compulsorily.

This aspect of self-determination is in fact encompassed in another highly significant formulation: the formula of Autonomy. Kant says that rational beings have to see themselves as law-makers as well as law-followers: 'every rational being must so act as if he were through his maxims always a law-making member in the universal kingdom of ends'.[6] This formulation recognizes the important aspect of choice or moral freedom by asserting that the will has to be seen as actually making the moral law which it follows. Other philosophers, Kant says, have espoused the principle of heteronomy; that is to say, they have tried to ground moral obligation on something extraneous to human will, and they have seen human beings as tied largely against their will to the moral law by duty; that is why they have always tried to show that they have some interest to gain in following their duty, or at least that it will lead to the fulfilment of some desire. In contrast, Kant's theory portrays the moral law as something made by human beings themselves, by a will which is given to them for that purpose. This means that morality and free will are inextricably connected.

While the hypothetical imperative requires very little explanation or justification, Kant recognizes that it is necessary to explain how a Categorical Imperative is possible. The Categorical Imperative has been presented as having opposed characteristics: it is at the same time both *synthetic* (that is, it is not tautological, but has real substance or content) and *a priori* (that is, it is not based on or derived from experience – on empirical evidence or sense-observation). This apparent contradiction needs explanation. In the final section of the Groundwork, therefore, Kant sets out this justification.

His argument starts from the position that autonomy, or freedom of the will, is the ground of the dignity of human nature, and freedom, according to Kant, is a matter of not being determined by alien or extraneous causes. This negative conception of freedom leads directly to the positive conception of freedom of the will as autonomy, the will as creating a law for itself. Thus Kant argues that a free will and a will under the moral law are one and the same. He goes on to say that freedom of the will is a necessary characteristic for humans, just in virtue of the fact that they are rational beings: the very conception of a rational being carries the guarantee of freedom. For a being without free will would be a creature determined by instinct, while a rational being is by definition a being governed by reason, not by instinct. Kant admits an apparent circularity in his argument – the moral law is the ground of freedom, just as freedom is the ground of the moral law. However, he seeks to avoid this circularity by turning to his broader metaphysical doctrines, which involve positing a world of *phenomena* (things as they appear to us) and a world of *noumena* (an inaccessible world of things in themselves).

The distinction between *phenomena* and *noumena* represents a division beween the sensible world which is variable, and the intelligible world, which is constant and unchanging. Humans, according to Kant, are members of the first of these worlds through their senses, and of the second through their intellect. Introspection shows them that they are possessors of reason, the highest function of which is to make this discrimination between the sensible and intelligible worlds. So humans can regard themselves as being both under the laws of nature (their heteronomy) and as belonging to the intelligible world and hence under laws which have their basis in reason alone (their autonomy). But as members of the intelligible world they can only conceive of their own will under the idea of freedom.

Through this reasoning Kant argues that there is, after all, no circularity in the inference from freedom to autonomy, and from autonomy to the moral law. His own summary is very clear: 'We see now that when we think of ourselves as free, we transfer ourselves into the intelligible world as members and recognise the autonomy of the will together with its consequence – morality; whereas when we think of ourselves as under obligation, we look upon ourselves as belonging to the sensible world and yet to the intelligible world at the same time.'[7]

It is in this way, then, that Kant answers the question, 'How is a Categorical Imperative possible?' He argues that if humans belonged only to the intelligible world, then all their actions would conform to the moral law; if they belonged only to the sensible world, then they would be entirely governed by the law of nature and so would be directed to the pursuit of happiness or to the satisfaction of their desires and inclinations. But the intelligible world, Kant argues, contains the ground of the sensible world and its laws, so that human beings find themselves subject to the laws of the intelligible world which appear to them as imperatives enforcing duties. Kant's answer, then, is that it is the mixed nature of a human being that makes the Categorical Imperative possible – that makes possible the existence of a moral 'ought'. He writes: 'The moral "I ought" is thus an "I will" for man as a member of the intelligible world; and it is conceived by him as an "I ought" only in so far as he considers himself at the same time to be a member of the sensible world.'[8]

But human beings cannot know the intelligible world; they are only aware of it as 'something more' setting bounds to the world of sense. 'The concept of the intelligible world is thus only *a point of view* which reason finds itself constrained to adopt outside appearances *in order to conceive itself as practical.*'[9] In fact, Kant goes so far as to say that we conceive of the intelligible world just in respect of its formal condition: that the maxim of the will should have the universality of a law. We cannot, after all, explain how pure reason can be practical or how freedom is possible. All we can do is to explain away the apparent contradiction in the idea of freedom, which is what Kant has set himself to do with his distinction between the sensible and the intelligible world.

Kant particularly insists that while people do have a disposition to obey the moral law, which may be called 'moral feeling', this is not what determines their moral judgements – it is simply a subjective effect of the law upon their will. Again, they may take pleasure in doing their duty, but this pleasure is not the ground of the validity of the moral law, which must be beyond both interest and feeling.

Kant says that he has here reached the extreme limit of moral enquiry, and that its end result has been to save reason from searching for a motive for morality in the empirical world. The ideal to which his enquiry has pointed he describes as 'a universal kingdom of *ends in themselves* (rational beings), to which we can belong as members only if we are scrupulous to live in accordance with maxims of freedom as if they were laws of nature.'[10] His final comment is that the failure to prove the necessity of the moral law may be grounded in its nature: for to prove it would essentially be to ground it on some underlying interest. It must, in fact, be self-supporting and independent of all considerations outside itself.

Problems with Principles

Kant's ethical theory provides a complex theoretical justification for a fairly simple and straightforward moral position: that morality consists of following faithfully certain universally valid principles of behaviour, and of not being swayed, or persuaded to deviate, by the special circumstances of particular cases. In a brief essay, 'On a supposed right to tell lies for benevolent motives', he carries this programme through to what many would consider to be an unacceptable conclusion: that even to save an innocent life, it cannot be right to lie – for example, by concealing someone's hiding place from a would-be murderer. Hence Kant is commonly accused of rigorism and legalism – of applying principles mindlessly and unsympathetically in a way that would generate, in practice, many 'hard cases'.

He is also criticized for his formalism – his refusal to allow the relevance of practical circumstances to moral decisions, and his dismissal of emotion or feeling as having any part at all to play in moral judgement. Kant would not have regarded these as criticisms, however, since his object was to insist that moral principles *must* be regarded as rigid and binding, whatever the circumstances, if hedonism is to be refuted. So he argued: 'All practical principles of justice must contain strict truths, and the principles here called middle principles can only contain the closer definition of their application to actual cases . . . and never exceptions from them, since exceptions destroy the universality, on account of which alone they bear the name of principles.'[11]

But while this thesis of universalizability – the criterion of universality as the test of moral maxims – has been accepted by many moral philosophers who do not necessarily accept the very rigid consequences of Kant's theory, it has also been the subject of criticism for reasons of a different sort: reasons which are logical rather than purely persuasive. Critics have pointed out that different results follow, depending at what level the test of universalizability is applied. In the case of lying, for example, it could be said that Kant arbitrarily selects a middle level and it is this that leads him to conclude that to lie would be wrong in any circumstances, whereas if he had applied the test at either a more general or a more specific level, the result would have been different. For example, the more specific principle 'lying-to-save-innocent-lives' may well be universalizable, while the *less* specific principle of 'engaging in conversation' is a morally inoffensive category of which 'lying' is merely a sub-category.

This means that, conceived as a straight logical criterion of moral action, the Categorical Imperative may work only negatively, not positively. It may not, after all, supply the material content of a working moral code. Indeed, a variety of moral codes might be compatible with it. Nevertheless, conceived of as a guide for someone already committed to the idea of acting morally, it works in a way which is not so far removed from the way Kant suggests in his four examples. It reveals what *cannot* be accepted as acting morally. Accepting even the most minimal interpretation, then, Kant has presented the case for impartiality as a necessary feature of moral judgements and demonstrated the logical incoherence of a purely egotistical morality. Put in today's terms, Kant aimed to establish that the notion of 'moral' necessarily involves the notion of being universally applicable. It is this aspect that constitutes a prime feature of the Oxford philosopher R. M. Hare's universal prescriptivism for, like Kant, Hare has consistently maintained that the moral 'ought' is, as a matter of logical necessity, a universal 'ought'. Although Hare sought to combine this Kantian insight with utilitarianism in his later work, this aspect is fundamental to his ethical theory.[12]

Varieties of Intuitionism

Many philosophers have shared Kant's conception of morality as a system of self-standing principles but, where Kant sought to base these on reason, they have looked to other sources for the support and justification of these principles. Amongst Kant's contemporaries, and in subsequent moral philosophy, too, an alternative to both empirical grounds and logical grounds was found in the notion of intuition or a moral sense. Indeed, faith in the ordinary person's moral capacity had already been expressed by an earlier thinker, too. Bishop Butler told his congregation: 'Let any plain honest man, before he engages in any course of action ask himself, Is this I am going about right or is it wrong? Is it good, or is it evil? I do not in the least doubt, but that this question would be answered agreeably to truth and virtue, by almost any fair man in almost any circumstance.'[13]

Twentieth-century philosophers, too, have found the 'plain man' to be naturally endowed with moral knowledge. As W. D. Ross (1877–1971) put it: 'The main moral convictions of the plain man seem to me to be, not opinions which it is for philosophy to prove or disprove, but knowledge from the start.'[14]

Ross's remark echoes the views of his contemporary H. A. Prichard (1871–1947) who, in a seminal article published in 1912 entitled 'Does moral philosophy rest on a mistake?' wrote: 'The sense of obligation to do, or of the rightness of, an action of a particular kind is absolutely underivative or immediate . . . The apprehension is immediate in the same sense in which a mathematical apprehension is immediate. Both apprehensions are immediate in the sense that in both insight into the nature of the subject directly leads us to recognise its possession of the predicate; and it is only stating this fact from the other side to say that in both cases the fact apprehended is self-evident.'[15]

The comparison with awareness of mathematical truth is common amongst intuitionists. It can be supported in the same way as a similar point made by the French philosopher René Descartes (1596–1650) about philosophical knowledge in general: that we do best to rely on what we clearly and distinctly perceive, for the longer the process of reasoning, the more scope there is for error to creep in.

Even before Prichard and Ross defended the role of intuition in determining moral obligation, however, a different form of intuitionism had been defended by G. E. Moore in a widely influential book, *Principia Ethica*. For Moore, the primary moral concept was not the right but the good. So he did not claim that moral *principles* were intuited; on the contrary, he thought that a faculty of non-sensuous intuition enabled us to recognize *good*, and that it was then our duty to seek to produce the maximum amount of good by our actions. Moore is therefore often classed, not as an intuitionist, but as a type of utilitarian. Since, in a famous chapter called 'The Ideal', Moore set out his conception of what constituted 'The Good' – truth, beauty and human affection – his theory is usually called *Ideal* Utilitarianism.[16]

Prichard, on the other hand, is a distinctive representative of the intuitionist school. No less iconoclastic than Moore, he believed that moral philosophers before him, including Kant and the utilitarians, had made the mistake of searching for *grounds* for doing your duty – something he believed you already know you ought to do without any argument at all. He compares this to the way philosophers in other areas of philosophy try to prove things they have always known perfectly well – whether about minds or about physical objects. All these things, he insisted, and moral truths as well, can be known either directly or not at all.

Nevertheless, Prichard shared Kant's view that showing something is advantageous is not relevant to the question of whether it is a duty. He, too, believed that the ethical 'ought' must be absolute and unconditional. Otherwise, as Kant pointed out, you are dealing with a hypothetical 'ought', not a categorical one. But unlike Moore, Prichard did not think 'good' could be the fundamental ethical concept: we can only have a duty to *do* some specific action, he held, not to bring about a state of affairs, and this kind of duty is known immediately, not through any process of reasoning. Prichard writes:

> Suppose we ask ourselves whether our sense that we ought to pay our debts or to tell the truth arises from our recognition that in doing so we should be originating something good, e.g. material comfort in A or true belief in B, i.e. suppose we ask ourselves whether it is this aspect of the action which leads to our recognition that we ought to do it. We at once and without hesitation answer 'No.'

Prichard suggests that one reason it may appear to be possible to ask for a reason for a duty is that the duty in question may have only been partially stated. People do sometimes make mistakes about what is their duty, however, and in a footnote, Prichard explains how this might happen. There are several possibilities: first, the obligation may be of a kind that only a developed moral being can appreciate; secondly, the person making the judgement may do it too hastily; or, thirdly, the person may lack 'thoughtfulness.'[17]

Finally Prichard suggests that if we ever come seriously to doubt whether we ought, for example, to pay our debts, the only thing to do would be to get into a situation where the obligation arises, or to try to imagine ourselves in that situation and then 'let our moral capacities of thinking do their work.'

Prima Facie Principles

A significant concession that Prichard was prepared to make was that 'obligation admits of degrees'. This means that it may be possible to deal with the problem of conflict of duties by asking, 'Which is the greater obligation?' This was a question which formed a central element in Ross's more elaborated and detailed ethical theory. Like Prichard, Ross held that 'right' and 'duty' are unique notions which cannot be defined. But Ross was aware of the problems that arose from an absolutist view of principles like Kant's – a view, that is, that allows no latitude for exceptions in special cases – and Ross sought to address this specific problem in a distinctive and plausible way.

He takes as an example the question of a possible duty to keep a promise when you may be in a position to avert a serious accident by failing to keep it. This leads him to introduce a new concept. There are, he says, two *prima facie* duties here: a duty to keep a promise, and a duty to relieve distress. The circumstances in a particular case can make the latter the greater duty. *Prima facie* duties, then, are different from absolute duties which hold in all circumstances. They could be called conditional duties.

So all *prima facie* duties *tend* to be a duty, but their shadow presence is a result of looking only at *part* of a situation; what is *actually* a duty depends on looking at the *whole* situation. A *prima facie* duty is self-evident in the sense that 'once we have reached sufficient mental maturity and have given sufficient attention to the proposition, it is evident without any need of proof, or of evidence beyond itself. It is self-evident just as a mathematical axiom, or the validity of a form of inference, is evident.'[18] So Ross, too, compares the moral laws to those of arithmetic or geometry – they would hold in any possible universe. However, Ross says that we can never be certain what our absolute duty is because we are not omniscient and so can never know all the consequences that will follow from particular courses of action.

Ross's theory has been criticized on the ground that there is no such characteristic as being a *prima facie* duty: to say something has the characteristic of 'tending to be wrong' is simply to say, 'Most acts like this are wrong, but some are right.' In other words, there is no universal characteristic here at all, and nothing therefore to be intuited. This might seem a plausible criticism, but the fact is that there is no particular difficulty in dealing with the notion of a tendency if it is interpreted as a claim that *other things being equal*, this will happen. For example, we can understand the claim that metals tend to expand when heated or that heavy objects tend to fall in precisely this way. At the same time, of course, we also understand that other things are *not* always equal, and that something may intervene to counteract the tendency.

Finally, it is common for critics to reject intuitionism simply on the general ground that there is no such psychological experience as having an intuition. Admittedly, too, there are conflicting views even amongst those who defend the idea of an intuition or a moral sense of some sort as to what it is that is intuited. And leaving aside those who, like Moore, think the quality *good* is recognized by intuition, there are other ambiguities in intuitionist writings which leave it unclear whether what can be intuited is a principle, a *prima facie* or conditional principle, or particular judgements in particular situations. Much the most common perception of intuitionism, however, would be the one that relates intuitive knowledge to knowledge of a limited number of simple moral principles. The two main objections to this are, first, that there is disagreement about some of these principles and, secondly, that the principles themselves can sometimes conflict in particular situations.

There are, however, a number of ways to avoid these difficulties. As for the first, moral disagreement can often be denied or explained away. To begin with, *factual* beliefs can make a difference to the way in which a situation is to be judged. For example, it has often been pointed out that the Eskimos – whose custom, it is said, was in times past to kill their parents when they approached old age – were not, after all, negating the widespread moral belief that children owe an obligation of care to their parents. On the contrary, it was because they believed that their parents would enter the afterlife with the bodies they inhabited at the end of *this* life, that they saw death before the faculties deteriorated as something that a good son should arrange for a parent. Similarly, even those who participated in the hated Inquisition did so believing that in burning the body of their victims they were saving them from greater and more prolonged pain after death.

There are other explanations, too, that can be found for apparent moral disagreements, some specific to a particular individual. For example, a deviant attitude may be traced back to some significant or traumatic personal experience in early childhood. Sometimes, too, it can be shown to be the result of pure intellectual confusion so that, if the confusion can be cleared up, the difference of opinion will disappear.

As for the second argument – that duties may sometimes be in conflict with each other – even if Ross's solution is rejected, it is still open to the intuitionist to recognize a hierarchy of duties; the intuitionist may allow for example, that it is better to break a trivial promise than to fail in a duty to save a life.

Admittedly, conclusions like these cannot be based on reason; if they are accepted, it is because they commend themselves directly to the unbiased judgement. So while Kant based principles on reason, the intuitionist agrees with Prichard that to ask for *a* reason is to make a mistake. This absence of a ground can be seen as an advantage or a disadvantage. If it is seen as a disadvantage, there are those who would turn to religion for a more substantial basis for their intuitive moral convictions. For these, an underpinning is supplied by the idea of God as the author and creator of the special moral sense which reveals to God's creatures what kind of actions are right, and which are wrong – or, indeed, tells them directly in particular situations what they ought to do. The notion of conscience, however, is not solely dependent on a religious basis; the idea of some such fundamental sense is a conviction shared by members of many faiths and none.

Interlude

I could see that Deon was interested in the views of the philosophers I had been describing and, indeed, had there been more time. I should have liked to go on to tell him that the view that there are moral truths that people can come to know in some sense directly, flourishes in the present day in the writings of a number of contemporary philosophers, in particular those who are described as moral realists. But these philosophers often follow in the empiricist tradition which recognizes only two types of knowledge: analytic or empirical. Since moral principles do not fit easily within this framework, they tend to apply their realism at the level of particular judgements rather than to speak of principles. As a result, they link the presence of a moral quality to some empirical feature of a situation. It then becomes a question whether moral qualities can be said to be supervenient on (to arise out of, or necessarily accompany) empirical ones, and if so, how we can know this to be the case. Not surprisingly, the New Zealand philosopher John Mackie (1917–81), as a hard-headed empiricist, rejected both the idea that there can be special moral qualities supervenient on ordinary empirical characteristics – these, he said, would be a queer kind of quality – and the idea that we could perceive them – this would be a queer kind of perception.[19]

Despite criticisms like these, there is something to be said for an intuitionism which relies not on principles but on an intuitive response to particular situations. It is no less logically respectable to base a judgement that some deed of murder or mutilation is wrong on an immediate and compelling perception that this is so, than to approach the issue from a more complex ethical perspective in which the particular judgement has to be derived from a more general, or indeed universal, judgement. What is more, the inferences used in the latter case are likely to be more doubtful than the immediate response. Of course, there are problems about the boundaries of incidents, but we have rough rules of thumb for marking these, and have no choice but to do the best we can with them. We can give weight to these immediate responses, and then use them to build up a more solid composite moral outlook, which can itself in turn be tested against new particular intuitions.

But earlier intuitionists, who might well have been prepared to consider this shift to the idea of an intuitive moral response to situations, would still have maintained that that judgement, no matter how complex, had universal application. The new defenders of real moral perceptions explicitly reject this possibility. Indeed, the British philosopher Jonathan Dancy chooses the term 'particularism' to describe his moral realism in his book, Moral Reasons.[20] *The kind of perception which is involved is distinguished from plain perception of a situation by the fact that it is intrinsically motivating. This is the thesis known as internalism. It means that, if you think you ought to do something, then you have a reason for doing it. The contrary view – that external considerations need to be brought in if a moral judgement is to be motivating – is called externalism.*

Although sometimes called 'neo-intuitionists', then, these moral realists need a different framework for their theories because they reject the universality that is the hallmark of principles. This framework, I began to suspect, might require more attention to questions concerning facts about human nature. For the intuitionist there is some faculty, whatever it may be called – conscience, moral sense, intuition, inner light – which makes it clear to a person what it would be right to do and which is part of ordinary human nature, so long as this has not been corrupted by special influences. For others, morality is seen as being in no sense natural, and in this case there is a need to appeal to more elaborate justifications – either to a hard-headed consequentialism, or to a rational derivation of morality. Perhaps, however, this awkward polarity is, after all, a result of failing adequately to consider the question: What are humans really like? And one member of the Alloi did indeed take that question seriously, as I discovered, and it became the focus of a very different ethical discussion. She had been listening to the latter part of our conversation and intervened at this point.

Notes to Chapter 6

1   Hume, *Treatise of Human Nature*, III i 1.
2   Kant, *Groundwork of the Metaphysic of Morals*, p. 55 (389). All quotes are from the Paton translation. Page number of the Prussian Academy edition in brackets.
3   Friedrich Schiller (1759–1805).
4   Kant, *Groundwork*, p. 84 (421).
5   Ibid., p. 91 (429).
6   Ibid., p. 100 (438).
7   Ibid., p. 113 (453).
8   Ibid., p. 115 (455).
9   Ibid., p. 118 (458).
10   Ibid., p. 122 (463).
11   'On a supposed right to tell lies from benevolent motives', in Abbott, *Kant's Critique of Practical Reason and other Works*, p. 365.
12   See Hare, *Moral Thinking*. Hare postulates two levels of moral thinking: at one level, simple, brief and teachable moral principles are used for routine decisions in ordinary life; this resembles the Kantian approach; at the second level, time and reflection may be applied to generate complex principles capable of solving difficult moral problems; this is in the end a utilitarian calculation. See also chapter 4 n. 17 above.
13   Butler, *Fifteen Sermons*, p. 36.
14   Ross, *The Right and the Good*, p. 21, n. 1.
15   Prichard, *Moral Obligation*, p. 7.
16   Moore, *Principia Ethica*, preface. See also the discussion of Moore in chapter 3, p.50.

17 Prichard, *Moral Obligation*, pp. 10–11.
18 Ross, *The Right and the Good*, p. 21 n. 1.
19 Mackie, *Ethics*. This is known as the 'argument from queerness'.
20 Dancy, *Moral Reasons*, ch. 4, pp. 60–72.

7

Virtue and Context

Seventh Conversation

Arete: The people you call intuitionists seem to be very confident about the goodness of human beings, unlike some of those you spoke about earlier who clearly assume that people can only be expected to make calculations in their own interest – even, perhaps, that they do no more than respond directly to the stimuli of pleasure and pain.

Traveller: Confident, perhaps, yes. But I would not say that intuitionists and their successors today *must* believe in the goodness of all human beings. True, they do believe that everybody *could* come to perceive situations in the right way. And they do, of course, say that there *is* a right way to view a situation. But they can allow for all kinds of distortion in people's perceptions. And what is more, it doesn't follow that they believe people will necessarily *do* what is right.

Arete: You mean, I think, that they can, after all, allow for the possibility of human wickedness, or simply for human weakness.

Traveller: Well, yes.

Arete: That suggests to me that you should take the question of character more seriously. And wouldn't you agree that there are traits of character that do themselves have an ethical description – good characteristics are what you call virtues; bad characteristics, vices?

Traveller: Of course. But I doubt whether you could build the whole of morality on that.

Arete: I would not suggest that you try to do that – rather that you supplement the intuitive convictions you have been discussing with some account of what it is to be a good person – a person who will naturally *have* the right sort of convictions.

Traveller: But what does 'naturally' mean here? Do you mean that a person's nature is something fixed and unchangeable?

Arete: Up to a point, perhaps yes. At the extreme ends of the spectrum, saints and sinners may be born, not made. But all the same, I think you are right to be cautious in making assumptions about the 'natural'. Human nature has a certain plasticity about it. It can be warped by the wrong sort of treatment, but it can also be changed for the better.

Traveller: Ah, so you agree with that Jesuit priest who said, 'Give me the child until he is seven, and I will give you the man.'

Arete: Well, not entirely. I don't say you can mould any child into any character but, all the same, I do think there is such a thing as moral education – seeking to develop children's better responses and to influence them away from the bad ones. So the question of how human beings *acquire* a morality is important. This takes account of something you have missed in your discussion with Deon as far as I heard it: that morality involves having the right attitudes and emotions. It is not just a matter of knowing something.

Traveller: I can see this would avoid some of the problems we have been talking about. It certainly has more flexibility than Deon's devotion to fixed principles. It would mean that being a good person would involve being able to pick out the features of a situation that are morally relevant. This would not, though, be just a matter of mechanical calculation.

Arete: It sounds as if you have already thought about this kind of approach. Perhaps it is not, after all, such a novel idea for you?

Traveller: Well, I have to admit that the notion of a morality centred on the virtues is an ancient conception in my own tradition. It has not been very influential in modern society until relatively recently, but certainly it now has its exponents amongst my contemporaries. It also fits – though this is not so often noticed – with certain feminist theories about these matters.

Arete: I would be interested to hear how that came about.

Traveller: I'd be happy to tell you. But I would need to begin by stepping back a little from the issue. Can you bear with me a little if I do that?

Arete: Of course. We have plenty of time.

Virtue and Vice

The moral philosophy of virtue was perhaps best put in the contemporary period, not by a philosopher but by a novelist, who wrote:

> Humans are caught – in their lives, in their thoughts, in their hungers and ambitions, in their avarice and cruelty, and in their kindness and generosity too – in a net of good and evil. I think this is the only story we have and that it occurs on all levels of feeling and intelligence. Virtue and vice were warp and woof of our first consciousness, and they will be the fabric of our last, and this despite any changes we may impose on field and river and mountain, on economy and manners. There is no other story. A man, after he has brushed off the dust and chips of his life, will have left only the hard, clean questions: was it good or was it evil? Have I done well – or ill?[1]

The essence of virtue theory, then, is a focus on character, and on seeing a human life as a whole – seeing it, too, under these larger dual categories of good and bad. It is in a framework of this sort that talk of virtue finds a place.

The discussion is not confined to the world of academic argument. It finds a place in the public arena, too, as political leaders, whether of conservative or communitarian leanings, promote improvement in standards of ordinary behaviour. And those politicians, of course, are only mirroring back to the people who elected them a more general rejection of the cult of life-style choice which was so influential in Western democracies in the late twentieth century – a rejection based on an increasingly widespread conviction that, economically and socially, personal irresponsibility about the consequences for others of one's actions, including the example set to the young, is a public, not merely a private, matter.

Amongst some political philosophers, talk of civic virtue is seen as an alternative to the liberal emphasis on rights and contract, and as a context more likely to foster a morality in which citizens will take their duties and responsibilities seriously. Other philosophers see an ethic centred on virtue as an *alternative* to such concepts as right, wrong, ought, duty, and so on, or at least as giving priority to the good over the right. This was a central theme of 'Modern moral philosophy' – a seminal article by G. E. M. Anscombe which appeared in 1958. In it, she recommended the replacement of talk about duty and obligation – the 'law conception of ethics' – with talk about virtues and character. Arguing that general references to moral obligation, including terms like 'ought', 'right' and 'wrong', are in a sense empty, since they carry no information about what it *is* that a person ought or ought not to do, Anscombe urged that these formal concepts should be replaced by terms referring to virtues on the one hand, and to vices on the other – terms which have a specific descriptive content.[2]

Alasdair MacIntyre picked up and developed Anscombe's theme in *After Virtue*. There he attacks liberal individualism, which he describes as a blend of Kantianism and utilitarianism, for placing individual preferences over substantial social and moral traditions. In contrast, MacIntyre argues that individuals are deeply rooted in particularities of character, history and circumstance. What is more, he argues that when such individuals attempt to pursue a universal culture and a universal morality – the Enlightenment ideal – this serves only to promote *anomie*, which is a kind of rootless cosmopolitanism.

MacIntyre's approach, which is essentially that of a sociologist, could easily lead to relativism and extreme individualism. He seeks to avoid this consequence, whilst rejecting such universal concepts as rights or moral absolutes, by locating virtue within some specific tradition that supplies firm guidelines for behaviour, and a way of life for its adherents.[3]

Some philosophers, however, *are* prepared to follow the path that leads from the rejection of a universal morality to a wholly particularistic ethics, and it is this that shapes their approach to virtue. For example, the Oxford philosopher John McDowell writes: 'If the question "How should one live?" could be given a direct answer in universal terms, the concept of virtue would have only a secondary place in moral philosophy. But the thesis of uncodifiability excludes a head-on approach to the question whose urgency gives ethics its interest. Occasion by occasion, one knows what to do, if one does, not by applying universal principles but by being a certain kind of person: one who sees situations in a certain distinctive way.'[4]

There are differences, then amongst contemporary virtue theorists. Most, however, have one thing in common, and that is the debt they owe to Aristotle (384–322 BC). Some therefore propose a return to the Aristotelian tradition, which they see as capable of giving meaning to the concept of an individual human life.

Aristotle

It is this concern with the practical and personal question of how to live one's life that bridges the gap of millennia between Aristotle's virtue ethics and the present-day interest in the subject. Aristotle writes: 'We are studying not in order to know what goodness is, but how to become good.'⁵ 'Becoming good' involves virtue in two ways: it involves being virtuous, and it involves displaying virtues. These are not necessarily the same thing. The first is a reference to character; the second to behaviour. On the other hand, it would be odd if these were not connected. A person could hardly be considered kind who never, or hardly ever, did a kind action. And it would be hard to deny the description 'brave' to someone who consistently behaved courageously.

But while these distinctions are important, they can only arise after a prior question has been settled. That is to say, it is first necessary to ask why anyone would *want* to be virtuous. In the *Nicomachean Ethics*, Aristotle supplies an answer to that question by defining the good, the essence of morality, as the ultimate end or objective of human beings, while all other ends, he says, can be seen as also means to something other than themselves. Aristotle's definition is 'that which is always choosable for its own sake and never because of something else.'⁶ But the only objective of which this is true seems to be happiness. Like Plato, then, Aristotle forges a strong link between virtue and happiness. But he is not prepared to go as far as Plato in saying that a just person who suffers extreme adversity is still happy – someone who says this, Aristotle declares, is talking nonsense.⁷ However, he does recognize that people can display virtues of character in the way they deal with their misfortunes, so that, after all, virtue is not totally incompatible with misfortune.

If virtue and happiness are identical, or even merely mutually supportive, there is no need to look for an extra justification for being virtuous. This has been noted, too, by more recent thinkers. The Anglican Bishop of Durham, Joseph Butler (1692–1752) told his congregation, anticipating that the pursuit of virtue might not directly appeal to all of them, that a well-thought-out policy of cool and carefully considered self-love would in practice coincide with a policy of pursuing virtue for its own sake.⁸ And Hume, expressing a similar sentiment, wrote:

> But what philosophical truths can be more advantageous to society, than those . . . which represent virtue in all her genuine and most engaging charms, and makes us approach her with ease, familiarity, and affection? The dismal dress falls off, with which many divines, and some philosophers, have covered her; and nothing appears but gentleness, humanity, beneficence, affability; nay, even at proper intervals, play, frolic, and gaiety. She talks not of useless austerities and rigours, suffering and self-denial. She declares that her sole purpose is to make her votaries and all mankind, during every instant of their existence, if possible, cheerful and happy; nor does she ever willingly part with any pleasure but in hopes of ample compensation in some other

period of their lives. The sole trouble which she demands, is that of just calculation, and a steady preference of the greater happiness.[9]

The conception of happiness implied here is clearly not a narrow hedonistic one, any more than was that of Aristotle. The term Aristotle used for happiness, *eudaimonia*, is often translated as 'well-being', and he is careful to distinguish it from pleasure. The view that a happy life is a life of material pleasures is, Aristotle says, a view that is held by the many, as opposed to the wise. Amongst those who succeed in avoiding this mistake, a further distinction exists: there are those who associate happiness with fame and honour, and this leads them to pursue public office or politics – a respectable intermediate conception. But there are also some who attain true wisdom; these are the few who find happiness in a life of contemplation – pursuing abstract thought to its limits and meditating on truth, goodness and God.

But Aristotle's most distinctive explanation of happiness and of moral virtue depends, not on this tiered judgement of different types of life, but on a more metaphysical doctrine which generates a conception of happiness of universal application to all human beings. This involves the notion of teleology. According to Aristotle, everything has a *telos* – an aim or point to its existence. In order to know what this is, it is necessary to know what its function (*ergon*) is. For example, the point and purpose of a knife is cutting; a good knife, then, is a knife that cuts effectively. Similarly, a good musician is one who plays his instrument well, since that is the point and purpose of being a musician.

By analogy with these individual cases, Aristotle argues that, irrespective of the particular category to which any particular human being belongs – that is, whether a musician, a carpenter, a general, or indeed anything else – there must be a function of man *qua* man. For Aristotle, this must be the exercise of the rational faculty that human beings possess (*to logon echon* – that which has reason) since reason is the distinctive and defining feature of a human being. But since to be a good member of a species or category is to fulfil that category's special function well, this means, in the case of human beings, expressing rationality in action – something that is summed up in the notion of virtue. So, Aristotle writes, the good for a human being is 'activity of the soul in accordance with virtue.'[10]

But then character, in the sense of a disposition to behave in the right way, is something that can be cultivated by the right sort of learning or training; it can be taught. This means that moral virtue is the result of becoming accustomed to doing the right things – a matter of discipline and practice, rather than any sort of inborn trait. Just as people can become good musicians by playing and practising, so people become just by doing just acts, brave by doing brave acts and temperate or self-controlled by behaving in a temperate or controlled manner. And because people can equally develop bad moral characteristics in the same way, Aristotle emphasizes the importance of early moral training designed to produce habits of morally good behaviour.[11]

So, for Aristotle, character is a result of the actions that a person freely chooses to make most typical of himself or herself. A virtuous character is marked by the choice of virtuous actions. It is still necessary, though, for a person to find a way to decide what *is* the right or the virtuous action. Aristotle's answer to this is that right actions are those which are in accordance with the right rule, and the right rule may be found by considering the damaging effects of both defect and excess. This is Aristotle's famous doctrine of the Golden Mean. Vices are seen by Aristotle as existing in pairs, one of which is the result of too much of a quality, the other the result of too little. The intermediate position represents the right course of conduct. Thus courage is the mean between rashness and cowardice, self-respect the mean between vanity and humility (a trait not considered a virtue by the ancient Greeks), while liberality is the mean between prodigality and illiberality.

There remains the question of why anyone should choose to pursue virtue, even when they understand intellectually how it can be achieved. Can merely understanding a rule provide a motive for following it? To answer this, it is necessary to go back to the question, 'What is happiness, and what is its connection with virtue and moral behaviour?' We have already seen that, according to Aristotle, happiness is a matter of acting in accordance with the highest and most distinctive aspect of human nature – the reason – and Aristotle adds that this is the part of a human person that shares most closely in what we conceive of as god-like or divine. He writes: 'If the intellect is divine compared with man, the life of the intellect must be divine compared to the life of a human being.' We must, he goes on to say, 'do all we can to live in conformity with the highest that is in us.'[12]

The idea that there *is* a best way of living, an optimal fulfilment, is summed up in the term 'flourishing'. This notion can best be understood by analogy with what it is for a plant or animal to flourish – to fulfil to the maximum its essential nature. It is a conception that is, perhaps, easier to grasp in reverse, by seeing how flourishing can be stunted or arrested; for example, the aetiolated plant in a dark cellar, the dog in the vivisection laboratory, the turkey bred for the table under intensive farming conditions, so plump that it cannot support itself on its legs.

This may seem like a claim that because these creatures or objects have these needs, the needs ought to be fulfilled – a thesis sometimes described as naturalism. But while the Aristotelian notion of teleology recognizes that a species has a *telos*, the flourishing in question here is not that of the species but that of individual members of the species. The claim, then, is rather this: they are the sort of creatures that do have these needs; one can conceive of their optimal fulfilment, and the vision of that fulfilment carries with it an intuitive conviction of its worth.

The same applies, then, in the case of human beings. As far as the world of human beings is concerned, Aristotle answers the question, 'Why choose virtue?' with the statement that for man the life according to reason is best and most pleasant, since reason more than anything else *is* man. He adds, however, that observance of social morality, the morality of interpersonal relationships, also brings happiness. Justice, courage, practical wisdom – the virtues with which Plato, too, was concerned – are also typically human, and bring their own happiness; although, since their exercise depends on so many contingent circumstances, the happiness they bring must be less perfect than the happiness that comes from the contemplation of truth.

If this view involves an element of hedonism, it is far from being a hedonism of immediate gratification. Aristotle's doctrine as a whole is an argument for a life lived according to principle rather than passion; for the idea of an ultimate end seems to necessitate living your life according to a rational plan. The doctrine of the Golden Mean gives an indication of the type of life a person who was guided by reason would choose, and Aristotle suggests that the logical case for planning rather than passion is made by recognition of the fact that a life *not* guided by reason is outside the scope of rational consideration:

> 'The man who lives in accordance with his feelings would not listen to an argument to dissuade him, or understand it if he did . . . In general, feeling seems to yield not to argument, but only to force.'[13]

Changing Conceptions of Virtue

The cardinal virtues recognized by the Greeks were limited and distinctive: the moral virtues of courage, justice and self-control, together with an intellectual virtue: wisdom (*phronesis*). When interest in Aristotle's philosophy enjoyed a renaissance in the thirteenth century, the Christian tradition added to these the theological virtues of love, hope and faith.

Later, Protestant Christianity brought a rather different conception of virtue, one which came to underpin what are often described as Victorian virtues: hard work, honesty, integrity, and doing good, either by benevolent giving or by personal and direct good works, such as tending the sick or educating the young. Victorian virtues also included family values, which, as Gertrude Himmelfarb points out, did not feature at all in the litany of the ancient Greeks, apart from the virtue of managing a household efficiently.[14]

Different virtues, then, may well fit different times and places, so that virtue is more relative than a concept like rights. Whether it can be as relative as today's moral particularists suggest is more doubtful. Aristotle's Golden Mean may have been relative to the individual – that is, courage might not be the same for a grown man as for a boy – but the Greek conception of virtue was put forward as having universal application and objectivity. The more recent developments of virtue theory have a more subjective emphasis, suggesting that there can be an appropriate individual response to any particular situation. Indeed, in the case of some of its exponents, it is hard to distinguish from what has been called 'situational ethics' – the view that there are no rules or common features relevant to moral judgement, only particular moral responses to particular situations. However, the claim, 'This is good for me' is no less relativistic than 'This is right for me', and both are versions of relativism, with all the flaws that that possesses.[15] Paradoxically, they represent the loss of the universalist vision, not only of modern liberal moral theories but also of the original virtue theory of antiquity, as it was conceived by Plato and Aristotle.

Living Well

The themes of modern virtue theory, however, are broad in scope. They include not only the analysis of virtue and of individual virtues, but also such related concepts as friendship, integrity, loyalty, shame, guilt and remorse. In addition, the frequent reference today to 'how to live well' suggests a way in which, as both Plato and Aristotle recognized, the notion of moral virtue connects with the intellectual virtue of wisdom. 'Living well' is not just a matter of being efficient or competent – of matching appropriate means to desired ends; it also means making good or wise decisions on such fundamental matters as career, marriage, or personal or family relationships. As Philippa Foot puts it, it means being able to judge what are the things that really matter. Foot adds that the virtues are also to be distinguished from arts or skills: virtue involves the will.

'Living well' also involves a certain notion of personal integrity. For example, someone may return a small sum overpaid in change, and this need not be because they think a serious wrong would be done if they failed to do this. They may even claim they would be justified in not returning the money because of the carelessness of the shop assistant who made the mistake. But let us suppose they do it nevertheless. What might be the reason? One possibility is that the person who is prepared to go to some trouble to return the money has a conception of herself as an *honest* person or, putting the same point negatively, as not being a petty thief. To keep the money would alter unacceptably her view of herself. The British philosopher Bernard Williams draws attention to this notion of integrity – a justifiable moral concern with one's own character and self-image – in two much-discussed examples: George, a young person who, while objecting to biochemical warfare on grounds of principle, is offered a job in a defence establishment working on such weapons, apparently to everyone's advantage, including his own; and Jim, a botanist who finds himself unexpectedly involved in a drama in which he is offered a chance to save the lives of a group of men who are about to be executed if, and only if, he personally shoots one of them.[16]

Williams' examples concern people who think about themselves under certain descriptions. Until his encounter with the execution squad, Jim had taken it for granted that he was not a murderer – not someone who would take a gun and kill a complete stranger – while George had seen himself as aiming to become a scientist working for the public good, not a creator of deadly toxins.

A preoccupation with self is sometimes criticized, but paying attention to one's self in this way is not the same as being selfish. The Victorians, while they did indeed stress self – self-help, self-control, self-discipline, self-respect – were far from promoting selfish behaviour. On the contrary, they believed that a liberal society required a moral citizenry. They recognized that the state might have to enforce compliance with its laws, but they valued the voluntary acceptance of moral laws. Himmelfarb cites Edmund Burke:

> Men are qualified for civil liberty in exact proportion to their disposition to put moral chains upon their own appetites . . . Society cannot exist unless a controlling power upon will and appetite be placed somewhere, and the less of it there is within, the more there must be without.[17]

Moral Education

These considerations bring up again in more acute form the question of moral development and moral education. The earliest recorded discussion of the theme occurs in Plato's dialogue, the *Meno*. There Socrates links the question, 'What is virtue?' to the question, 'Can virtue be taught?' and, as the *Republic* also shows, Plato clearly saw that such questions could not be separated from an understanding of human nature. In the present day, the attempt to reach this understanding has tended to be the preserve of psychologists rather than philosophers. Modern theorists – in particular, the structuralist psychologist Jean Piaget (1896–1980) – have used empirical studies rather than *a priori* reasoning in order to identify a common pattern of moral development from the pre-moral state of the very young child to a stage of autonomy in which the individual has made the requirements of morality his or her own.

Piaget's theory, which was concerned with the *form* of moral reasoning rather than its content, was part of his more general account of cognitive development – a theory of knowledge whose biological roots are reflected in the term 'genetic epistemology' which is usually applied to it. This attributed cognitive as well as moral development, like physical development, to an invariable sequence of maturational processes. For example, children learn to crawl before they learn to walk, although there is wide variation in the age at which they attain these skills – the sequence, though not the timing, is fixed. Similarly, Piaget set out to prove that the sequence of moral development, though not its pace, was invariable. According to the theory he developed, the child, once it has passed the pre-moral stage, passes through a stage of heteronomy in which morality is seen as derived from authority, first of elders, then of peers, before reaching the stage of autonomy – a progression from an egocentric position, through a societal one to a universal perspective.[18]

Lawrence Kohlberg (1927–87) sought to refine and develop the broad picture painted by Piaget, identifying initially three levels of moral development – Preconventional, Conventional and Post-Conventional. Each level consists of two stages, making a sequence of six stages in all.[19] Kohlberg's stages of moral development are usually described as a progression from lower to higher – itself an inbuilt and at first unrecognized value-judgement. The early or lower stages are: first, a stage in which children's thinking is rooted in obedience to adults, fear of punishment and acceptance of authority; then a stage of an essentially self-interested acceptance, for the sake of reciprocity, of a principle of fairness between peers; then a further stage of seeking approval and desiring to be well thought of by one's community or group. At this stage relationships between persons and the role they occupy as spouse, mother, father, citizen and so on are of key importance.

Later comes a stage of respect for justice: recognition of the importance of rules for community living, followed by an awareness of the universality of some of these rules and their embodiment in principles of individual human rights applying across varying cultures and societies. Kohlberg speculated about the existence of a seventh stage in which the universal human perspective is replaced by a holistic cosmic perspective which might have a religious or even a pantheistic orientation.

The Idea of a Female Ethic

Kohlberg's research was framed in gender-neutral terms, but it appeared to reveal that women often failed to reach the later stages of moral development; instead, they were disproportionately clustered at the third stage, conceiving of morality in terms of interpersonal responsibilities, with an emphasis on personal relationships and on helping, caring, and seeking to please. Initially, researchers engaged in the development of Kohlberg's theories considered that this simply showed that women were less advanced morally than men – that is, that they were in many respects deficient. However, this struck one psychologist, Carol Gilligan, who was investigating the relation between moral judgement and action, as worthy of comment and also of further research. As she later wrote:

> Herein lies a paradox, for the very traits that traditionally have defined the 'goodness' of women, their care for and sensitivity to the needs of others, are those that mark them as deficient in moral development.[20]

As she listened to women's explanations of how they approached difficult moral decisions, Gilligan began to feel she was hearing not a stunted level of development, but rather 'a different voice' on morality. The idea that there might be a difference in the way in which the sexes approach morality or morals is not, of course, entirely new. Sigmund Freud (1856–1939) wrote in 1925: 'For women the level of what is ethically normal is different from what it is in men', and went on to say that 'women show less sense of justice than men, that they are less ready to submit to the great exigencies of life, that they are more often influenced in their judgements by feelings of affection or hostility.' At about the same time, the novelist Virginia Woolf wrote: 'It is obvious that the values of women differ very often from the values which have been made by the other sex.' But in the 1980s, Gilligan summed up her conclusions in more theoretical mode, making them not an apology for the female perspective but a statement of what was to become a new concept of feminist ethics, the ethics of care. As she put it:

> The moral problem arises from conflicting responsibilities rather than from competing rights and requires for its resolution a mode of thinking that is contextual and narrative rather than formal and abstract. This conception of morality as concerned with the activity of care centers moral development around the understanding of responsibility and relationships, just as the conception of morality as fairness ties moral development to the understanding of rights and rules.[21]

What Gilligan found was that, describing their moral reflections in relation, for example, to the issue of abortion, women did not discuss whether the fetus was a person, or try to negotiate the competing rights of woman and baby; rather, they said such things as, 'My mother-in-law was terminally ill and my husband unemployed. It would have been wrong to bring a baby into such a situation.' In other words, they saw themselves as key persons with responsibilities for defined others who depended on them for their care, and they saw this as dictating their course of action. They were, after all, offering *moral* reasons, but reasons of a different sort from those involved in either the Kantian or the utilitarian presumptions of impartiality, universalizability and formal rationality.[22]

The female 'voice' in ethics shares with virtue ethics a preference for seeing the moral self as embedded in its concrete particularity – called by some philosophers a 'thick' not 'thin' concept of a person – and as a self already bound by responsibilities and ties. Other people, too, are seen as having specific characteristics, and as being located within specific situations, rather than featuring as examples of universal categories such as 'person needing help', 'person who will die if not rescued' and so on. Nell Noddings puts this more strongly still: caring is the natural basis of morality, but people can only care for particular others with whom they are in some specific relationship, and who can therefore reciprocate or at least appreciate this care.[23]

In place of a morality of rules, then, many feminists defend, like some virtue theorists, a morality of context. For them, this is a morality of care, responsibility, and responsiveness to specific situations, with an emphasis on the traditionally 'feminine' virtues of kindness, generosity, helpfulness and sympathy. Gilligan calls this 'a particularist moral epistemology'.

The contrast between the ethic of care and the ethic of justice is summed up in two stories in the Old Testament which might seem to carry conflicting messages. The first of these is the story of Abraham, a father who was put to the test and triumphed morally by being willing to sacrifice his son to God (although in the end this sacrifice was not required of him) – essentially the archetypal sacrifice of person to principle. In contrast, the mother in another Biblical tale, the story of the judgement of Solomon, was willing to sacrifice justice (Solomon having judged that the child claimed by both herself and another woman should be cut in half and divided between them) to save the life of her son.[24]

Interlude

As I discussed these two stories with Arete, I found myself asking, if there are some key differences between men and women in their approach to morality, what might be the causes? Would these lie in the different biological facts about men and women, particularly the fact that women bear children, with the various life-transformations that can bring? Or can they be accounted for in terms of differences in upbringing and in environmental and cultural influences? Or, again, are those feminists right who argue that patriarchy – male oppression of women across all cultures – explains all?

Arete was interested in these questions, which we went on to discuss at some length, but in the end we agreed that the issues in which we were interested in fact transcended the differences between the sexes. There was a sense, which we both shared, that the two different emphases – justice and care – were not really alternatives, but that each was appropriate in its own sphere. We agreed, too, that, if there was a difference between the sexes, this might be a reason for each to learn from the other and to seek to adapt their responses in a suitable way.

But it was becoming clear to me from the way in which my conversation with Arete was developing that many of the theoretical questions of ethics we had been discussing might find a particular focus in the deepest and most intimate of personal relationships, especially those that involve bringing into being new people, and fostering their development as members of the community of moral beings. I wondered how the Alloi led their lives in these matters, whether they had an institution of marriage or its equivalent, and how they raised their young. It was clear, too, that the Alloi were anxious to have answers to similar questions about me and the society from which I came. But Arete seemed anxious to dissociate herself from the aspect of interrogation which seemed to colour some of

*my conversations with her compatriots, so she left me to discuss this with
Gyna and An – two wise people who were, it seemed, often sought out
by members of the group for practical advice on personal matters of this
sort.*

Notes to Chapter 7

1 Steinbeck, J., *East of Eden*, p. 459. Quotation supplied by Duncan Boswell.
2 Anscombe, 'Modern moral philosophy', 1958.
3 MacIntyre, *After Virtue*. See also the discussion of liberalism and communitarianism in chapter 10 below.
4 McDowell, J. 'Virtue and reason', pp. 347–48.
5 Aristotle, *Ethics*, p. 72 (10966b26–1097a14).
6 Ibid., p. 73 (1097a35).
7 'Those who maintain that, provided he is good, a man is happy on the rack or surrounded by great disasters, are talking nonsense.' Ibid. p. 254 (1153b).
8 See Butler, *Fifteen Sermons*, particularly sermon 11.
9 Hume, *Enquiry Concerning the Principles of Morals*, p. 279.
10 Aristotle, *Ethics*, p. 76 (1098a17).
11 Ibid., p. 92 (1103b).
12 Ibid., p. 330 (1177b).
13 Ibid., p. 336 (1179b 25).
14 Himmelfarb, *The De-moralization of Society*. The author writes that the idea of virtue was not confined to the middle or upper classes. 'Respectability' was a particular virtue of the working-class: 'Working-class memoirs and the evidence of oral history testify poignantly to the efforts to remain respectable, to have a good character (in both senses of that word), in spite of all the difficulties and temptations to the contrary. For men it meant having a job, however lowly, and not being habitually drunk; for women, managing a clean, orderly, and thrifty household; for children, being obedient at home and school, doing chores and contributing, if possible, to the family income. For the family as a whole, it meant staying "out of the house" (the workhouse) and off the dole, belonging to a burial club or Friendly Society so as to be spared the ignominy of a pauper's burial, having a "clean" (paid up) rent book, wearing clean if shabby clothes and, for special occasions, "Sunday best," and giving no cause for disgrace (such as being arrested for drunkenness or having an illegitimate child.)', pp. 32–3.
15 See chapter 4, especially, pp. 57–63.
16 In Smart, and Williams *Utilitarianism: For and Against*, pp. 97–118.
17 Himmelfarb, *The De-moralization of Society*. She comments: 'Today, among the disciples of Nietzsche or Foucault, it is precisely this self-induced morality, the internalized conscience, that is regarded as most coercive and tyrannical. This point of view would have been incomprehensible to virtually all Victorians', p. 51.

18   See Piaget, *The Moral Judgement of the Child*.
19   Kohlberg, *Essays on Moral Development*.
20   Gilligan, *In a Different Voice*, p. 18.
21   Gilligan, 'In a different voice, p. 482.
22   See, however, the discussion of feminist arguments on abortion in chapter 9, pp. 152–4.
23   See Noddings, *Caring*.
24   For comment on these stories, see Gilligan, *In a Different Voice*, p. 104.

8

Personal Connections

Eighth Conversation

An: We have been told that you come from somewhere further away than any of our people have ever travelled. Now, as you can imagine, that has aroused some curiosity here. There are many ways in which we would like to know how your society is arranged, and how it differs from our own.

Traveller: I'd be happy to tell you, though indeed you should understand that, if we are talking about personal relations, there is no *one* way of life where I come from – there's a good deal of variety both in opinion and practice. All the same, I could give you some idea of those variations and – more important – of the broad principles that lie behind these differences.

Gyna: That's just what we want to know. Perhaps others will come to you for the facts – the details about your institutions and practices – but we are really more interested in what lies behind them. Do you have rules, for example, governing personal relations? Are these seen as ethical matters? And what happens when people decide to have children? Who is responsible for them? Are all these matters of personal life left to the individual, or is it a matter for law and regulation?

Traveller: Well, some people certainly believe that personal relation-ships are a private matter and we see it as very important to draw a firm line between the public and the private sphere. But – call it a paradox if you like – if what you want to discuss is relationships between the sexes as they affect the founding of families, then I have to tell you that, as a matter of fact, there have been almost no societies where these most intimate aspects of life have not in fact been made the subject of law and regulation, although the arrangements enforced have varied from time to time and place to place.

An: Interesting. Perhaps, then, *we* should tell *you* that here amongst our people, there is very little regulation of relationships. If you are wondering about the reason for that, I would say it is because our scientists are skilled in the cultivation of plants and essences for medicinal purposes. This has in effect given us entire control of the reproductive processes, and it means that we have been able to separate both sex and sexual relationships completely from the business of producing children.

Traveller: That must have given your people a great deal of freedom in their personal lives.

Gyna: In some ways, yes. But it also gives our Ruling Committee more scope to regulate these apparently 'personal' decisions. Here women must apply to our Children Committee for permission to bear children, and an unregulated birth would be seen as a very serious matter. As for men, they have very little to say on such things. It is up to them, if they are interested, to find a woman willing to bear them a named child. Mostly they do not bother, and the children are anyway allocated at birth to all-day crèches at public expense.

Traveller: But why should women *want* to have children, if they have so little to do with them?

Gyna: I can see why you think that might be a problem. But many women *do* want to have at least one child. And then, we also have people we call 'Birth Women' who make a career out of having children and are well-paid for it.

Traveller: I hope you will tell me more about this some time. There are many ways in which what you say reminds me of trends in my own society and of rumours I heard before I left of practices in other parts of the world. I might add that something of the sort was also a feature of Plato's ideal Republic, but there things were not left to chance. Mating festivals were arranged, and behind the scenes the rulers arranged who would have access to them. But after that necessary pairing, no bonds were allowed to continue between the couples or between parents and children.

An: It's certainly interesting to hear about these differing practices and ideas. But we are really more interested in the underlying principles, and surely the starting-point for *that* discussion would not be these various practical arrangements but rather the close relationships people form with each other, which you mentioned to begin with.

Traveller: Agreed. So I should, I think, say that I was using the term 'relationships' very broadly to cover anything from a slight acquaintance, through companionship and comradeship, to friendship and finally to love. Perhaps, though, since 'love' has become something of a devalued currency in my part of the world – an excuse for betrayal as much as a mark of commitment – I should really say, that what I am talking about is that unity of persons that goes beyond love.

An: I'm not sure we'll be able to follow you in such high-flown regions. We are, I suspect, thinking of something a little more down-to-earth.

Traveller: All right. But even if you narrow the topic down to sexual relationships, these, too, lie on a scale that extends from a single anonymous and purely pleasure-seeking encounter to the life-long pairing of two individuals.

Gyna: One moment. Could I just ask, are you talking now about relations between male and female?

Traveller: Not necessarily. Because, of course, there are many kinds of relationship between people of the same sex. The commonest of these is simply friendship, and in the past friendship would usually have been between people of the same sex – no doubt for practical reasons as much as anything else. Today a preoccupation with physical contact has made the idea of friendship – even same-sex friendship – more difficult, and more prone to misunderstanding. On the other hand, same-sex sexual relationships are no longer taboo.

An: A little complicated. But, then, this is a broad area – too broad, I suspect, for a single conversation. So let me say that while we, here, are indeed interested in all these matters, it is what you have to say about relations between male and female that interests us most – especially since, in the end, this bears on the matter of child-making and child-raising. For, as Gyna has already told you, here we try to keep these thing apart.

Traveller: Well, then, I'll do my best to guide you. But even narrowed down to this, the subject is vast.

Sexual Morality

In the past, the term 'morality' was often used to mean nothing more than sexual morality. The wheel has now turned full circle, so that many people think that sexual morality is not an area of morality at all. The influential moral philosopher Peter Singer (b. 1946), for example, begins his book *Practical Ethics* by saying that 'sex raises no unique moral issues at all . . . Accordingly, this book contains no discussion of sexual morality.'[1] This is a view that is by no means confined to philosophers. It is in fact widely held, and it owes much to the advent of reliable contraception, which, before the appearance of rampant sexually transmitted diseases like AIDS, seemed to create the possibility, for the first time in history, of consequence-free sex.

However, while the desire to avoid being moralistic in this area is understandable, it has to be recognized that morality is, in a sense, bound to feature here, for it involves having a view about what is right, what is good, what is wrong and what is evil. This is not, of course, to say that people are obliged to force their views on others, or to pass laws which compel others to live by their standards. All the same, they *are* obliged, just as moral beings, to have views on these matters in a more general sense, and there is no reason to exclude the area of sexual and personal relationships from this general truth.

In tandem, too, with new doubts about the biological consequences of sexual freedom – the fear of new diseases and renewed uncontrollability of old ones – the experience of sexual freedom has brought reappraisal of sexual mores on a deeper level, as many have become convinced that intimate relations between people, and the institution of the family that depends on these, are the bedrock of community and civility.

If this is correct, and if sex is not, after all, a moral no-go area, then it is reasonable to ask, 'What *should* be the moral basis of sex and sexual relationships?' One possibility is to take as a standard what is natural and normal, for 'abnormal' and 'unnatural' are already often used to condemn certain kinds of behaviour in this area. But the idea of what is 'normal' is no more than a way of referring to what most people do, and that is difficult to establish with any certainty. And even if the truth *could* be established, what the majority do would remain just a plain matter of fact without necessary moral implications.

On the other hand, it is true that knowledge of what is normal can be useful indirectly; for normal behaviour may in practice provide a guide to what is natural, and this is more convincing as a foundation for a fulfilling and therefore ethically sound human life. The idea that what is natural for human beings is also good for them is particularly associated with some religious perspectives – for example, Christian, Jewish and Islamic – but it has much wider appeal than this. In its narrowest form, the view that takes nature as a guide is the view that only those acts that can lead to procreation are natural. However, procreation is a rare event in most people's lives, so, interpreted like that, doing only what nature dictates would require very little in the way of sexual activity. A more generous and more realistic understanding of the natural would be that it extends to anything that continues to serve the purposes of procreation by securing and reinforcing the bond between individuals during the long process of child-raising. While this greatly extends the scope of the 'natural', it also implies some restrictions excluding, for example, adulterous relationships, and multiple partners on an exploitative basis. Off the moral scale altogether, too, would be a range of practices expressing the darkest side of human nature – rape, sadism and the abuse of children.

The 'nature' criterion might also seem to exclude homosexual activities, but these, when based on biological differences – a matter of orientation and not simply a matter of choice – could be said to be conducive to and supportive of some people's lives, and so natural in a different sense. The notion of the 'natural', then, is not without implications as far as sex is concerned. But as in the case of the 'normal', there remains a gap between establishing the facts and drawing a moral conclusion. Humans do not, after all, always believe that it is right to follow nature, although they would be unwise to discount it altogether as a guide. So while it would be absurd to ignore the importance of nature's requirements – in the sense of what is necessary for the survival and continuation of the human species – there is a case for exploring as well some less directly biological considerations. Here there are a number of possibilities.

Personal hedonism

First there is the possibility of a wholly selfish ethic – that of hedonism, egoism, or the pursuit of personal gratification. While personal hedonism is not usually thought to be an adequate basis for ethics in general, many people think it is acceptable within the narrower field of sexual behaviour. But it is difficult to project this, or to recommend it, as a universal policy, for it would necessarily involve willingness to be used by others solely as an object for gratification as well as to use them in this way. In other words, if everyone takes the selfish pursuit of personal pleasure as a guide to behaviour, the area of sexual relations becomes a kind of Hobbesian 'state of nature' – a 'war of every man against every man' – or, in this case, between man and woman, woman and man. This would mean that relations between the sexes would be governed by a sexual *caveat emptor* principle, and inevitably lead to the exploitation of the weaker parties. If their interests, too, are to feature, then it seems that the goal of generating happiness or pleasure cannot be limited to a purely egotistical basis.

Maximizing happiness

One way to avoid these difficulties would be to widen the basis on which pleasure can be considered a legitimate goal, adopting a broadly utilitarian position and considering consequences on a broader basis. In this case, what is right is what will make people happy. But judging what this is, is not as simple as it looks. Do you include in the calculation only those directly affected? Or should the results for the community as a whole be assessed? Even if only those directly affected are considered, in many cases this includes not just couples but also children, and there is no shortage of evidence that children suffer from shifting adult relations, and particularly from parental splitting. By every measure – health, academic and social – children brought up securely and in the long term by both father and mother do better than others. Nor are the effects of family breakdown confined to children. For older family members, too, it can destroy their settled expectations of old-age security, friendly domestic care, and contact with their grandchildren; for the pivotal partnership itself, too, there may be an important contrast which the partners are inclined in the heat of the moment to neglect, between immediate and long-term happiness.

There is a 'whole community' perspective, too, that is readily discounted when it comes to personal life, and yet it seems likely that the move within liberal societies from settled relationships to more atomistic life-styles involving divorce, splitting of families, social change and geographical mobility, takes a heavy toll in terms of emotional and economic security.

It would be rash, then, for anyone to claim firm knowledge of the 'balance of happiness' outcome from all possible points of view. A simplistic view of what is at stake is too short-sighted, and the broader considerations are so complex and so extensive that a utilitarian approach is clearly limited as a way of settling questions of sexual mores.

Principled morality

It is considerations like these that make a simple appeal to principle a more attractive option than debating practical outcomes. This is the viewpoint of the major religions, but it does not necessarily depend on religion for support. For while religious believers base their principles on authority and revelation, principles can also be defended on a non-religous basis as self-evident or, alternatively, they can be argued for on rational grounds. Nevertheless, a morality that recommends living by strict principles in the area of sexuality is unpopular and is often attacked for a variety of reasons. To begin with, there is a general charge that this is too rigid in practice; and it has to be admitted that, historically, a good deal of human misery has resulted from the strict application of principles untempered by compromise in those intimate and private areas where emotions and feeling rule.

There is also another and more specific charge levied against an absolutist or principled approach: that talk of principles may ignore the undoubted limitations of human nature. For example, one important principle that often plays a role here is the duty to keep a promise. But in the context of personal relationships, people often make promises concerning what is strictly outside the promisor's control – a situation which would in all other cases be held to invalidate a promise. In particular, it may be said, people cannot realistically promise to retain the same kind of personal feeling for another person for ever. It might seem that this would immediately invalidate the concept of marriage but it could equally be taken as demonstrating that marriage should not be confused with a promise to love someone for ever. There is a place for principles, then, albeit tempered by humanity, and, of course, many ordinary moral principles can play a role here, too: fairness, consideration of others, lack of exploitation, honesty, openness and the degree of commitment involved in at least *intending* to keep a promise.

Passion or Promises? Duty or Inclination?

These brief considerations , however, say nothing about what the role of the law should be in this area. A brief essay by the poet Percy Bysshe Shelley (1792–1822) expresses very well a long romantic tradition which anchors the relationships between the sexes in the powerful personal feeling known as love. Shelley believed that the institution of legal marriage damaged this ideal foundation. As he put it: 'Love withers under constraint: its very essence is liberty.'[2] In saying this he was following the anarchist spirit of his father-in-law, William Godwin (1756–1836), author of *Political Justice*, whom he greatly admired.[3]

The cause Shelley is pleading is that of passionate attachment. On the other hand, however, there has been a long philosophical tradition which rejects emotional attachment altogether, seeing it either as dangerous – Plato, in the *Phaedrus*, depicts the passions as horses out of control, putting the charioteer in danger – or as making a person hostage to life's changing fortunes. Another of Plato's dialogues, the *Symposium*, which is a discussion on love, extols the virtues of relationships which, while they may involve sentiment and attachment, are non-physical. It was the Stoics, however, who most strongly believed that the grief that you risk by attaching yourself to what you cannot keep for ever could be avoided by keeping yourself free from deep attachments. Epictetus wrote:

> Whenever you grow attached to something, do not act as though it were one of those things than cannot be taken away, but as though it were something like a jar or crystal goblet, so that when it breaks you will remember what it was like and not be troubled. So too in life . . . remind yourself that the object of your love is mortal; it is not one of your own possessions; it has been given to you for the present, not inseparably nor for ever, but like a fig, or a cluster of grapes, at a fixed season of the year, and if you hanker for it in winter, you are a fool.[4]

Views not unlike these are represented in modern times by existentialist philosophies, and by the postmodernist and feminist views that have succeeded them. In the case of the French existentialist thinker Jean-Paul Sartre (1905–80), his philosophical views were reflected in his personal life in his relationship with Simone de Beauvoir which, for both of them, epitomized the ideal of non-ownership – of making no claims on another person. As subsequently emerged, however, some whom the couple separately or together took up in this way came to see themselves as victims; it is unclear, too, whether de Beauvoir herself was in the end happy with her lot, although many contemporary feminists have uncritically taken her life as a model of desirable freedom.[5]

Today's sexual free-thinkers are not necessarily arguing, like the Stoics, against passion; rather, they argue against passionate attachment or permanency. But this position conflicts with people's desire – often strongly felt – for strong connections, not merely with contemporaries, but with the past as represented by parents and grandparents, and with the future, through children and grandchildren.

Apart from considerations like these, the aspect of passion or romantic love, even if for many people the dominant aspect of their relationship, is something which, of its nature, belongs to the private world of personal experience and cannot easily be taken as a factor in the public realm where law and economics rule. In this sense, then, Shelley was right to say that it is essentially beyond the reach of any regulation.

This is why, under most jurisdictions, there are external sanctions imposing through law a more formal conception of marriage as a public and certified relationship. Of course, societies do not have to wrap the relations between the sexes around in formal bonds. Common law marriage and *de facto* relationships provide a less formal but still workable structure even within the setting of a complex modern society. But in developed modern societies, quasi-marital arrangements themselves depend upon a primary conception of marriage as an institution, of which they are a shadow with little or no legal substance.

Marriage

It follows that the question, What is marriage? is fundamental. And it may be necessary to approach this question initially in ethical rather than legal or social terms. Typically, in Christian and Jewish traditions in the West, marriage is the name given to an exclusive relationship in which two people give up freedom to develop other relationships on the mutual understanding that the other does the same. It also involves at least an intention of permanence, with the stability that that creates, not only for the children of the marriage, but also for the partners themselves.

Nevertheless, there is widespread acceptance of sexual relationships outside marriage in the present day, and the ending of marriages by divorce is common and widely accepted; it is also true that increased life-span and better long-term health have made a difference to what might be expected of an early-contracted marriage. But making it possible to cut free from a marriage by easier divorce has serious drawbacks in practice. In the long run, the freedom of those who cut free often turns out to be less rewarding than anticipated, leaving them, as well as their abandoned partner, at risk of loneliness, mental breakdown and illness triggered by the collapse of a network of connections which have in an important sense created each partner's identity and self-image.

These are, of course, practical considerations, but there is another and more philosophical objection to easier divorce – especially divorce by consent, in which the fact of breakdown alone is accepted for the legal ending of a marriage. This is a matter of the way the *concept* of marriage is to be understood. Just as you could not have an institution of promising if it was universally the case that promises were kept only if convenient, so you cannot in fact have an institution of marrying in which there is universal understanding that the agreement lasts only as long as a feeling in favour of it persists. A marriage promise is a kind of Ulysses contract – it says, 'Trust, me, whatever I feel in the future.'[6]

Nevertheless, there are many advocates of a form of marriage which is by mutual agreement open from the start. The contemporary American philosopher Richard Wasserstrom argues that a commitment to sexual exclusivity cannot be regarded as being either a necessary or a sufficient condition of marriage.[7] This places the burden of argument on what the *concept* of marriage entails, but, for two people to agree a notion of marriage which leaves both as much freedom as they had before is to reduce the concept to incoherence. Mutual freedom in effect denies the contract. But without that agreement and that openness, the partners must resort to old-fashioned deception, the negative features of which are well-known: trust betrayed, secrecy, lying, a retreat from joint to solo enterprises and the risks of disputed or concealed parentage.

So marriage, in its formal sense, is a relationship entered into publicly, and authenticated by legal arrangements which have been carefully considered and understood by the parties concerned. And while mutual love might have more immediate appeal to the parties involved, from the community's point of view, the piece of paper certifying the marriage contract indicates simply an economic and sexual union.

This relatively dry and formal description can nevertheless be linked to a more full-blooded and less mercenary conception of marriage as life-long companionship – something that has, whether cynically or realistically, been described as an insurance policy for life. It is a view implicit in the words of the Christian marriage service which describes the union as lasting 'in sickness and health, for better for worse, for richer, for poorer.' Notions of mutual support and tenderness, friendship and joint enterprise, are more amenable than passion to the long-term promise that is involved in entering into a marriage relationship. And it may well be a promise in these terms that is the special and defining feature of the relationship.

Unions for many purposes can be assisted by the parties concerned having sought and specified a suitable legal framework – the common acquisition of property, for example, would on its own seldom be approached without any regard for the legal implications. But people are less cautious when it comes to the common bond of children. And yet, for an enterprise of this kind, requiring years for its fulfilment, a promise of mutual commitment provides a rational justification or underpinning of the project. This is a particularly important consideration for those who would offer an even simpler account of marriage as being primarily a union for the having and raising of children.

It is considerations of this kind that have influenced the views of certain philosophers, in particular Locke and Kant, who have seen marriage as essentially a contract between individuals, mainly for purposes of sexual satisfaction, but also for the founding of families. Locke took a narrow and relatively limited view of the contract, which is closer to many contemporary ideas on marriage: he saw the roles of husband and wife not as involving a lasting transformation of identity, but as external social roles which could be taken on for a time and then abandoned when the purpose for which the marriage was entered into – the raising of children – was fulfilled. Kant, in contrast, emphasized the judicial status of the partners and the rights, which he saw as lifelong, that they establish with respect to each other. In a sense, he suggested, each becomes the possession of the other.

In contrast to this, the German idealist philosopher, G. W. F. Hegel (1770–1831), found Kant's emphasis on contract offensive. He held that, on the contrary, the contract involved in marriage goes beyond the prosaic nature of ordinary legal contracts: it creates a spiritual unity between two people who come to constitute an organic system, and it creates in their two selves, and in their children, a common world.[8] He wrote: 'though marriage begins in contract, it is precisely a contract to transcend the standpoint of contract, the standpoint from which persons are regarded in their individuality as self-subsistent units.'[9] Despite these apparent differences, both the liberal individualist views of Locke and Kant, and the organic holism of Hegel, stand in opposition to the romantic conception which links the marital or quasi-marital relationship to transitory whim or a preoccupation with personal gratification.

Of course, Shelley was right to say that you cannot discipline the indisciplined feelings of the heart. But people may nevertheless be expected to live by the commitments they take on. And the function of the state is to make long-term agreements possible by either enforcing them, or by guaranteeing compensation for an injured party if they are breached. This may seem an anti-libertarian sentiment, but, as far as the desire to limit the encroachment of the state in private life is concerned, there is a reciprocal relationship between the strength or weakness of families and the state's detachment from or involvement in private life. State involvement expands to fill the vacuum left by individuals, for genuine dependency must be covered one way or another in a modern society. Widely accepted, too, even from a libertarian point of view, is the principle that the rights of the weak are to be protected; since children must count as weak in this context, their interests, too, justify the upholding of a relevant contract by the state.

Family

For after all, there are practical needs to be catered for, and the idea of a family, which stems from the even older and simpler conception of the household, implies a certain network of connections: common residence, economic co-operation, sexual relationships, reproduction and raising children. The irrationality, power, and arbitrariness of sexual passion can cut across this prosaic framework. This has been recognized even by philosophers such as Rousseau who attach a particular value to freedom, but nevertheless argue that friendship and mutual respect are a better basis for marriage than sexual passion.[10]

Other philosophical views, however, are less sympathetic to the idea of the family. Marxists take their lead from Friedrich Engels (1820–95) who projected a view of the family as a device for perpetuating and making possible capitalist patriarchy – a way for men to hand down their property to children who could be identified as their own.[11] Radical feminists have accepted the essentials of this analysis, but have substituted gender for class as an explanation of exploitation. They have extended the analysis to a general thesis of patriarchy as applying under *all* economic and social systems, since they see the dominance of men over women as an important feature of *all* social orders, not only of capitalism. The nuclear family in particular – one man, one woman and their dependent children – is seen as repressive, preventing women fulfilling their potential, uncluttered by child-care responsibilities.

These are questions of power and control and the fact is that women have always been at a disadvantage in relation to men, not only because they are on average physically smaller and hence weaker, but also because of the unremitting and debilitating cycle of child-bearing and child-rearing that was their lot in the past. With pregnancy and childbirth drastically reduced as part of women's lives, necessary dependency, too, may seem to be reduced. For women in some occupations this may well be so. For others, it is often taken for granted that the dependency of women around childbirth and early child-rearing is removed by state support. At the same time, the concept of illegitimacy – once a feared stigma – has almost evaporated, with the one-parent family in some areas and groups the norm rather than the exception. However, it is a mistake to imagine that women's dependency is genuinely removed, and their liberty increased, if the state rather than an individual man assumes economic and practical responsibility for them at this stage. Practically speaking, a woman receiving 'state' support is supported by others through the compulsory levy of taxation. Her support is more diffuse and those who supply it do not have any personal care from her in return, but this does not mean that the dependency relation has been eliminated.

Nevertheless, these changes have also brought changes in the moral basis for judging these matters, and to liberalization both of moral judgement and of law. Predictably, too, they have led to an increasing participation of the state in the family in other ways as well, as more and more of the traditional responsibilities of parents are assumed by the state. The state as parent, though, has many limitations. It cannot threaten, cajole or inspire the teenage rebel, and the loss of parental pressure, particularly that of a father, leaves room for peer pressures to create a less than civil society.[12]

Individual and personal freedom, then, pushed to its limits leaves the state to take over the private freedoms of family life, but, paradoxically, since it can do this only inefficiently, it may lead in the end to a loss of personal freedom in the wider community.

Interlude

An and Gyna could see from my account that the family in my society was subject to many pressures, although I doubted that they could really understand the complexity of the kind of community I was describing to them. Indeed, I could see from their reaction that they thought it would be no bad thing if we were to follow their own pattern of living which, of course, they considered ideal. I was not able to pursue these questions with them as far as I would have liked, for at this point a new participant joined our conversation. This was Jatros, one of the scientists of whom some of my interlocutors had spoken. He had other aspects of the family in mind, and indeed, it struck me that some of the problems concerning families and relationships that I had described were influenced as much by developments in biological science and technology as by social factors.

These highly significant technological changes include developments in contraceptive methods, in techniques and possibilities of early abortion, and a whole range of developments in reproductive technology which have struck at the very root of the notion of relatedness. It seemed to me that it might be rewarding to pursue these questions with Jatros, for whom these scientific matters were of considerable interest.

Notes to Chapter 8

1   Singer, *Practical Ethics*, 1993, p. 2

2   Shelley, 'Against legal marriage', p. 45.

3   Godwin was married to Mary Wollstonecraft (1759–97), author of *A Vindication of the Rights of Woman*. They married in spite of their shared conviction that the need for a companion for life was a cowardly illusion, but Mary died a few days after giving birth to their daughter (subsequently Mary Shelley), leaving their sadly truncated relationship, the impact of which influenced Godwin for the rest of his life, as a symbol or monument to love. For a subtle and sympathetic account of these relationships by a philosopher, see Don Locke's biography of Godwin, *A Fantasy of Reason*.

4   Epictetus, *Arrian's Discourses of Epictetus*, Book III xxiv, pp. 84–7.

5   See *The Second Sex* and *The Prime of Life*.

6   Ulysses had himself bound to the mast of his ship so that he might hear the dangerous and seductive song of the sirens without falling victim to their allure and following them to his own destruction. He instructed his crew in advance not to release him whatever he appeared to want at the time.

7   Wasserstrom, 'Is adultery immoral?'

8   For discussion of the views of these three philosophers, see Trainor, 'The state, marriage and divorce'.

9   Hegel, *Philosophy of Right*, p. 32. Quoted by Trainor, 'The state, marriage and divorce', p. 142.

10 See Pateman, *The Sexual Contract*, who quotes Rousseau as saying: 'people do not marry in order to think exclusively of each other, but in order to fulfil the duties of civil society jointly, to govern the house prudently, to rear their children well.'

11 Engels, *The Origin of the Family, Private Property, and the State*.

12 See, for example, Dennis, and Erdos, *Families without Fatherhood*, London, and Dennis, *Rising Crime and the Dismembered Family*.

9

Matters of Life and Death

Ninth conversation

Jatros: I hear that you have scientists who have achieved some remarkable feats.

Traveller: Yes. That's true. But it sounds to me as if your own knowledge and skills have provided you with many of the things we have achieved in our science-based society – control of fertility, and the management of reproduction, for example. There are also aspects of illness, injury and death over which we have gained some control, but I expect there are ways you, too, can affect those.

Jatros: Yes, indeed. Human biology is well understood by us, and we have people who are experts in a variety of healing techniques.

Traveller: I understand that you are yourself one of those experts.

Jatros: Well, yes. I am a doctor. People come to consult me about their problems, and I generally have some idea how to deal with them, or at least I can tell them what they may expect in the course of nature. For sometimes, of course, I can only point to an inevitable progression to death.

Traveller: You would tell a person that, then?

Jatros: Oh, yes. Why not? For one thing, it gives them the chance to end their life before things get too bad. Indeed, we rather encourage that. And I can always help them along with it if necessary.

Traveller: So you don't have any scruples about killing?

Jatros: No. Or at least not when there's a good case for it. We put criminals to death, for instance, if we think their crimes are serious enough.. And we are very proud of our killing record in the wars we wage with the out-groups who lurk in the deep forest. So why should we hesitate when it's a matter of sickness – of someone who *wants* to die?

Traveller: Or even, perhaps, from what you say, someone who doesn't? And what about children, or babies, who are sickly or misformed?

Jatros: Well, I would certainly like to hear what you would do in such cases.

Traveller: It's a difficult area – there's a good deal of dissent about this in my society. But let's not lose sight of our starting-point. We began by talking about controlling reproduction, and, to my mind, questions about the beginning and end of life are interconnected. From what I have already heard, it seems that you have reliable means of contraception, but now I wonder what happens if someone becomes pregnant without permission, or unwillingly, or unintentionally. I presume you have ways of ending pregnancies easily? And, if so, is that allowed, or are there rules against abortion?

Jatros: We see no problem with any these things. But from your question, I can see there are doubts in your mind. Obviously, these must reflect sentiments in your own society, so why don't you come out with things openly? Tell us what's worrying you, and how you come to think any of this is problematic.

Traveller: All right. But these are very diverse issues, and I suspect I will just have to take them separately and in turn.

Jatros: No need to apologize. That suits my way of working, too.

Producing New Lives

One of the most striking aspects of scientific intervention in the biological life of human beings is the possibility of creating new life in the laboratory – a development that raises deep ethical questions. New life begins, of course, with the fusion of elements – gametes – supplied by male and female. It is not difficult to find ways of transferring male gametes – sperm – from man to woman without the necessity for sexual intercourse – and, in many countries, this is a relatively well-established way of dealing with certain kinds of infertility. But advances in the field of embryology mean that it has also become possible to transfer female gametes – eggs – from woman to woman and indeed to transfer embryos, or to freeze them and keep them in storage. The fertilization process itself can be carried out in the laboratory in a test-tube or glass dish – hence the term *in vitro* fertilization. In general, these developments have been welcomed, not only as a way of solving the problem of infertility, but also as a way of avoiding passing on inherited diseases.

They are developments that have been common for some time in animal and plant husbandry, but, initially at least, it was thought that transferring such practices to humans would be ruled out on ethical grounds. Indeed, one of the pioneers of test-tube baby techniques, Robert Edwards, writing in 1966, at the very beginning of research in this area, remarked:

> If rabbit and pig eggs can be fertilized in culture, presumably human eggs grown in culture could also be fertilized, although obviously it would not be permissible to implant them in a human recipient.[1]

That 'obviously' was soon abandoned, for humans tend to operate on the principle, 'If it *can* be done, sooner or later, somewhere or other, it *will* be done.' Only a very few years, then, separated Edwards' cautious ethical assessment from the birth of the first test-tube baby in 1978. A decision to move forward in this way does not, however, mean that the ethical doubts have been settled. On the contrary, it is widely acknowledged that almost every step in the rapid advance of the new technologies of reproduction poses ethical questions of an unfamiliar nature. These questions owe their importance to the fact that arrangements around sex and reproduction are, in most societies, central to social order and convention. Often, too, they are surrounded by mystique, taboo and religious and moral significance. But even for a sophisticated modern society which has sloughed off many of its traditional beliefs and attitudes as encumbrances from an unenlightened past, there are important social implications.

These social implications do not always feature strongly at the front line where practical advances are being made. For most of the new procedures are carried out within the framework of medicine and health care, and there is a general presumption in favour of medical advance. The medical problem they are primarily intended to alleviate is the problem of infertility. There can be a concealed ambiguity, though, in the term 'fertility treatment'. It is generally used not only to refer to methods of assisting people to have children of their own where some identifiable physical difficulty stands in the way, but also to describe the transfer of gametes or embryos to people who are not genetically related to them. Religious groups, including Jews, Catholics and Muslims, see this distinction as important. But they are not alone in this; nor is it just a religious issue. On the contrary, while helping people to have children who are biologically and genetically their own is a medical procedure with few, if any, wider social consequences, the transfer of gametes and embryos to non-related hosts changes the possibilities surrounding the family – children and their parents – in ways which can impinge on society in general, as well as on the people directly involved.

The reasons for this are complex, and may perhaps better be sought within the depths of the subconscious mind rather than in any reasoned judgement. The myth of the changeling has haunted literature and legend since the beginning of history. The 'Cinderella' experience, too – stepparent and stepchild relationships with their tensions and threats – has been a common and recurring theme. And where doubts about paternity have long been a feature of human life, these new capabilities make it possible for people to experience doubt about their parentage on both sides in a radically new way. Is their mother really their mother? Are their parents really their parents? Is this person to whom I am attracted really a forever-to-be-unidentified half-sister or half-brother? These questions could come to haunt even those to whom none of these doubts applies in reality. They have become possible, however, because previously unified roles are now susceptible of division.

To begin with, the simple notion of a father may be split into its separate aspects: a man may be a biological father, a legal father or a social father. This, indeed, is not new, for men have, it seems, always been capable of dissociating themselves from their biological offspring in certain circumstances. Over the course of history, for example, in many parts of the world, there have been men who have rejected unwanted daughters and connived at sexually selective infanticide; and during the period of slavery in America, there were slave-owners who unfeelingly consigned their own offspring, born of enslaved mothers, to the rigours of slavery.[2] What is new today, then, is not this paternal indifference, but the sheer impersonality involved in the collection and distribution of sperm under conditions of anonymity and medical confidentiality.[3]

New, too, and more striking in its impact, is the proliferation of maternal roles which in the past would not have been separated: a mother may now be the originator of the embryonic raw material which supplies the child's genetic heritage (the genetic mother); or she may be the woman who carries a child to term and gives birth to it (the gestatory or birth mother); or, in the case of someone who arranges or pays for a surrogate to bear her a child, she may be a commissioning mother, who hopes as a result of the arrangement to become the social or nurturing mother.[4]

So what is one to conclude in face of these multiplying possibilities? On one side are those who would say that the family has not been diminished, but renewed and regenerated in myriad new forms. They welcome the new possibilities for single parents, lesbian couples, gay couples, groups or communes, to create new kinds of 'family' to add to the 'traditional' nuclear family – two persons of opposite sex raising their own (biological or adopted) offspring. In relation to the biological possibilities alone, these would agree with the Oxford philosopher Jonathan Glover who, in a Report to the European Commission, expressed the view that the future shape of the family should be allowed to evolve experimentally – that we should view positively the possibility of 'taking control of our own reproductive processes.'[5]

They might perhaps defend this goal on the basis of a 'right to procreative liberty.'[6] But it is worth noticing that liberties of this sort do not come free; an IVF baby, for example, is an expensive commodity, and in societies with health cover or insurance, this is often funded by others rather than the individuals concerned, and so must compete with other, possibly more pressing, medical needs. Questions of costs in money terms are not, however, the only considerations. More important are the personal and social costs of developments which are often superficially viewed as carrying only benefits. For if gametes are regarded as being no more than raw material for the medical manufacture of children, a whole dimension of human reproduction is lost – in particular, the network of kinship relations that provides the key to an understanding of a society's culture and practices.

On the other side, then, are those who view matters from a wider social perspective than the interests or preferences of just the individuals directly concerned. As the social anthropologist Marilyn Strathern puts this broader picture:

> Until now, it has been part of most of the indigenous cultural repertoires in Europe to see the domain of kinship, and what is called its biological base in procreation, as an area of relationships that provided a given baseline to human existence.' She adds: 'It is an extraordinarily impoverished view of culture to imagine that how we conceive of parents and children only affects parents and children.[7]

Apart from parents, then, children are linked to a wider kinship network of grandparents, siblings, cousins, aunts and others – a network of connections that constitutes the social space within which they find their original identities. To break the genetic link is to remove that important network of relationships. It is also, from an individual point of view, and when carried out under conditions of strict medical confidentiality, the violation of what in some countries is regarded as a basic human right: access to knowledge of one's genetic or biological parentage.

Genetics and Identity

Progress in the biological sciences has brought other possibilities, too. These include not only the capacity to create new life in the test-tube but also to change the nature of that life by gene-splicing – the alteration of genetic characteristics. These are awesome capabilities for fallible human beings. On the one hand, there is a fear that scientific advance divorced from ethical sensitivity may become a Frankenstein monster capable of destroying its creators. On the other hand, there is the lure of being able to fulfil previously impossible aspirations, immeasurably increasing the sum of human welfare. But while to say of a practice or procedure that it creates happiness or reduces unhappiness will often seem a good reason for undertaking it, it cannot be the *only* consideration. As the British philosopher Mary Warnock insists: 'No-one's morality consists of nothing but a calculation of benefits and harms.'[8]

The doubts that are involved here are of two kinds: doubts about knowledge and doubts about practice. The first kind of doubts arise from the problems created by increased understanding of existing genetic characteristics, particularly when that understanding is applied to specific individuals; the second kind of doubts arise when the new knowledge is used to change the nature of life in its microscopic form: for example, by altering or eliminating existing genetic characteristics, or by introducing new ones.

As far as the first kind of problems are concerned, there is nothing particularly objectionable or upsetting about discovering that blue eyes or brown hair, or even musical or mathematical talent, or a sporting physique, are a result of genetic endowment. But there are other characteristics – criminal tendencies, for example, or a disposition to violence – that people have been held to account for in the past, and where the discovery of a genetic origin seems a direct challenge to people's conception of their own identity, affecting their belief in free will and self-determination. What is more, knowledge itself is not neutral, so if it is possible to predict, by identifying a gene, the probability of the early onset of breast cancer, or the late development of Huntington's chorea, this can generate problems of a different sort. People may be haunted or acutely distressed by the knowledge of their own potential fate, or feel impelled to take drastic pre-emptive action, such as a premature and possibly unnecessary resort to surgery. They may feel unable to decide to have children of their own, and may also find it difficult or impossible to obtain insurance, a mortgage or employment.

As far as the second kind of problems – the problems of application – are concerned, it would be hard to object to changing genetic material so as to avoid illnesses and dispositions to illness, such as cystic fibrosis or muscular dystrophy. But the question in this case is how far this should be taken, and where the process of improvement should stop. Drastic interference with a genotype – the attempt to mould the so-called 'designer baby' – is widely considered objectionable. Even more problematic is the possibility of germ-line therapy – that is, changing a genetic characteristic so as to alter not just an individual, but that individual's descendants as well. On the one hand, it is tempting to take a step which could mean that some hereditary illness could, perhaps, be completely eliminated; on the other hand, knowledge is always imperfect, and it makes sense to hesitate when the results of actions are long-term and irreversible.

In both cases, there is the problem of deciding *what* to change and *what* to preserve: manic depression is a psychotic illness, but paradoxically, the world might *not* be better off without it; many artists and writers have produced their best work as a result of, rather than in spite of, mania or depression. Sexual orientation, too, would be a dubious case for interference. For if it turns out, as some investigators have claimed, that there is a gene for homosexuality, it does not follow that it is an illness; to call it an illness is to make a different kind of judgement. In general, then, the term 'gene therapy', when used to describe attempts to change genetic characteristics, begs some important questions that need to be asked first, about what is good or bad, desirable or undesirable in human nature.

There is nothing irrational, then, in recognizing a special taboo when dealing with human genetic material, since what is at issue is not just what some individuals now may want or find convenient, but a view of human nature on a much broader scale: what humans are; what they may become; and how they may best find their fulfilment. As the philosopher Leon Kass has put this: 'At stake is the *idea* of the *humanness* of our human life and the meaning of our embodiment, our sexual being, and our relations to our ancestors and descendants.'[9]

In practice, however, gene therapy is not the easiest or most likely way to attempt to eliminate undesired characteristics. It is much easier to take advantage of the more Darwinian possibility of recognizing diseases or defects in an embryo, possibly *in vitro* before implantation, and then selecting for future development only embryos without an inherited illness, or embryos possessing some desired characteristic. At first sight, this might seem even more manipulative of character and identity; but in fact no interference with genetic material is involved. This does not mean, though, that there are no ethical problems. Indeed, the selection of 'good' and 'bad' embryos has disturbing ethical overtones, which become even more acute when applied to later stages of development, where what is involved is abortion rather than selection for implantation.

Partly, this is because having a notion of the 'normal' and condemning what is seen as a 'defect' involves a controversial value judgement – a judgement that certain kinds of life are not worth living, especially a life with some mental or physical handicap. More generally, too, there is the sense of some boundary which is overstepped by the sheer exercise of power to choose to give or withhold existence – of becoming the arbiter of life and death. This is a consideration that features centrally in relation to the issue of abortion.

Abortion

Positions on abortion are often characterized as conservative or liberal – terms which may be misleading if they are taken to imply that abortion is part of some well-defined political package. Alternative terms are pro-life (or anti-abortionist) and pro-choice. These terms, too, can be misleading, for the issue is far more complex than these single-word summaries suggest, and there is a whole spectrum of possible opinions. Few of those, for example, who favour legalized access to abortion would favour it in all circumstances and at all stages of pregnancy; while few of those who *oppose* abortion would wish to see it ruled out even in extreme circumstances – for example, when the life of the mother is threatened by physical features of the medical situation, or in cases of rape, incest or the diagnosis of serious handicap in the fetus.

All the same, the debate – which is, politically as well as personally, a potently divisive issue – tends to be defined in terms of the two extreme positions, rather than the moderate or qualified ones. Conservatives are often depicted as holding that there is no dividing line in the process that leads from conception to birth – sometimes, but not necessarily, on the basis of the theological view that the soul exists from conception. And because they hold to the principle of the sanctity of human life, it is assumed that they must believe that it is wrong to kill, whatever stage of development of a human being is involved. The strongest element of the conservative position is its unwillingness to discount the claims of a vulnerable incipient human being. Its weakest is its failure to take into account the serious demands that pregnancy makes upon a potential mother.

Liberals, on the other hand, are perceived as arguing that decisions about having children should be a matter of free choice by the individual concerned, and that law should not interfere in what is essentially a private matter. They may also argue pragmatically that legalized abortion is necessary to prevent the scourge of illegal or 'backstreet' abortions. Perhaps the strongest liberal argument in favour of access to abortion is that a law against abortion is a law that compels an unwilling woman to continue the process of pregnancy, that is, to undergo a physical experience which is dangerous, lengthy and arduous. Its weakest, on the other hand, is that if abortion is not available, this results in the birth of unwanted children – it is the weakest because, first, children can be wanted by people other than their parents; secondly, because children who are unwanted in anticipation may well become wanted and loved once they arrive; and, finally, because in no other circumstances would being unwanted by others be accepted as a morally sound reason for ending someone's life.

As far as terminology is concerned, then, complex issues are ill-served by one-word summaries of positions. In particular, while it makes sense to define a conservative as one who wishes to preserve life, it is wrong to regard a liberal as one who is indifferent to it. For a liberal in the true and original sense sets an equal value on all human beings, including the most vulnerable. But this is a consideration that moves into the heart of the abortion debate – a debate which turns to begin with on the question of the moral status of the unborn. Does that incipient entity count as much as an existing human being? At one extreme is the view that what is removed in abortion has no more significance than a bad tooth or a hair clipping; at the other is the view that it matters just as much as a baby or full-grown adult.

The Potentiality Argument

Many of those who favour abortion are reluctant to concede that the entity involved in the abortion debate *is* a human being. For this concession makes it harder to approve of its deliberate destruction. So they draw a sharp distinction between an *actual* human being and a *potential* human being. While they concede that the fetus, or indeed the embryo, is a potential human being, they deny that this carries with it the same moral claims as if it were already a human being.

So does a potential *x* have the same rights as an actual *x*? Can a merely potential being have actual rights and interests? Those who think the answer to these questions must be 'no', often point out that a potential king does not have the same rights as an actual king; and that it does not seem necessary to give the same respect to an acorn as to a mature oak tree. This argument, though, overlooks the fact that value can attach to potentiality itself. The heir to a throne is accorded special protection and respect just in virtue of what, all being well, he will become. And in a world in which all existing oak trees had fallen victim to some uncontrollable disease, an acorn would have extraordinary value – again, because of the ability it possesses to become an oak tree and even, of course, to furnish the world with oaks if that should turn out to be necessary!

The principle involved here is that having the potential to be something important – something that matters – sheds reflected importance on the thing that has that potential. In contrast, the potential to become something trivial is itself of trivial concern. Given this, the potential to become a complex entity like a human being *is* important, and it is certainly important *to* a human being. Even more important to any individual human being, one might add, is the potential to become that person's son or daughter. The argument that dismisses potential altogether, then, is based on an out-dated and limited empiricism which recognizes nothing that is not currently detectable by the senses.

If potentiality is not morally negligible, however, then it is not difficult to see that abortion may well be a bad thing. Indeed, this is usually conceded by its supporters as well as by those who oppose it, when they argue that it is simply, in certain circumstances, the lesser of two evils. The lesser evil in this case will be defined in negative terms that again relate to potentiality; it is the evil involved in the loss or sacrifice of something valuable.[10]

This point may well be met with the claim that the same could be said about even earlier genetic material, eggs and sperm. Don't these also have value, it may be asked, since they, too, have the potential to become human beings? The question, however, is misleading. As long as they are separate, no identifiable x – actual or potential – exists. And for this reason, it would be unreasonable to regret their passing away too greatly. Even so, a woman may have a different attitude to her eggs than a man has to his sperm. For the first are an identifiable and limited collection; the second are generated at a moment of time in million-fold quantity. Nevertheless, it is not until the genetic material from both sources are combined that there is a unique, identifiable individual.

A potential human being, then, is not without moral importance, and this importance may well be judged great enough to require respect for embryo and fetus from the earliest stages. The claim that only a potential human being is involved is not, after all, an adequate defence of abortion. But while the Argument from Potentiality fails to justify abortion, rejecting that argument does not necessarily close the debate, for both moral importance and the respect it generates may be a matter of degree. It is worth considering, then, whether there is some identifiable stage of development when the 'something' involved in the development of a human life becomes uncontroversially an entity which matters, not merely potentially, but for its own sake and in its own right. In other words, *when does an individual human life begin?*

The Stages of Development Argument

For some people, it will seem obvious that a human life can only begin at birth. Before that event, what exists is indeed an entity – a being – and it is indeed human, but it is not 'a human being'.[11] This fits with the view taken by the law in many countries, which usually prefers to recognize the landmark event of birth as the transitional point for claims of wrong. For the law allows a living child to sue retrospectively for pre-birth damage it may have suffered, for example in a car crash, but does not allow a fetus to make any claim at all, not even for the loss of its future life in abortion.

The law, however, must in the end be based on convenience and feasibility. From a moral and practical point of view, birth seems too late a point at which to suggest there is a transformation of status. A late fetus may be older and more developed than a premature baby, and it is hard to see why an eight-month fetus should be cut off from the rights and protections afforded to a six-month premature baby, simply because the latter is in an incubator in a hospital and the other is still *in utero*. But if birth is not a convincing cut-off point, where else might the line be drawn? The most widely defended suggestions are, first, conception, secondly, quickening, and, thirdly, viability.

Conception

It would be natural to trace the beginning of an individual human life all the way back to the moment of conception. However, there is a case for saying that the entity that exists during the first fourteen days of development is not yet an individual life. The reason for not regarding the newly conceived entity as an identifiable human being is that, up to the fourteenth day approximately, that entity may still divide, giving rise to twins or a multiple pregnancy. Only after that point is passed is it possible to be sure that there is one unique entity.

The Warnock Committee, which reported in 1984 on these matters to the British Government, suggested the use of the term 'pre-embryos' for these early entities and recommended that they be given only limited protection in law.[12] Paradoxically, this means accepting, in the case of one's own existence, that two weeks which would in the past have been regarded as the first part of one's own life history are missing.[13] The alternative, however, is equally paradoxical: it is to accept that, in some cases, the early existence of two or more individuals coincided for those fourteen days. These are interesting metaphysical puzzles which may perhaps be left unresolved. But in practical terms, the Warnock recommendation would remove many of the moral problems associated with the very earliest stages of pregnancy, particularly those surrounding such 'abortive' devices as the coil, the morning-after pill and RU486 (an early abortifacient pill), opening the way to leaving them entirely within the discretion of the woman concerned, without the need, practically, legally, or morally, for the involvement of doctors or other authorities.

Quickening and viability

Later stages of embryonic development could, of course, be more signifi-cant than this but, in practice, if conception is rejected as the start of an individual human life, the next clear demarcation point comes at a much later stage, when a woman becomes aware of the fetus moving on its own. This stage, which was traditionally called quickening – a term which actually *means* the coming of life – would be around the fourth month of pregnancy. Although it has few contemporary supporters, this is in many ways the most natural point at which to judge that there is a new life in existence, and in medieval times some theologians believed this was the moment when the fetus acquired a soul. It is also the point at which a woman is likely to recognize the changes in her body as the presence of a new life, rather than as changes in herself. Despite this, quickening is fairly summarily discounted by most present-day theorists because scientists have found that the child has begun to move independently much earlier than previously thought and before the mother is aware of it.

If quickening is rejected, then the next clear transition point is the stage when the child is able to survive independently of its mother, if it is born prematurely. This is the stage described as 'viability ' – around the twenty-fourth week. Although this has been used as the basis of law in some countries, this, too, is sometimes discounted as a possible demarcation point on the ground that viability varies with the available level of technology in different places. In one part of the world, a premature baby will have to survive on its own and its mother's physical resources; in another, it will have the whole panoply of high-tech survival aids to see it through to the normal infant stage.

Both quickening and viability, then, are rejected by critics as significant points of change because they are not accurate or exact. But how effective is this argument? A grey area like this is common for any changes that involve living things. So, first of all, as far as quickening is concerned, how significant *is* the discovery that what the woman perceives may not actually *be* the child's first movement? The fact is that when the pregnant woman becomes aware of movement, she is right to think her pregnancy has entered a new phase, even if that new phase started, unknown to her, a few weeks earlier, before she was aware of it. Secondly, how significant is it that viability varies with the presence or absence of neonatal intensive care units? Again, it would seem that the difference available technology makes is simply to create another possible demarcation point a little earlier. The stage when the child can survive independently remains a significant point, even if it is a shifting one. So the objections only blur the line where a turning-point is reached; they do not show that no such line exists.

Indeed, this is part of a general problem about the way in which minute quantitative changes can become a change in quality. Who can say, for example, when a few grains of sand become a heap? But nevertheless there is a certain arrangement of particles which are indisputably a heap, and a scattered small number which could not possibly be regarded as one. So, one might say, a fetus which kicks, and which moves in response to stimuli, has become a separate living entity, in a way that a motionless embryo, whatever its potential, has not yet done. And a fetus, or a pre-birth infant which, if delivered, would survive as a living baby, is certainly at a different stage of development from one which could *not* be delivered as a living baby.

In general, then, nature tends to provide only vague boundaries. Law, in contrast, operates with fixed definitions, not only in the early stages of life, but later as well, necessarily ignoring individual differences to specify an age of consent, a voting age or an age for military service. Hence, if the intention is to distinguish between something that deserves the full protection of the law and something that does not, key stages of development *can* be taken as turning-points for judgements about abortion, even if in practice there will be a few ambiguous weeks of transition. As it happens, this corresponds quite closely with the legal position in a number of jurisdictions in which the conditions attaching to abortion become increasingly stringent at points roughly coinciding with these stages. Following this principle, since the weakest case concerns the earliest stages of embryonic life, the first twelve weeks might be free of control, allowing women ready access to safe, reliable means of curtailing an unwanted pregnancy and re-establishing the menstrual cycle without the need for formal authorization; serious medical – not social – considerations might be needed for second trimester abortions; while hardly any considerations would justify the deliberate destruction of the fetus in the third trimester of pregnancy.

The Personhood Argument

Although a scheme of this sort harmonizes with both logic and law, many philosophical writers on the subject reject the attempt to find a demarcation point in the stage of development a fetus has reached. This is because they attach moral importance only to a much later stage – one not attainable by a fetus at *any* stage – when something could be said to have become a *person*.[14] In order to be a 'person' in this sense, certain essential conditions must be met. These are likely to include such factors as consciousness, a sense of self, rationality, and the capacity to want to continue living, as well as a sense of past and future through memory and anticipation. Those who accept this account of what it is to be a person hold that only persons in this sense have, first, interests and, secondly, rights. The Oxford legal philosopher Ronald Dworkin writes: 'It makes no sense to suppose that something has interests of *its own* . . . unless it has, or has had, some form of consciousness.'[15]

According to this account, then, 'person' and 'human being' are radically different notions. This has two rather surprising consequences: first, that the term 'person' need not be restricted to human beings; and secondly, that it is not necessarily the case that all human beings are persons. So for example, an animal could be a person, as could a corporate body like General Motors or ICI. At the same time, a newborn infant, or even a young child, or someone at a later stage of life who has become unable to function mentally or physically – perhaps as a result of permanent coma – might not be a person.

One of the main architects of the Personhood Argument, the Australian philosopher Peter Singer, is explicit in judging that being a member of the human species is not, on its own, relevant to the wrongness of killing, and that animal lives may be more valuable than the life of a human fetus. Strikingly, while it would not be unusual to see something inconsistent in being a vegetarian who supports abortion, Singer takes the rather more surprising view that unless you *are* a vegetarian, it is inconsistent to *object* to abortion: 'Even an abortion late in pregnancy for the most trivial reasons is hard to condemn unless we also condemn the slaughter of far more developed forms of life for the taste of their flesh.'[16]

Many people would regard these conclusions as so unacceptable that they could in themselves be taken as a refutation of the Personhood

Argument. A precedent for treating unacceptable conclusions in this way was set by the philosopher G. E. Moore (1873–1958), who argued that when philosophers appear to have established improbable and counter-intuitive claims, this is a sign that the philosophers have made a mistake, rather than that the conclusions are true.[17] The same might be said of the Personhood Argument and its consequence. The main argument against it, however, is that 'personhood' is a wholly artificial construct, replacing in some ways the historic concept of the soul, but freeing it from its theological connotations. Applied in the biomedical area, it ignores deep questions in the philosophy of mind about the complex relation between consciousness, brain development and individuality.

Despite his rejection of the personhood of the fetus, however, Singer does acknowledge that after about eighteen weeks, it may have a degree of consciousness and therefore some intrinsic value. But he argues that even then a woman's serious interests override the rudimentary interests of the fetus. This last argument, though, shifts the ground from the Personhood Argument to a very different kind of consideration, since it suggests that even 'personhood' can, in certain circumstances, be overridden. So, supposing that what is involved in abortion is, after all, a person, are there still circumstances in which abortion would be justified? The most likely ground for answering 'yes' to this question is respect for the wishes or interests of the woman involved.

The feminist argument

The view that gives priority to a woman's claims is part of a broad feminist position that emphasizes women's rights. In the case of abortion, those rights must be set against those of the incipient being she is carrying. Even so, there is a fairly broad consensus, reflected in the law governing abortion in many countries, that a woman's rights take precedence over those of the fetus in the case of rape, incest, disability or disease of the fetus, and the woman's own serious interests – for instance, a threat to her life or health.[18] The American philosopher Judith Jarvis Thomson goes beyond this to argue that any lack of intention or consent to pregnancy on the part of a woman gives her a right to abortion – not only rape, but also error, or contraceptive failure. She illustrates the point with a story in which someone is unwillingly turned into a life-support system for another adult and argues that there would be no moral obligation to maintain the connection, even if they knew that the other person would die as a result of their decision.[19] The root of this position is a feminist claim for women to have control of their own bodies, and a moral judgement that no one has an obligation to support another life at serious cost to themselves (although they may be morally admired for doing so).[20]

This emphasis on the woman's position, as against the claims of the fetus, is strengthened by the consideration that some of the exceptions the law already allows are not based on anything to do with the status or rights of the unborn child, but are rather a matter of the circumstances surrounding conception. On the other hand, it is possible to concede that very strong claims of a woman (for example, the claim of a thirteen-year-old victim of gang-rape not to have to continue a pregnancy) can outweigh the claims of a fetus, without allowing a mere preference to do so.

Nevertheless, the case for abortion on feminist grounds is not as clear-cut as is often assumed – if 'feminist grounds' are grounds that give priority to the interests of women. For outside the wealthy nations, abortion often works *against* rather than *for* women's interests. Where it is widely used as a birth-control strategy, as it was in Eastern Europe under communism, free access to abortion can have a devastating effect on the health of women, who may experience repeated abortions throughout their child-bearing years.

There are countries, too, such as China and India, where the ready availability of abortion can result in the widespread aborting of female fetuses. And despite the fact that feminist theorists often support the Argument from Potentiality and discount the claims of merely potential people, there must be something remarkable and regrettable from a feminist point of view about the loss of girls and women resulting from prenatal sexing and selective abortion. Those who defend it may do so reluctantly, only as preventing the worse evil of female infanticide.[21] On a gender basis, then, the argument that a valuable life is lost in abortion is strengthened by the sheer scale of the disproportionate loss of female lives.

While these are broad political and social considerations rather than individual ones, women's interests are not necessarily served even on a more personal level by easy access to abortion. For if a woman later comes to regret an abortion decision, or to see it as a moral error, the error is disproportionately bad as compared with other possible moral errors – for what could be worse than to come to believe you have killed your own child? And it is not only the central figure – the woman herself – who may experience this kind of shift of perspective. Dworkin reports that some prominent American Republican politicians declared that in certain circumstances they would support their own daughter or granddaughter if she decided to have an abortion, and he comments: 'They would hardly do that if they really thought that abortion meant the murder of their own grandchildren or great-grandchildren'.[22] But what if they later *did* come to see it as precisely that – perhaps because their daughter had no later opportunity to become pregnant, for example, or became infertile, or died? In other words, the politicians' comments, whatever they intended, reinforce the point that abortion resembles those trick diagrams used by psychologists in which the same picture, looked at in one way, shows a vase, and, in another, a pair of human faces. A mere blink of the eyelid can effect the transformation. Similarly, abortion looked at in one way is the termination of an awkward or unwelcome condition; looked at in another way, it is the snuffing out of an independent life rich in possibilities.

Even so, it might still seem that women are best served if the choice is left to them. But choice can also, in a paradoxical way, be a different kind of constraint.[23] For the availability of abortion changes attitudes to pregnancy, so that it is increasingly seen as voluntary. This can affect the situation for both the central persons: a woman may be reluctant to accept pregnancy until some ideal moment later in life, but find herself trapped in a series of childless partnerships which take her beyond her child-bearing years; a man, on the other hand, who might in times past have bowed gracefully to the inevitable, may feel he cannot be held responsible for a child which he sees as its mother's voluntary choice.

Women's interests, then, are more complex and harder to assess than straightforward talk about 'choice' suggests. And as far as women's rights are concerned, there is a distinction that is too often blurred between claiming a right to terminate a pregnancy and claiming a right to terminate a potential life. The distinction becomes important in the later stages of pregnancy when it may involve taking direct steps to bring about the death of the fetus in the womb to ensure that abortion does not result in an unwanted live birth. It was also strikingly illustrated in a controversial case in a London hospital which involved the abortion by lethal injection of a healthy twin at the request of a mother who felt she could cope with one but not two children.[24] In this case, since her pregnancy continued, it was clear that what was at issue was not a right to end a pregnancy, but a right to end a life, even in circumstances where the continued development and eventual birth of the remaining twin would provide a living demonstration of the nature of the loss involved in that decision.

The wider political context

In spite of, or indeed *because* of all this, it might seem that these are personal considerations which are best left to individuals. It is possible to think that something is wrong, it may be said, but still not want a law against it. In the case of abortion, there may well be no public consensus, at least in the short term, so the question may reduce to asking, 'Who should decide'?

But *should* the state leave morality to individuals? Dworkin argues that an important legal judgement in the USA, *Roe* v. *Wade* (in 1973), which was widely taken to have established women's right to abortion, was really an assertion that this question has to be answered in the affirmative. 'Should *any* political community make intrinsic values a matter of collective decision rather than individual choice?' he asks.[25] Dworkin's own view is that, despite the fact that abortion would have struck the Founding Fathers themselves as abhorrent, freedom of choice about it is part of the religious freedom guaranteed by the First Amendment. Apart from the general implausibility of this as a defence of abortion, it reinforces an erroneous view of the issue as a religious one, rather than as a moral issue of much more general significance. The fact that Catholics and other Christian groups have a well-defined absolutist position on the matter is, of course, important, but it does not make this broad ethical issue, with its implications for people of all religions or of none, a narrowly and exclusively religious or theological question.

Whatever the historic position, however, even where religious requirements are concerned, someone's *belief* that something is a duty is not necessarily a conclusive reason for it to receive the backing of the law. For example, the law would not support in the name of religious freedom someone who believes he has a religious mission to kill unbelievers. The question of who should decide, then, cannot pre-empt the wider ethical and philosophical questions. And it is only if there is a public decision in favour of permissive legislation that the question of whether women alone may decide, or whether others are necessarily involved, can be raised. Since it is doctors who must carry out what is decided, even when the law is permissive there will continue to be a tension between the woman and her reasons on the one hand, and the doctor's own conscience on the other.

Infanticide

Many of those who favour abortion from a philosophical point of view, despite all its problematic aspects, do so on the basis of a utilitarian ethic. Utilitarians, it seems, find it easier to discount the taking of life in abortion because they only need to look at the resulting happiness of those who are alive. The problem with this position is that, while it simplifies the abortion issue, it is too strong for its purpose. Once someone or something is dead, it ceases to feature in the happiness equation. So utilitarians really have no satisfactory answer to the question, 'Why not kill?' in the case of adults either, since killing leaves its victim unable to harbour grief or regrets. This means that they are forced to fall back on the defence that arbitrary killing is wrong because it may make *other* people sad, or that it would make everybody nervous, in case they, too, were killed in this way.

Not all of these considerations will apply, however, in the case of infants or very young children, and so some of those who defend abortion are willing to extend the scope of their arguments to cover infanticide in certain cases. Singer argues that there are no direct utilitarian arguments against infanticide – it cannot arouse fear in an onlooker, and the newborn infant cannot itself have a conscious desire to live. He suggests that a period of a month after birth should be legally available for consideration of infanticide and that, following the practice of many primitive people, and also of the Greeks and Romans, it should be possible to end the lives of handicapped infants if their parents and doctors agree that this is the best option.

Where the killing of infants *is* wrong, Singer believes the wrong is mainly to those who were prepared to love the child. But in general, it is worse, he suggests, to kill an adult than a child. This is a strange position to hold, for the murder of children usually arouses particular horror, and within most human beings there is a deep instinct to protect the vulnerable and helpless. Singer sees such reactions as a sentimental response to children's physical attractiveness, and comments that laboratory rats are attractive, too. As in the case of abortion, he presses for a reinterpretation of 'person' and argues that only 'continuing selves' have a right to life. Moreover, he writes: 'The wrongness of inflicting pain on a being cannot depend on the being's species: nor can the wrongness of killing it. The biological facts upon which the boundary of our species is drawn do not have moral significance.'[26]

Apart from these considerations, some key arguments of a different kind are commonly advanced in favour of infanticide. One of these is what might be called the Replaceability Argument.[27]

The Replaceability Argument

As far as the Replaceability Argument is concerned, abortion and infanticide may be justified as ways of trading a life for a life. If a handicapped child is born, or is allowed to live, it is argued, this may deprive the world of a later normal baby – a baby the parents might go on to have in its place. So what if they put back something for what is destroyed? What if it is a matter of replacing the worse with the better?

This is very much a speculative argument. For, of course, it is quite possible that they would not do so. And how soon would they have to do so for this to count as replacement? Or what if someone *else* – a relative, for instance – had an extra child instead? Would this be a 'replacement'? It is by no means certain, either, that someone who has a handicapped child would not go on anyway to have another child in the hope that it would be healthy and meet their disappointed aspirations.

Apart from such considerations, there are two main arguments against the Replaceability Argument: first, if replaceability works at the stage of the newborn infant, why should it not come to be applied more widely? You can always hope to create someone better, so the Replaceability Argument could be drafted in to do double service as an argument for getting rid of the old, the infirm or the disabled. The only utilitarian argument offered is that this would worry ordinary people who were not old, infirm or disabled, but might become so; and worrying a person in the prime of life is widely accepted as wrong by a large number of philosophers who happen to fit this description!

Secondly, when the Replaceability Argument is used to justify abortion, the case most often cited is that of children diagnosed as being likely to be handicapped; in practice, however, instead of replacing handicapped with healthy children, abortion is frequently used to postpone child-bearing. The real 'replacement', then, is of children of mothers in their prime child-bearing years – their twenties – with children of mothers in their thirties who are statistically more likely to have children with various kinds of handicap, thus *adding* to the problem of handicapped births.

The Replaceability Argument is also applied socially, geographically and internationally, and here questions of costs come to the fore. Singer argues that even if a child could be placed in an institution, there is a question about how much it is realistic to expect a community to spend on this form of care. He also suggests that the care of handicapped infants in the wealthy nations should be compared with alternative ways of spending the money, and particularly with the needs of children in Third World countries. Here, however, as is so often the case, economics and ethics seem to part company.

Nevertheless, even if many of the arguments in favour of infanticide are objectionable, this does not mean that there is not a real problem about the treatment of severely handicapped newborn infants. Advances in neonatal intensive care mean that many babies who would have died in the past can now be kept alive, even though their medical prognosis is tragic and their condition cannot be improved or remedied.[28] The concerns of adults, including financial considerations, must take second place to this central fact. And as long as only consideration for the welfare of the child is operative, it may be that the practical conclusions of a more restrictive ethics will not be so different from those of the utilitarian philosophers. This is particularly likely if the issue turns not on direct killing but on choosing not to embark on heroic treatment. If it *were* to turn on killing, however, there would still be still a question about whose responsibility this is. In the early days of the thalidomide crisis, a Belgian mother faced court proceedings for killing her own baby, born without arms or legs. Love can take different forms, but killing in such circumstances could certainly be an act of love, although it would be very different from routinized clinical killing. So even if there is a case for infanticide, there is still a question about whether what is right or at least condonable when prompted by personal feeling should come to be viewed as a matter of ordinary medical practice.

Euthanasia

This last case brings the issue of infanticide within the broader framework of euthanasia, often described as mercy killing. The most significant difference is that an infant is not aware of its situation and cannot participate in the decision about its life, whereas an adult can. This is an important aspect of the wider debate in which a distinction is usually drawn between voluntary and non-voluntary euthanasia. Voluntary euthanasia covers those cases in which the patient chooses, or has expressed a wish in advance, to be helped or allowed to die; non-voluntary euthanasia covers those cases in which the possibility of choice does not exist, either because it has never existed – as in the case of infants – or because it has been lost through physical or mental incapacity, particularly the complete loss of sentience involved in coma (the so-called Persistent Vegetative State, or PVS). Some also include a category called involuntary euthanasia, covering both the case of someone who would be capable of choosing if asked, but who is not asked; and the case of someone who would not consent, but who is killed against their will to prevent them suffering.[29]

Voluntary euthanasia is a response to the increased technical ability to prolong life in cases where, in the past, death would have been relatively quick. Two developments in particular have changed the situation: first, the discovery and development of antibiotics, particularly penicillin; and, secondly, the whole technology of terminal care: respirators, dialysis, artificial feeding and hydration. The effect of both is to 'save' people from relatively easy and quick deaths, probably at home – pneumonia was once called 'the old man's friend' – leaving them to endure lengthier and more painful terminal conditions in the depersonalized surroundings of the modern hospital.

Not all countries adopt the same attitude, however. In Denmark, for example, doctors must abide by patients' 'living wills' and must check on a central register whether their patient has made one. ('Living wills' or 'Advance Directives' are documents drawn up earlier in life which specify how a person would want to be treated if difficult decisions were to be needed in their care.) In Holland, euthanasia is not legalized, but it is agreed between the government and the medical profession that no criminal prosecution will result if it is carried out by a doctor, with the support of a second opinion, under certain conditions: first, that the patient is incurably ill and suffering pain, and, secondly, that the patient makes a considered request for euthanasia and does not change his or her mind at any point.

The moral principle cited by those who favour voluntary euthanasia is autonomy – the right of people who are ill to make informed decisions concerning their own care or treatment. Rights, choice and preferences, the preservation of the faculties and the desire for death with dignity all play a part here, together with what many would consider a rational preference for a shorter rather than a long drawn-out process of dying.

Within these areas, which generate many practical dilemmas, theologians and moral philosophers have drawn some distinctions which are intended help to resolve questions of responsibility.

Double effect and acts and omissions

Sometimes an action undertaken for one purpose (usually good) has an unavoidable further consequence (usually bad). Many procedures carried out within medicine fall into this category. For example, it could be necessary to amputate someone's leg in order to save his life. The principle of double effect means that the surgeon in this case is not to blame for making the patient lame, since this was not his intention – that was to save the person's life; rather, the patient's lameness was an unavoidable consequence of doing this.

There is also a distinction between taking active steps to bring life to an end and simply discontinuing treatment or not treating a condition at all. This general distinction between acts and omissions underpins the contrast between active and passive euthanasia. There is a strong sense that while people may rightly be held to account for their actions, blame does *not* attach in the same way to their omissions. However, the distinction between killing and letting die is not always clear – for example, discontinuing technological interventions such as artificial feeding, hydration and respiration might be regarded as killing; but they might, on the other hand, simply be regarded as not artificially prolonging a painful life, or one which is useless to its owner. Nevertheless, from the point of view of the person responsible for treatment, giving a lethal injection will seem very different from failing to carry out some major surgical intervention to keep a person alive, even though the outcome is the same in both cases. The utilitarian preoccupation with outcomes obscures what initially looks like a clear distinction, which can also be supported by distinguishing between ordinary and extraordinary means of preserving life.

However, not all bioethicists accept these distinctions, some of which have their origins in the reflections of medieval theologians rather than in contemporary philosophy. Utilitarian philosophers, in particular, dismiss them as being based on an unthinking commitment to the principle of the 'sanctity of life', rejection of which is often presented as the key to resolving the issues of abortion and euthanasia. Of this commitment, Singer and Kuhse write:

> The principle of the sanctity of human life is a legacy of the days when religion was the accepted source of all ethical wisdom . . . Now that religion is no longer accepted as the source of moral authority in public life, however, the principle has been removed from the framework in which it developed. We are just discovering that without this framework it cannot stand up.[30]

In place of a commitment to the sanctity of human life, then, a number of contemporary secular thinkers – not only philosophers, but also health economists and medical practitioners – would put straightforward judgements about *quality* of life. These, they argue, would justify direct killing in many cases. But is it so unreasonable to retain a commitment to the sanctity of life? At the very least, it is worth bearing in mind that a taboo against killing – or, put the other way round, a belief in the right of any human being not to be killed by others – is harder to reinstate, reinforce and preserve than it is to ignore or set aside. Hesitation on the matter is therefore a reasonable reaction to proposals to make changes in the law, even if this leaves difficult decisions for individuals.

The hospice movement can avoid many difficult decisions and offer, for some people, a more acceptable and gentler solution. But autonomy is about what the patient wants, and this may not always be comfort. Some people may place a higher priority on avoiding mental deterioration, incontinence, total dependency or the loss of faculties like sight or hearing.

One way to avoid these difficult decisions would be for individuals to be freed to make their own choice at an earlier stage through suicide or assisted suicide.[31] In the Christian tradition, suicide is regarded as wrong, but other cultures, including the Stoics in ancient times, and the Japanese in the present day, make a virtue of suicide under certain circumstances. A Japanese patient is quoted as saying: 'Suicide is not a very difficult thing . . . it is like going to another room by opening the door because the air of the room I am in is not fresh.'[32]

But would a more supportive attitude to suicide, assisted suicide and euthanasia lead to a slippery slope in which health fascism ruled and only the fit would be tolerated? The Nazi euthanasia programme of the 1930s stands as a dreadful warning of how things may deteriorate once killing becomes an accepted norm. This programme started long before the Second World War. It was based in clinics where the mentally and physically unfit were systematically killed by the medical staff who had charge of them. On record is a Christmas party at which staff celebrated their 1,000th 'euthanasia'. It is not enough to dismiss this as part of a wider racial policy, for, while it is true that it led on during the war to the killing of Jews, gypsies and others, it was 'racial' at this early stage only in the sense of aiming at creating a healthy population – an apparently worthy goal which seems to provide an innocent underpinning to policy in biomedical areas.

These are complex considerations, then. They can best be resolved by relatively complex solutions, in particular by distinguishing between the very different practices subsumed under the general heading of euthanasia. These include:

1 *euthanasia* in the sense of direct killing by medical personnel;
2 *medically assisted suicide*;
3 *positive abstention from interference* – non-interference in a patient-initiated attempt to commit suicide;
4 *negative abstention from interference* – refraining from high-tech interventions to preserve life, particularly bearing in mind that these can keep people 'alive' for decades. The right to be asked for informed consent to treatment carries with it a right for a lack of consent to treatment to be respected. It also carries with it a less obvious right to be fully informed about condition and prognosis, as well as alternative treatments and the consequences of non-treatment. This right can be juxtaposed alongside a long medical tradition of putting a brave face on an illness for the sake of the patient's morale. Being lied to is the historic lot of patients, but it prevents them being empowered to make their own decisions and from facing up to the truth, which is concealed from them. And even if they guess that they are dying, they may be

compelled to join in a general charade of optimism with relatives and friends.

5   *advice only* – advising a person about suicide without supplying assistance or the means to carry it out. Advice in this case could be limited to: (a) *timing*, in the sense of advising a patient as to what point in an inevitable process of decline is likely to prove the last opportunity to carry out a self-sufficient act of suicide; and (b) *means*, in the sense of what would be effective, and what, on the other hand, would carry the risk of worsening conditions without ending life.

A different ethical assessment, and hence a different legislative approach, may well be appropriate in these different cases and indeed, changes in the law in various countries could well be more easily achieved if campaigners were to agree to limit their claims to the less radical changes. There is a strong sense, which limits political and social willingness to make legal changes, that it is not only wrong but also unreasonable to ask medical staff to kill; but at the same time, it may be equally wrong to bar people from competent help and advice, and from access to efficient means to take their own life if their circumstances warrant it and that is their preference. There are now a number of jurisdictions, – for example, Washington and California – where voter initiatives which would have allowed such moderate changes have been only narrowly defeated. In parts of Australia, they have already been introduced.

On the other side, apart from religious considerations, there is only an argument of a more personal and tenuous nature: that it is, in some sense which may be hard to pin down, our human fate to suffer. In support of this argument, it may be pointed out that the desire to avoid pain is a late development of a secular Western civilization – utilitarian rather than Christian, for the Christian tradition values suffering. Unlike the abortion issue, however, euthanasia and suicide involve an individual judgement in which it is easier to argue that others have no legitimate concern.

Interlude

After I had finished my account, Jatros looked thoughtful. He asked me, first of all, for my personal reactions to some of the matters I had been describing, and I said that I believed a strange reversal has taken place. Outside the philosophical world, a hard core of moral considerations have in the past seemed relevant in these areas: in particular, that the mature care for and protect first of all the young and immature, even sacrificing themselves to do so; that both of these respect and care for the old; and that the vulnerable from whatever cause – illness, disablement, sex, age or youth – are in special need of protection and help. True, these were Christian values, so rejected by some non-believers, and by other major religions, too, and explictly treated with contempt by the philosopher Friedrich Nietszche (1844–1900). Nevertheless, they tacitly shaped responses within Western societies. It turns out that philosophy's utilitarian spokespersons in the bioethical debate seem to have generated a consensus which exactly reverses these tacit assumptions. Those who count are those who are mature – identified as persons, they must be already rational, vocal, and have plans and purposes, to qualify for consideration. The younger and less capable of self-preservation human beings are, the less claim they have to consideration and, if they are at the most incipient stage of all, may be treated only as material for the purposes of the mature. (This could be called 'maturism' by analogy with racism, sexism and speciesism.) But having passed maturity, or lost health and the ability to fend for themselves, humans, according to this account, become less and less deserving of consideration.

I briefly explained to Jatros the story of Faust, who sold his soul to the devil. The moral of the story is that you can have your desires but that there is a price to pay. So it is here, I suggested. Advance in these areas has not necessarily given happiness – reproductive freedom, for example, brings for many people emotionally unsatisfying serial relationships and childlessness. Even, I went on to say, a relatively neutral advance like the ability to prolong life by transferring organs from those who have died in accidents carries an unexpected downside, for the need is greater than accident can supply, so that Indian or Turkish villagers are driven to offer their own or their relatives' organs for money, while the unscrupulous anywhere in the world will arrange murder or organ theft to save a life that they value. In other words, this life-giving potential puts a bounty on the head of every human being. This is only one example of the way in which medicine, it seems, is the modern world's Pandora's box, and it cannot put the wonders it has released back in the box.

Jatros looked still more thoughtful at my reply, and then went on to ask me some more questions of a technical nature about ways and means but, not having been trained in medical science myself, I was unable to give him as much help as he wanted.

In point of fact, I was quite pleased about this, since I could see that the part of my account that interested him was the part that dealt with the technical possibilities so familiar in the developed world, but as yet unknown in his own. But I could also see that he had no sympathy at all for my reservations and doubts, nor for the moral constraints that were so uppermost in my mind.

In the discussion that followed, we returned to the point that there are many difficult decisions in a society about what to do. And yet it seems that not everybody's opinion carries the same weight, and even that there may be groups in society that have more power and influence than others. As we began to discuss this point, we were joined by Isos, a colleague of Jatros who seemed to be, as far as I could judge, rather an important person in the community. At least he had a very firm and confident way of addressing the issues, and made me feel quite uncomfortable at times, particularly in the rather cold way in which he fixed his gaze on me.

9

Notes to Chapter 9

1   Quoted in Gunning and English, *Human In Vitro Fertilization*, p. 7.

2   See the account of his own upbringing by the black abolitionist leader Frederick Douglass in *Narrative of the Life of Frederick Douglass, an American Slave*.

3   Practices differ, however, in different countries. Some jurisdictions, e.g. Sweden, New Zealand, and the state of Victoria in Australia, recognize a child's right to know the identity of its father in the case of children born of AID (artificial insemination by donor). France limits the number of children who may be conceived by an individual donor to two or three, and seeks donors who are mature married men with families, and have a full understanding of what parenting means. Britain, on the other hand, recruits largely young donors, who are permitted to father up to ten children, itself a recently imposed limit.

4   British law is not entirely clear about the way in which these different roles are to be regarded. For example, sections 27 and 28 of the Human Fertilisation and Embryology Act 1990 define a mother as the 'carrier ' (that is, the one in whose body the embryo grows to term) of the child, whether or not that child is genetically hers. However, under section 30 of the same Act, a woman who carries a child, but hands it over to a couple as a result of a surrogacy agreement, ceases to be the legal mother, just as in the case of adoption.

5   Glover, *Fertility and the Family*, p. 35.

6   The phrase 'right to procreative liberty' is used by Max Charlesworth in *Bioethics in a Liberal Society*. He provides a figure of about $40,000 (£20,000) as the cost of an IVF baby, calculated by dividing the cost of cycles of treatment by resulting live births. Even the simple prescription of fertility drugs resulting

in a multiple birth could cost up to £1m. in intensive care for up to two months per infant.

7   Strathern, *Reproducing the Future.*

8   Warnock, 'Do human cells have rights?'

9   Kass, 'Making babies revisited', p. 345.

10 For a defence of this point of view, see Marquis, 'Why abortion is immoral.'

11 It is no solution to use the term 'fetus', for the general use of that term has only developed as a response to the wide availability of abortion. Before changes in abortion law in various countries, the term was hardly to be found outside medical textbooks.

12 They might, for example, be used for scientific experiment and then destroyed. See Warnock, *A Question of Life.*

13 An article which explores this rather counter-intuitive conclusion is Holland, 'A fortnight of my life is missing'.

14 Tooley, Glover, Hare, Singer and Harris, for example.

15 Dworkin, *Life's Dominion*, p. 16.

16 Singer, *Practical Ethics*, p. 151.

17 Moore, 'A defence of common sense'.

18 Unusually, the British Abortion Act 1967 adds to this list the physical or mental health of a woman's existing children.

19 Thomson, 'A defense of abortion'.

20 See, however, the discussion in chapter 7, pp. 119–21 above, of ethics and gender. It is interesting to note that Gilligan's theory of an ethic of care was at least partly suggested by women's comments on their own abortion decisions which did not, in general, turn on consideration of rights.

21 See Kumar, 'Should one be free to choose the sex of one's child?' and Warren, *Gendercide.*

22 Dworkin, *Life's Dominion*, p. 20.

23 See the discussion of this point by the feminist writer, Christine Overall, in *Human Reproduction.*

24 'BMA backs doctor over twin's abortion', *The Times*, London, 5 August 1996.

25 Dworkin, *Life's Dominion*, p. 26.

26 Singer, *Practical Ethics*, p. 88. This judgement of the relative value of animals and children cannot, of course, be established by argument. See discussion of this issue in chapter 12 below.

27 This argument is presented by many biomedical philosophers including Glover, Hare, Harris, Singer and Kuhse.

28 The issue certainly needs to be discussed. There has been, however, understandable resistance to discussion of such questions in certain European countries, particularly Germany, because of the way in which the programme to eliminate the handicapped – the 'unfit' – was developed in that country in the 1930s. For the controversy about freedom of discussion on the issue, see 'A German attack on applied ethics' by Singer.

29 See, for example, Singer, *Practical Ethics*, p. 179.

30 Singer and Kuhse, *Should the Baby Live?* pp. 20–2.

31   The distinction was blurred in thes case of Dr Jack Kevorkian who invented a suicide machine which allows the person himself or herself to control the administration of lethal drugs. This nevertheless left Dr Kervorkian to face charges of murder or manslaughter. It is similarly blurred in the case of computer-controlled self-administration of a lethal dosage of drugs, as happened with legal sanction in 1996 in Queensland.

32   Cited by Murayama, 'A comparison of the hospice movement', p. 120.

10

Equality and Diversity

Tenth Conversation

Isos: I have just come from an interesting conversation with my friend Polydox. He was telling me that your society contained many views about right and wrong, good and bad. I think, though, that you hinted that it also contained many differences of a more concrete nature.

Traveller: That's true. Apart from the differences that exist here too – the difference between male and female, for example, or differences in physical capacities – it has been common where I come from to see society as divided into classes: the rich, the poor, the aristocratic, the working class.

Isos: I see. But what exactly *is* a class?

Traveller: Well, perhaps the most useful thing I could say is that it is determined by the job you do or don't do! And although some now regard class as an out-dated concept, the fact is that it lies at the base of a political ideology, Marxism, which has been and still is very influential in our world.

Isos: Ideology?

Traveller: Well, yes. I suppose that is a tricky concept too. I would say it is a way of describing something that is both a theory and a movement. For example, as a *movement* Marxism is committed to advancing the cause of the working class in all countries, while as a *theory* it explains economic and political change through an analysis of society in terms of social class.

Isos: I think I see what that might mean, although the fact is we don't have that kind of division here. We have rulers, but they change so often – and everyone has a turn – that you could not talk about a

ruling *class*. But are these the *only* differences in your society, then?
Or are there others?

Traveller: Oh, yes. Today the kind of societies I know – those in Europe,
North America and Australasia – are even more radically mixed. They
are not closed societies like yours. People travel; they migrate. And
there have been major historical events – a vast slave trade in people
across continents, for example – that have also resulted in huge
displacements of people. So most modern societies are plural, not
just in the sense of containing different opinions – something I
discussed with your friend Polydox a little while ago – but also in the
sense of containing different races and ethnic groups. There are also
religious groupings which are themselves often also linked to culture
and race.

Isos: So how does that affect the matter you mentioned at the end of
your conversation with Jatros? I mean, how does it affect questions
about the relation of individuals to the society and community they
live in – their commitment to their 'own' group , which, from what
you have told me, could be a matter of race, nation or culture? And
how far do all these differences *matter*? Are there privileges or
disadvantages depending on who or what you are?

Traveller: I am interested that you should ask these questions. For it
sounds to me as if you are hinting at something I have heard people
call social justice. Perhaps even a presumption in favour of equality?

Isos: Put it that way if you like. Here we have a very simple notion of
equality. We make no difference between women and men; both
fight and hunt, and children belong to us all – we assign people, both
male and female, to look after them till they are old enough to fend
for themselves. Didn't you say that one of your philosophers, Plato,
also recommended a system like that?

Traveller: Yes indeed. But what about the other differences we mentioned? What about the weak? And what about those of a different
race?

Isos: We have no sick, old or ailing people. Since we cannot look after
them, we take them out and leave them to the care of the gods in
the woods. And we have no racial divisions either, because we do not
admit strangers –

Traveller: But you've admitted me!

Isos: Ah, yes. That's true. Maybe you should give that fact more thought
than you seem to have done so far . . . But anyway, enough about

the way *we* live. I have been sent here to ask you rather more about those plural societies you say are the rule rather than the exception where you come from. There can be little equality in them, I suspect, and surely that must make them very unstable.

Traveller: I can only answer that at greater length. Do you have the time to listen?

Isos: Why, yes. There is no problem about time as far as *I* am concerned. **,**

Equality

Equality is a principle most modern societies endorse, often together with other ideals such as justice and freedom. It is a basic principle of democracy, not usually seen in isolation, but more often set against some kind of privilege. The root idea was put by the English philosopher John Locke (1632–1704) in these terms:

> a state of nature is a state of equality, wherein all power and jurisdiction is reciprocal, no-one having more than another, there being nothing more evident that that creatures of the same species and rank, promiscuously born to all the same advantages of nature, and the use of the same faculties, should also be equal one amongst another . . . all being equal and independent, no-one ought to harm another in his life, health, liberty or possessions.[1]

This principle of equality was later to be enshrined in the American Declaration of Independence and also became one of the demands of the leaders of the French Revolution. In these contexts, the claim that all are born free and equal is a denial of inherited privilege, caste or position. Aside from that understanding, the phrase, 'All are equal' cannot be taken literally, for patently everyone is different from everyone else in many factual ways. Locke was right, then, to treat the assertion, 'All are equal' as a moral recommendation. Politically, it is a demand for universal suffrage, expressed in the principle, 'One person, one vote'. Legally, it is a claim for justice in the sense of equality before the law. It can be summed up as prescribing that all should be *treated* equally unless there are relevant grounds for treating them differently – that is, that there should be no discrimination between people on irrelevant grounds.

But what are *relevant* grounds? When justice is said to be blind, this usually means that it pays no attention to class, race, wealth or position in society. But it is not expected to be blind to more material differences – for example, that one person has committed a crime and another has not.

And so it includes such notions as desert and entitlement, often expressed in the language of rights. These are rights to be enforced by the public authorities and they give rise to public laws, enforced by a system of sanctions or punishments. A network of social institutions supports this system – law courts and prisons, as well as the bureaucracy needed to administer them.

The notion of formal justice, then, treats the state as an umpire, whose limited functions include guarding citizens against interference in their liberties, and protecting their contracts and agreements. For a sense of justice that would involve something beyond these limits, another notion of justice is needed: justice in the sense of 'fair shares'.

Social or Distributive Justice

Justice in this second sense is concerned with the allocation of goods and benefits. It deals with the question of what kind of considerations might justify differences in the goods or wealth that people hold or enjoy. It can consider this question of fairness from two different points of view: first, how fair is the process or procedure for handing out goods? or alternatively, how fair is the outcome of the process? What sort of distribution of goods within a society will count as just?

Another way to put this second question would be to ask, 'How many should have how much?' And there are several possible answers to this question: one answer would be that there should be an absolutely equal distribution – everyone should have the same. However, this is a Procrustean proposal.[2] That is to say, given that differences will keep emerging between people, it will always be necessary for the state to interfere to correct this, taking from those who gain and giving to those who lose. In other words, it involves continuous monitoring as well as social engineering on a massive scale. It is the antithesis of liberty.

Apart from this objection, it is far from clear that an equal distribution would, in any case, be accepted as morally satisfactory in practice. For individual needs vary, and a system of distribution that failed to take account of those needs would strike many people as unfair. Indeed, it suggests a different way of answering the question altogether. This would involve bringing the matter of needs forward and giving it priority: that is, accepting an unequal distribution as long as it is based on need.

However, this, too, is open to criticism, for it might seem right or just to consider not only that someone *is* needy, but also *why* or *how* they have become needy. If one person has worked hard and made sacrifices, for example, and another has thrown away every opportunity, it might well seem unfair to meet their needs in exactly the same way, even if those needs *are* identical. There are also, more contentiously, differences in intelligence and competence, as well as determination, which might seem to justify differential rewards.

These last considerations are summed up in a principle formulated by Aristotle: that it is as unjust to treat unequals equally as to treat equals unequally. If this is so, what is needed is a principle of a different sort altogether: one that involves distribution that is in proportion to desert or to merit. But a meritocratic principle of this sort – one that involves giving to those who are deserving and holding back from those who are not – is not really an *outcome* criterion at all, since what it says is, again, that only relevant differences should be allowed to count. The difference lies only in what is considered to be relevant. This means that a principle of distribution in proportion to desert comes close to the principle of formal justice, so bringing the discussion of equality full circle.

Even so, the meritocratic principle itself does not go unchallenged. Some argue that it is unfair to relate rewards to merit or even effort on the ground that skills, ability and moral character are all a result of genetic endowment. Since we cannot alter our character – our genetic endowment – they think it unfair to make it the subject of punishment or reward.[3] As Rawls puts it: 'Even the willingness to make an effort, to try, and so to be deserving in the ordinary sense is itself dependent on happy family and social circumstances.'[4] But there is something unsatisfactory about this argument, for it seems to carry with it the idea that there might be a person within a person – an inner controller of character, who is the product of neither heredity nor environment. The fact is, however, that people are simply who they are, as defined by character, abilities, disposition, potentialities and so on. Apart from the logical issue of identity, there seems, too, to be something inconsistent in claiming that intellectual and moral qualities are valuable while at the same time insisting that society should be arranged so as to deny them any reward.

If the attack on the meritocratic claim can be resisted in this way, then the moral case for equality can be put in terms of the principle of equality of opportunity – ensuring simply that everyone starts on a common basis to compete for the prizes of life, without unfair advantage or disadvantage. This is still not the end of the matter, though, for it may be that equal opportunity itself can be affected by a variety of factors which, unlike ability, initiative and hard work, are clearly irrelevant to the question of what people deserve. Amongst these factors two characteristics are often seen as unfairly affecting an individual's success in life: the first of these is gender; the second is race or ethnicity. Invidious treatment on either of these grounds is widely condemned as, in the first case, sexism and in the second as racism. Both of these, it is argued, can lead to unfairness in the distribution of social goods. Before either of these charges or their remedies can be discussed, however, it is necessary to be clear about the meaning of the terms themselves.

Racism and Sexism

Both racism and sexism are disputed concepts. One standard way to interpret them is to link them to certain *beliefs*, particularly the belief that there are differences in abilities and capacities either amongst racial groups, or between the sexes.

A typical example is provided by the policy document of a British educational institution, which defines the two concepts like this:

> racism is a system of beliefs, attitudes and concepts which rest upon notions of racial superiority and inferiority.

It continues:

> sexism refers to the belief that gender determines intrinsic worth, capacities and role in society, and that sexual differences produce an inherent superiority of a particular sex, usually the male.[5]

There are a number of problems with this way of defining the two concepts. To begin with, it fails to distinguish between, on the one hand, believing that there *are* differences related to race or gender, and, on the other, taking those differences as measures of superiority or inferiority. To take a neutral illustration of this, if someone were to claim that men are superior to women because they are heavier, they would be claiming, first, that they *are* heavier, a factual claim which is true or false, and, secondly, that being heavy is superior to being light, which is a matter of judgement. Moreover, even if there *are* on average differences between groups in some respect, whether racially or gender-based – perhaps, for example, in their tendency to appreciate classical music, or in respect of height, or of sporting skills, or success in orienteering – this does not mean that *all* members of one group will perform better in that respect than members of the other group. Indeed, the very notion of an average entails that some will be above the median line and some will fall below it. So, for example, even if women on average are not as tall as men, some women may still be taller than some men.

There is, too, an objection of quite a different kind to interpreting racism and sexism as factual beliefs: this is the moral consideration that it leads to a conflict with one of the most important of liberal principles – freedom of thought and belief. If it extends further to a ban on *bona fide* research or investigation into factual differences, then it also clashes with freedom of academic enquiry – the right, or indeed the duty, to pursue truth without constraints. The only ground on which such restrictions could be justified would be if the exercise of these freedoms were to lead to actual physical harm to some individuals. In this case, even someone committed to the principle of individual liberty could accept restrictions, but this would be for the sake of the liberty of those who were threatened. The issue would then turn on this matter of fact.

Whatever the facts, however, there is a case for looking more carefully at the question of definition. And indeed, on reflection, it is clear that racism and sexism have much more to do with behaviour than with belief. That is to say, they concern the way people treat other people rather than the way they think about them. According to this alternative view, then, racism and sexism involve treating some people adversely because of their sex or race. Shifting attention to *actions* in this way brings the issue into an arena that has long been recognized as a legitimate area for law. What is more, the implicit demand behind this way of defining the issues is for impartiality of treatment where irrelevant factors are concerned, and this is a very generally recognized moral requirement. As R. M. Hare has argued, it is a requirement that can very readily be applied to an issue such as race, which stands out as an irrelevant criterion for differential treatment.[6] To treat people well or badly because of their race, then, or because of their sex, is, apart from everything else, to fail in the duty to treat people as independent, autonomous beings – as Kant put it, as ends in themselves.

But these are theoretical considerations, and in practice, impartiality of treatment may turn out to raise problems of its own. In particular, it may result in some groups noticeably falling back in relation to others. Statistics about the make-up of bodies like legislatures, boards of business enterprises, professions or student bodies often show a disparity in the number of women or members of ethnic minoirities they contain in proportion to their number in the population as a whole. It is often assumed that if a group is not proportionately represented in every desirable occupation or course, this must be because of some underlying institutional or personal bias.[7]

As far as this charge is concerned, it first has to be said that, while it is true that there can be structural arrangements which make access harder for some particular group, the notion of 'institutional bias' itself should be treated with some caution. This is because institutions, not being persons with minds and desires, cannot in fact have intentions or moral attitudes for which they can be praised or blamed. The idea, then, can only be taken as a metaphor, or as a way of pointing to the attitudes of individual people who happen to have institutional roles and responsibilities.

Even so, it is beyond dispute that certain groups are indeed sometimes the subject of bias or prejudice, and have also suffered unfair discrimination in the past. There is therefore a case for seeking to find some way to balance that injustice. Since formal justice and equality rule out discrimination *against* people, it has seemed to many people that an appropriate way to do this is to adopt the reverse procedure – to discriminate in *favour* of members of the disadvantaged groups. This has been a significant policy in the USA for some years, but has recently been challenged by renewed proposals to outlaw taking race or sex into account in awarding jobs, college places or public contracts, *whoever* this is intended to benefit.[8] Many have pointed to the paradox that while the Civil Rights Act 1964 outlawed ascriptions of people in terms of 'race, color, religion, sex, national origin', in order to carry out this 'race-blind' policy people find they are obliged to label themselves for public record in terms of these categories – something which many find offensive in itself.[9] Reverse discrimination, then, is a controversial issue, and this is compounded by the fact that discrimination itself is morally ambiguous.

The Discrimination Issue

There are many contexts in which being discriminating is thought to be a good thing. These included situations as diverse as choosing a meal in a restaurant, ordering a beer in a pub, buying a painting or novel, choosing a partner or awarding a research grant. However, the case for positive discrimination is usually based not on this general observation but on a specific view of gender and race inequality.

First, though what *is* positive discrimination? According to one interpretation, it means that if there are two equally well-qualified people who are being considered for a place or a job, one of whom belongs to the group regarded as disadvantaged, selectors should prefer the member of the disadvantaged group. Alternatively, positive discrimination may be interpreted as meaning giving preference, in some circumstances, to a less well-qualified member of the disadvantaged group. Both of these are to be distinguished from the policy known as affirmative action, which is a less contentious approach and which simply involves making an effort not to overlook people in the under-privileged groups – or, more positively, to seek them out and encourage them to apply.

The situation envisaged in the first interpretation of positive discrimination is so rare, and absolute parity so difficult to establish that, in practice, the issue has tended to become identified with the second policy. Hence it has resulted in a number of famous court cases in the United States which have involved white applicants being turned away from courses to which they applied in favour of black applicants with lower qualifying scores than they themselves could offer.[10] Those who believed themselves to have lost out as a result of these policies argued that they were being treated adversely simply because of their race.

Nevertheless, despite the sense of injustice felt by some individuals in these circumstances, positive discrimination has been widely defended on different moral grounds. Two kinds of argument have been advanced in its favour. One is a backward-looking argument – that it seeks to compensate for past wrongs and to cancel out past injustice by permitting preferential treatment now and in the future in respect of jobs or education. Alternatively, it may be seen as an attempt to redress *present* deprivation or handicap by the same means. In either case, the principle being applied is that of compensation for a wrong done. The other argument has a different moral basis. It looks to the future rather than the past, and seeks to break the cycle of deprivation, for example, by providing role models for younger members of the disadvantaged group, or securing proportionate representation in desirable professions or educational settings. This is an essentially consequentialist or utilitarian principle of justification, which is sometimes supplemented by a claim that considerations like these make being a member of the disadvantaged group a qualification for the job.

A number of difficulties, both practical and moral, are raised by these arguments. First, there are those who believe on psychological grounds that the attempt to privilege groups could in fact create the very racial or gender-based tension that it seeks to correct. Secondly, the whole enterprise seems to depend on actually assuming the natural inferiority of the groups in question, since it takes it for granted that they cannot be trusted to achieve success for themselves. What is more, it makes life difficult for members of the under-privileged groups who *do* achieve advancement – people may wrongly assume that their success is a result of lower standards being applied in their case, or that they are not as good as the more typical (usually white male) applicant or job-holder.

Fourthly, there is a problem about treating *groups* in this way. The notion of compensating an individual is clear, both morally and practically. But it is less obvious that compensation for the ill-treatment of a group can be achieved by kindness to a different individual member of that group who may not personally have been disadvantaged at all – this is particularly so when both the individual members who suffered injustice, as well as the individual members of the group which ill-treated them, are long dead.

The arguments which have been applied in respect of race, ethnicity and gender, may also be extended to the disabled, and to groups distinguished by minority sexual preferences. But there are significant differences when it comes to applying positive discrimination in these areas. In the UK, legislation following the Second World War recognized disability as a handicap in many kinds of employment, but sought to help those who had lost limbs or faculties in the service of their country by imposing a shared obligation on all large employers to take on an agreed proportion of disabled persons. This reasoning is different from the more recent arguments concerning race or gender, for whereas the argument in those cases is usually based on a claim that all are equally competent, the reverse is assumed in the case of the disabled war veterans or ex-service personnel; it was precisely because they could not compete with the able-bodied in an open market that an employment niche was to be reserved for them. Of course, many disabled people can overcome their personal difficulties and so perform as well as the able-bodied in certain contexts; nevertheless, it remains the case that particular disabilities preclude particular competences – for instance, a blind person cannot scan reading-matter at speed like a sighted person, and a deaf person cannot deal with mumbling members of the public.

As for sexual preference, if this is not overt, it is unlikely to lead to discrimination in the workplace or by the selection panel since they will not be aware of it; but if confirmation that it is *not* being used adversely is demanded, knowledge of sexual orientation becomes essential; thus an intrusive form of monitoring is needed, in which an employee's sexual preferences are declared and possibly held on file. For these very different reasons, then, the path to abolishing discrimination in these areas is strewn with practical obstacles.

Whatever the particular arguments, however, there is one general principle that is hard to refute: if discrimination is wrong, then it must be wrong to *use* discrimination to counter discrimination; and if racism and sexism are wrong, it must be wrong to use racism to counter racism or to use sexism to counter sexism. Two special cases deserve separate consideration.

Punishing Racially-motivated Crime

In a number of countries, the desire to eliminate the evil of racism has been expressed in legislation that adds a statutory extra penalty to punishment for crimes that have been inspired by racial motives. At first sight, this seems an effective way of expressing society's special abhorrence of racist violence in particular, and of deterring groups which aim to commit crimes of violence against members of other races.

However, despite these good objectives, legislation of this kind is bound to offend against the principle of equality before the law by creating different classes of victims, and hence of criminals. The world of crime becomes racially divided, giving the police reason to collect and record information on racial aspects when investigating a crime. There are a number of ways in which this might be found offensive. If the law says that violence from a racial motive is worse than violence from other motives, then it must in a sense also be saying that other motives for violence are better. But once this path is entered, it is hard to know where to stop. After all, there are other vulnerable groups in society – children, women, gays, the elderly, the infirm. To be selected for violence because you are old and vulnerable is no less unpleasant for the victim of violence than to be selected as a member of a racial group. If, on the other hand, it is suggested that what is offensive is that the attack is for ideological reasons – if it is the organized nature of the violence that creates the special nature of the crime – racism is not the only root from which this can spring. Religion, for example, has, for most of recorded human history, provided another potent motive for persecution.

Laws that respond to motive in this way also offend against democratic notions of the limits of law, which have traditionally been set at the boundary of action, so that speech and thought, except in specially defined circumstances, are off limits for law. Totalitarian regimes that seek to control the mind are hated by those who value freedom – and in a sense, of course, thought cannot be controlled and motive is notoriously difficult to prove. But the attempt to do so sits ill with liberal regimes. These principles are even more clearly seen in relation to the issue of directly banning racist talk.[11]

Outlawing Racist and Sexist Talk

If freedom of thought is an absolute claim, but freedom of action can rightly be constrained or limited by the claims of others, freedom of speech provides a half-way house between these two. It is closely connected to freedom of thought, for of what value is it to have ideas, thoughts and beliefs if you cannot publish, communicate or discuss them with others? And yet speech is in the public, not private domain, and can undoubtedly be mischievously and dangerously employed. Hence a case exists for constraining speech which could provide a bridge from thought to action of a harm-threatening kind. This is particularly so where race is concerned, given the history of persecution associated with it.

The American Constitution rules that Congress may make no law abridging freedom of speech. Nevertheless, racist and sexist talk are not in fact free of sanction in America, since both sexual and racial harrassment are crimes that can be taken as applying to speech. Speech is also constrained in British law, where the Race Relations Act 1976 established the offence of publishing or distributing written matter that is threatening, abusive or insulting; or of using words that are threatening, abusive or insulting in a public place or at a public meeting in a situation where racial hatred is likely to be stirred up. It can be argued, though, that this is not necessarily an unjustifiable infringement of liberty, but a situation precisely like the one recognized by J. S. Mill in his classic essay on liberty, as constituting a justifiable exception to the principle. In that essay, Mill argued on a number of grounds for freedom of thought and freedom of speech. To suppress an opinion is, he suggested, to assume infallibility. It may also be to set back the cause of truth for centuries. Even a false opinion, Mill believed, should be allowed to be aired, for those who hold true opinions need the challenge of opposition and criticism if their beliefs and ideas are not to become 'dead dogmas'.[12] Nevertheless, he argued that while people should be free to express the view that corndealers were thieves, they should not be free to express that opinion before an angry mob outside a corndealer's house during a famine.

So while classical liberalism does not demand absolute freedom of speech, it nevertheless takes a clear threat to the physical safety of an identified human being as the kind of justification needed if freedom of speech *is* to be abridged. This puts laws outlawing racist or sexist speech in a morally sensitive position. In so far as they are justified, this can only be on the basis of the empirical assumption that they will in fact lead some people to harm or indeed kill others.

Multiculturalism

The discussion of racism has presupposed that there is an unambiguous way of marking people out by race. This in itself is questionable, sometimes necessitating a return to a dark past in which racial identities have to be established by an exploration of family history to grandparents, great-grandparents or yet more distant ancestors. But in any case, race and gender are not the only social divisions, and the term 'multicultural' is used in a way that points to some extra dimensions of difference – in contemporary discussions, these differences may include religion, language, skin colour, and sexual orientation, as well as gender, race and ethnicity. Not all of these, however, mark out genuinely 'cultural' groups, for the notion of 'culture' has a well-established connotation. This includes two primary senses: first, that of culture in relation to literature, art, music and the sciences as 'the best that has been thought and known' – so-called 'high culture' – and secondly, the notion of *popular* culture in the sense that involves the features of a common life, such as entertainment, food, life-styles, customs and habits, which mark out the distinctive way of life of a community.[13] Apart from reflecting differently these two primary senses, the term 'multiculturalism' can also take on a different meaning in different geographical locations. While in Europe, for example, pluralism and multiculturalism suggest mainly religious and ethnic differences, often reinforced by differences of language, in the United States diverse 'cultural identities' may be attributed to women, gays or groups defined by skin colour.

But while religion and language are indeed important cultural markers, sometimes extending to a whole way of life, the colour of people's skin, their sexuality or gender are less reliably linked to culture in either of its primary senses. This is not necessarily a bad thing, as the Nigeria-born Harvard philosopher K. A. Appiah observes, pointing out that to construct one's identity out of being gay or black may in the end be the opposite of liberating. He writes: 'If I had to choose between the world of the closet and the world of gay liberation, or between the world of *Uncle Tom's Cabin* and Black Power, I would, of course, choose in each case the latter. But I would like not to have to choose. I would like other options.'[14]

Gender, too, is not a *cultural* marker. For women are not a culturally distinguishable group. They live amongst the population at large, seldom in separately located communities. While there have been significant changes in the position of women since Simone de Beauvoir wrote *The Second Sex*, for the overwhelming majority of women worldwide it is still true, as she wrote then, that women 'live dispersed among the males, attached through residence, housework, economic condition, and social standing to certain men – fathers or husbands – more firmly than they are to other women.'[15]

So societies contain, and always have contained, many differences, but not all differences are a matter of culture. In Europe, essentially homogeneous cultures, woven over millennia from Jewish–Christian influences and the historical legacies of the Greeks and Romans, have only recently met with a number of significant influences: large-scale immigration by groups with other historical and religious traditions, the ubiquitous influence of international media, particularly those based on contemporary American culture, a decline in traditional Christian religious belief as a result of a more sophisticated understanding of science and history, and the influence of previously neglected groups – the marginalized voices of minorities of various kinds.

If, at a factual level, multiculturalism is a suspect concept, it is even more so in its normative implications. Multiculturalism in political terms is based on doubt that it is right for the state to endorse any particular moral, cultural or religious position. The principle that government should be morally and ideologically neutral is understandable in an immigrant society like that of the the USA, which has welcomed individuals and groups with strong cultural and religious differences, as well as people of different races and ethnic backgrounds. But European history leads in a different direction. In Europe, it has in the end, after many struggles, been generally accepted that the anti-colonialist movements of the twentieth century were based on a sound moral principle: that groups, and particularly national groups, should be free to propagate and perpetuate their own distinctive culture and values, and to reject those imposed by alien outsiders.

These two principles of state neutrality on the one hand and a right to a national cultural identity on the other are in direct tension with each other. As far as a right to the affirmation of culture is concerned, it is not always recognized that the principle, if accepted, has at least equal legitimacy when applied to the liberal democracies themselves. Instead of accepting this, the liberal democracies are plagued by self-doubt, fostered by a misconception of what liberalism actually involves. In recognizing the liberty of individuals to choose the kind of life they want to lead, they have neglected the liberty of those same individuals to choose the kind of community in which they would wish to exercise that freedom. They have assumed that the liberal state must be neutral between different cultural ideals and different conceptions of the good. This issue has become encapsulated in the debate between liberals and communitarians.

Communitarian Ideals and Liberal Individualism

Communitarianism is based on affirming the essential value of communities, although the nature of a 'community' is ill-defined; it can vary in scale from a small sub-group within a state to the nation state itself, or may even be understood in global terms. Communitarians may prefer to define the term 'community' in terms of commitment to a set of shared values, norms and meaning, and one version of the movement which emphasizes this perspective has been developed by the American theorist Amitai Etzioni under the name of 'responsive communitarianism'. This term is meant to convey a flexible and adaptive political approach directed at maintaining a balance between the needs of the community and individual rights. For example, in the USA – where, communitarians believe, there is too much emphasis on individualism – responsive communitarians are expected to emphasize community responsibilities; in China where there is too little, it may be more important to defend individual rights. Like sailors on a sailing ship, then, responsive communitarians will move from side to side, keeping the ship of society safely afloat.

This explains, perhaps, why communitarians find themselves subject to attack from two very different directions. On the one hand, they may find themselves charged with conservativism and nostalgia – and perhaps, too, with a totalitarian desire to enforce conformity to the opinions of the majority. On the other, they may be charged with a desire to promote welfare provision, state subsidies and socialism. Communitarians themselves would prefer not to be typecast in traditional terms; they see themselves as putting forward a position which involves a number of closely related theses:

1   The thesis of 'the embedded self' – this is the doctrine that individual human beings are identified with their own particular language, culture and tradition and that choice can only be meaningfully understood within this 'thick' identity. Autonomy is interpreted in a non-Kantian non-universal sense, as authenticity.[16]
2   The retreat from the notion of universal rights, at least when these are divorced from responsibilities and duties, in favour of a policy of empowerment. Rights are seen as belonging to the (liberal) domain of justice – an abstract conception which fails to take account of each person's particularity. The communitarian view is expressed in terms of a plurality of incommensurable values rather than universal principles.

3   The preference for particularity. For example, instead of relating duties to universal claims, individuals are expected to think of their own position in relation to their own particular context and their own personal responsibilities.

This contrasts sharply with the political stance of liberalism in its classic form, which is humanistic and universalistic in its emphasis. That is to say, it is based on faith in a common human identity which generates common, universal, human rights and freedoms. It is this conception that gives liberalism its moral authority, and its moral ideals are an integral part of its history, lying in a rejection of religious persecution and authoritarian government, especially that of a hereditary aristocracy. Liberalism prefers reason to authority; it bases political obligation on the free consent of the individual, and interprets moral obligation in terms of autonomy. The ideals to which the liberal is committed could be summed up, then, as:

- the ethical ideals of freedom, toleration, and justice;
- the intellectual ideals of rationalism and universalism;
- the political ideal of individualism, with consequent limitations on the power of government;
- the social ideals of pluralism and tolerance of difference;
- the economic ideals of *laissez-faire* and the free market.

In the United States, this form of classical liberalism is more likely to be called libertarianism, while the term 'liberalism' has become linked there to welfarist goals and tendencies.

Critics of Liberalism

The idea of a state that is committed to a particular view of the good life and that seeks to impose it on its citizens, is sometimes described as perfectionism. This tendency, represented by political thinkers as diverse as Plato, Aristotle and Marx, has been condemned by some philosophers as illiberal and totalitarian.[17] But the idea that the state can or should remain neutral is equally problematic. Today many societies contain genuine cultural minorities and cultural membership is seen by many as a primary good. Faced with the accusation that it is insensitive to the needs of minority communities, and unable to associate itself officially with any of them, a liberal state may seek to empower all equally to pursue their own conception of the good life. This may well seem an incoherent goal, but the Canadian philosopher Will Kymlicka, defending a liberal theory of minority rights, embraces the paradox that people may need a stable cultural setting to make their individual choices meaningful.[18] This is a view that is also put forward by Alasdair MacIntyre, but MacIntyre has no wish to retain the liberal concept of rights, which he dismisses as 'fictions'.[19] Instead, setting individualism as it is traditionally understood in opposition to community – the natural ties of family, neighbourhood, ethnic and national identity – MacIntyre proposes a return to an Aristotelian tradition of civic virtue.

Nevertheless, in practice the content of some cultures and the practices of some communities will be unacceptable to the liberal; and there are liberals who believe that the value of freedom depends on the moral worth of what a person is free to do. The Oxford philosopher Joseph Raz writes:

> since autonomy is valuable only if it is directed at the good it supplies no reason to provide, nor any reason to protect, worthless let alone bad options.'[20]

This leads to a further series of charges against liberalism in its classical or libertarian form. It is often portrayed as being responsible for the emergence of a rootless privatized individual who is psychologically and emotionally isolated in a mass society. This in turn produces, it is claimed, a moral and cultural vacuum which leads, in the end, to other widespread evils: crime, pornography and the decline of the family.[21]

These charges might be justified if the social evils currently afflicting the liberal societies – an aggressive international drug-trade, HIV, pornography and the degradation of taste and manners – were indeed to be defended in the name of liberalism. But if there is an erosion of the common environment of public and social institutions – if society has indeed become 'uncivil' – the fault may lie not with liberalism itself but with the interpretation that has been put on it, and the strains to which it has been subjected internally by those who have taken advantage of the freedoms it offers to test and push against its limits.

However, the fact is that a classical liberal is under no obligation to support acknowledged social evils in the name of freedom. To take only one example, drug-taking can be condemned on purely libertarian terms: for to use addictive drugs, it can plausibly be argued, is the equivalent of selling yourself into slavery, something no libertarian can defend; in addition, the social costs of drug-use and abuse are high and must be borne by others. Undoubtedly, J. S. Mill, in defending the freedom of individuals to harm themselves if they so chose, underestimated – or, rather, failed to anticipate – the economic costs of self-damage on a massive scale. In contemporary terms, these may involve the decline of whole neighbour-hoods and the breakdown of family networks of mutual support which used to provide the cement of fragile human relationships.

Liberalism, then, has been accused of converting a lack of ethos into a principle for living and of elevating choice to the highest good.[22] But liberalism does not, after all, mean permissiveness or indifference to the good. While it is often interpreted as a philosophy of positive rights and negative or neutral morality, it is better seen as a philosophy of negative rights and positive morality. Nevertheless, it must be admitted that its emphasis on universality – the idea of a common humanity – is for many people too broad a perspective; people do, it seems, seek the congeniality of smaller units, searching for a sense of belonging; it is this, after all, that produces the strength of family, tribal and ethnic allegiance and ultimately, perhaps, nationhood and the sense of patriotism that engenders.

Interlude

> I went on talking to Isos for some time. He asked me about the world I came from, which he was hearing about for the first time. I had to tell him that it had in many places broken down into tribal wars. I described secession movements in some parts of the world, the shaking off of colonial rule in others. Just then someone else arrived. This was Polemos, a heavily built man who wore all the signs of the warrior class – indeed, apart from his general manner, I could hardly have overlooked the fact that he was more adorned with weapons than were any of the other people I had so far met. Polemos observed that some of the matters we had been discussing could be given an application even within the Alloi's own experience. He said that they, too, valued their group but hated their enemies – indeed, he felt that their very identity was defined in relation to the enemy or outsider. So he saw no value in peace, but valued friction or conflict for its own sake.
>
> We went on to discuss some of these issues, and also the question of how the Alloi dealt with people from their own ranks whom they regarded as enemies of their own society. In general, Polemos argued strongly for the Alloi's right and duty to protect their way of life by punishing those who broke their rules, and also to maintain their independence from interference by the warring groups living in the depths of the unknown forested land that lay beyond their home territory.

Notes on Chapter 10

1   Locke, *Second Treatise of Civil Government*, ch. II, sec. 4. See also ch. VI, sec. 54.

2   Procrustes was said to have tortured his victims by placing them on a bed and then, according to their height, either stretching them or cutting them down to size. The British philosopher Antony Flew used the term Procrustean to describe radically egalitarian social policies in his book *The Politics of Procrustes*.

3   See, for example, Feinberg, *Social Philosophy*, pp. 112–17.

4   Rawls, *A Theory of Justice*, p. 74, n. 11. See also the discussion of Rawls in chapter 5, pp. 76–9.

5   PNL policy statement on equal opportunities, pp. 4–5.

6   Hare, *Freedom and Reason*.

7   This issue is very clearly discussed by Antony Flew and Antony Skillen. See Flew, 'Three concepts of racism' and Skillen, 'Racism: Flew's three concepts of racism'.

8   Proposition 209 in California, which echoes in its wording the Civil Rights Act 1964. Report in *The Times*, London, 23 December 1996.

9   This is discussed, for example, in Moynihan, *Pandaemonium*, especially pp. 55–6.

10   Probably the best known of these was *Regents of the University of California* v. *Bakke*, 1978, and *De Funis* v. *Odegaard*, 1974.

11   Both these issues are discussed by Erik Wals in an unpublished dissertation, 'Hate in the United States and Europe.' The author cites a number of cases in Europe and the USA which have turned on this issue and prompted diverse responses from the courts.

12   Mill, *On Liberty*. See also chapter 4, pp. 68–9.

13   See Eliot, *Notes toward the Definition of Culture*.

14   Appiah, 'Identity, authenticity, survival', p. 163.

15   De Beauvoir, *The Second Sex*.

16   See the discussion of Kant's view of autonomy in chapter 6, pp. 96–8.

17   See, for example, Popper, *The Open Society and its Enemies* and Talmon, *The Origins of Totalitarian Democracy*.

18   Kymlicka, *Multicultural Citizenship*.

19   Kymlicka, *Liberalism, Community and Culture*.

20   Raz, *The Morality of Freedom*, p. 251.

21   See Beiner, *What's the Matter with Liberalism?*

22   Ibid. p. 36.

11

Freedom, Justice and Conflict

Eleventh Conversation

Polemos: Earlier you mentioned two kinds of justice, but it seems to me there are wider questions about this than the ones you discussed. For example, do you believe that it may be just to take someone's life?

Traveller: Well, I suppose that, where I come from, the answer to that would be that it depends on the situation. Most people would accept that the state can order you out to war, where you might very well be killed, and you yourself are authorized to kill in these circumstances. But *private* killing is outlawed, whether by the criminal within society or the terrorist without. Some states feel justified in taking the lives of those society members who break this rule; and some would kill terrorists in confrontations, but the spirit of liberal democracy is marked by its reluctance to take life.

Polemos: So you don't execute murderers?

Traveller: Ah, now you are jumping to conclusions. I didn't mean that you would never find capital punishment in a democratic country; indeed there are places where it has been reinstated after a period of abolition.

Polemos: So why is there this reluctance that you mention? We don't have any problems with killing our enemies here, whether internal or external enemies.

Traveller: I am glad that you mention enemies. You wouldn't kill *innocent* people, of course, would you?

Polemos: That's another matter. But let's stick to the point. We don't really recognize the distinctions you have drawn. Here only the outsider may be killed, but we believe that one of our own people makes himself an outsider if he takes the life of one of us.

Traveller: That's certainly a way to avoid inconsistency. But it seems in fact as if you aren't too concerned about setting limits.

Polemos: You might say that, but I am beginning to think you make too much fuss about killing, especially when you bother so much about killing people who actually *want* to die for one reason or another. On the other hand, it sounds as if you remove all these restraints when you go to war.

Traveller: Well, yes. I can understand your puzzlement. And I am sorry to say that, for those who abhor the excesses of war, time and civilization have not brought about any improvement. Indeed, in the twentieth century the whole world was drawn into two world wars which resulted in slaughter on a massive scale. But excuse me – not *quite* the whole world. Of course, hidden away in this remote place, you and your people could have known nothing of those events.

Polemos: True. We did not. So how could such wars have happened? Is there some general explanation, or is it only possible to explain war in terms of particular circumstances?

Traveller: Well, there are certainly people who look for general explanations. Some find an answer in the machinations of rulers or the vested interests of aristocrats; others in jingoistic nationalism or the greed of armaments manufacturers. There are those, too, who think the causes of war lie in the quest for territory and resources, very often because of an expanding population. Indeed, in the eighteenth century, Thomas Malthus (1766–1834) argued that unless there was a balance between a population and its food and resources, nature would supply the deficit through famine, disease and war.

Polemos: I have a colleague who would find what you have to say on that subject very interesting. Perhaps I can bring him to meet you later. But tell me first, does everyone where you come from think that war is a bad thing?

Traveller: Certainly there are those who refuse to fight under any circumstances, but most people believe that there can be situations in which there is no other choice. And historically, war has been regarded as a noble art and the role of the soldier as an honourable profession.

Polemos: Of course, if you have enemies, they must be prevented from injuring you and your children. That is, after all, what we say in the case of *internal* enemies.

Traveller: You mean criminals.

Polemos: That's right. And surely in their case you think it is right to do what you can – even if that means killing them – to prevent them doing harm.

Traveller: True, they have to be restrained in some way. But as I said, many people object to killing people who have committed crimes, even the most heinous crime of murder.

Polemos: Why is that?

Traveller: Well, let me explain.

Crime and Punishment

Political theorists of left and right acknowledge the right to life of the individual, and the individual's right to be free from physical harm deliberately or carelessly inflicted by others. This is the starting-point for political institutions, and for civil society. The state has at minimum, then, a double duty: to preserve public order within its boundaries and to protect its citizens from enemies without. This means, however, that there may be circumstances in which these individual rights may be set aside. One such circumstance is provided by conventional warfare; another is the requirement for an institution of punishment, possibly including capital punishment. For it is no denial of freedom to say that each person's freedom must be constrained both by the requirements of justice and by the competing freedoms of other people.

Nevertheless, punishment may need some wider justification than this. For a utilitarian, who is willing to allow that the end can justify the means, this will be a matter of showing that by inflicting the harm of punishment on some people, you prevent greater harm to others. On the other hand, for those who reject utilitarianism and hence any justification in terms of future gains, it may be necessary to seek a justification for punishment in what has happened in the past. Indeed, the principle of retribution – the Old Testament law which demanded an eye for eye, a tooth for a tooth – is probably one of the oldest justifications of punishment. In the present day, this particular principle of justice has been modified by a stronger dislike of the crude or the barbarous, so that a direct response of like with like would not generally be acceptable.[1] Instead, the equivalent of the damage done has to be worked out in terms of something that *is* acceptable, whether fines, imprisonment, community service or some other alternative. Nevertheless, the principle of just retribution continues to find its expression in the demand that a balance should be struck between punishment and crime. Beyond this lies a yet stronger claim: that a crime should not be left unpunished. This second aspect was put by Kant in uncompromising terms:

> Even if a civil society were to dissolve itself by common agreement of all its members . . . the last murderer remaining in prison must first be executed, so that everyone will duly receive what his actions are worth and so that the bloodguilt thereof will not be fixed on the people because they failed to insist on carrying out the punishment; for if they fail to do so, they may be regarded as accomplices in the public violation of legal justice.[2]

More strongly still, Hegel held that punishment was required even from the point of view of the criminal. This is because it is needed to cancel out the crime that has been committed; and since this annulment is the only way to restore the moral balance, a criminal has a *right* and even a desire to be punished. So, as Hegel puts it: 'the injury which falls on the criminal is not merely implicitly just – as just, it is *eo ipso* his implicit will.'[3]

Strong metaphysical claims of this sort, however, are not essential to the view that seeks to justify punishment as retribution. For in its simplest and most convincing form, it amounts simply to the belief that the question, 'What right have we to punish other people?' is adequately answered by the retrospective statement, 'They have knowingly and deliberately done wrong.'

The force of such a retrospective justification is in strong contrast to one that looks to future gains as a reason for punishment. A utilitarian justification is bound to look forward in this way. For since the starting-point for utilitarian moral theory is the belief that pain is evil, the practice of punishment can only be justified if it can be shown that, by inflicting that limited pain, greater pain can be averted in the future. The utilitarian view is that there are three respects in which this may be the case.

1   It may act as a *deterrent*, both to others and to criminals themselves, inducing them to avoid repeating the crime.
2   It may *prevent* crime by removing the criminal from society, at least temporarily.
3   It may result in genuine *reform* and *rehabilitation* of the offender.

These three objectives are not necessarily consistent with each other, although it is often optimistically assumed that they are. In particular, while the first two objectives require as punishment some process that is unpleasant and unwelcome, it is quite possible that the third requires treatment of a more positive and sympathetic nature. This contrast causes a tension between humanitarians and disciplinarians even within the context of an approach which takes it for granted that punishment must achieve some future good.

The formula for a utilitarian approach was most fully worked out by Bentham who, in the late eighteenth century, set out a comprehensive theory of punishment within the framework of his general utilitarian philosophy.[4] His was a practical as well as a theoretical interest for it led him to devise a scheme for a new type of prison, the Panopticon, in which prisoners were to work and be rewarded for their labour. The scheme came close to fruition, having gained the support of the British Parliament, but it was cancelled at a late stage. Bentham's contribution to the *theory* of punishment, however, was more enduring. It was a theory that required of any system of punishments in a society a close and precise calculation of future gains to be secured and future losses averted. Bentham recognized that laws were essential for public order and civil society, and that laws, to be effective, needed the support of the sanction of punishment. But he argued that punishments must be precisely calculated so as to outweigh the attraction of a crime by just enough to make the crime not worth committing; in other words, they should be neither too heavy nor too light. The calculation involved would be complex enough to take into account not only the severity of the threatened punishment in comparison with the rewards of crime, but also the probability of being caught and, if caught, of being found guilty.

But while Bentham strongly advocated this pragmatic approach, it was as strongly repudiated by Kant who wrote:

> Judicial punishment can never be used merely as a means for promoting some other good, for the criminal himself or for civil society, but instead it must in all cases be imposed on him only on the ground that he has committed a crime; for a human being can never be manipulated merely as a means for the purposes of someone else.[5]

Kant's objection points to two requirements of any just theory of punishment.

1 That it should entail that only the innocent should be punished: At first sight, it might seem reasonable to ask, 'Why punish only those who have committed crimes?' After all, unscrupulous rulers have in the past often found it more effective to punish the relatives of offenders than the offenders themselves. What is more, it is not always possible to identify the person who has actually committed a crime and, in the absence of a suspect, it could be useful, for the sake of public order, to pin the crime on *any* plausible individual. The retributivist has no difficulty in saying that either of these courses of action would be wrong, for only the guilty deserve retribution; the utilitarian, on the other hand, has more of a problem.

For some utilitarians it is a problem that can be solved by resort to a technical solution: to make it a matter of *definition* that only those who are guilty can be punished – that punishment is a term that only applies in the case of guilt. This was called by the Oxford philosopher of law, H. L. A. Hart (1907–92), the 'definitional stop' argument.[6] The very meaning of punishment, it might be said, is that it is a matter of the infliction of pain by an authority on an offender for an offence. The advantage of this solution is that including the guilt of the person in the definition of punishment in this way gives the term 'punish' something of the self-guaranteeing quality of words like 'know' or 'remember'. The drawback, though, is obvious: that it does not relate to any matter of fact; instead, it remains in the area of stipulative definition. In other words, if this definition is accepted, it will follow that someone who is genuinely punished is indeed guilty, but, of course, there is no guarantee that everyone who is charged with a crime and found guilty is not in fact being 'punished' for a crime they did not commit.

If the conceptual solution is not available, however, the utilitarian must fall back on the practical argument that punishing the innocent is unlikely to be effective in reducing crime in the long run, and that even its temporary success would have to depend on the unlikely condition that most people remained in ignorance of the policy.

2 That it should not treat people as puppets: Utopian thinkers have, like Bentham, frequently devised schemes in which society functions smoothly just because people have been encouraged to function like well-oiled cogs in a machine. Some famous allegorical novels of the twentieth century – Skinner's *Walden 2*, Huxley's *Brave New World*, Orwell's *Nineteen Eighty-four* – have in common the idea of rulers who secure a docile citizenship by the use of punishment and reward. It seems that utilitarian justifications of punishment, too, have a tendency to treat people as puppets to be manipulated by rulers. Indeed, the theologian and writer C. S. Lewis (1898–1963) saw the humanitarian approach favoured by liberals, although mooted with the best of intentions, as having much in common with the way dissidents were treated in the Soviet Union during the communist era.[7] Under that system, there were people who, for largely political reasons, were held in psychiatric units indefinitely for treatment for their 'crimes', rather than being given determinate sentences in the courts. An approach that substitutes treatment for punishment, then, is one that says: 'Let us, your rulers and betters, put you right. We don't accept that you could really *want* to be a deviant, a nonconformist, or a criminal; so deviance can only be a sign of illness, and for that you require help rather than punishment.' In contrast, a retributive approach recognizes the criminal as a person and an equal – someone whose deeds may be condemned, but whose personality is no one else's business. As far as justice is concerned, then, it is no small consideration that retributive punishment has clearly defined limits, while the process of making someone a better person is open-ended.

Capital Punishment

The idea of retribution is often dismissed, however, as no more than a crude theory of revenge – and it is true that it may well be difficult to distinguish these two sentiments on the part of someone who has lost someone in a vicious murder whom they loved or cared for. But in discounting what may seem a negative sentiment, it is worth remembering that official institutions of punishment are set up to replace the anarchic system of private revenge and vendetta that characterizes a society without formal institutions of punishment – a situation in which there is no impartial hearing of an accused person's defence, no cool assessment of guilt and no measured appraisal of what would be an appropriate punishment. But if a state that does have such an institution fails to exercise its punishment function adequately, that is, to the reasonable satisfaction of those who have been wronged, the need for private vengeance remains unsatisfied – a situation that risks undermining civil society. From this point of view, there are crimes for which only capital punishment may seem adequately to match the feelings of anger or pity felt by others on behalf of a victim. This is an aspect often lost in the utilitarian approach to the issue of capital punishment – an approach which tends to focus on numerical comparisons, looking, for example, for empirical evidence to support the view that capital punishment does or does not reduce the number of murders.

The question of figures may seem irrelevant or beside the point, however, not only to those who favour capital punishment, but also to those who oppose it. These latter might, for example, condemn it on the ground that it is a relic of past barbarism – a cruel and unusual punishment that depends on methods of execution each of which carries its own particular horror, to which is added, of course, the long horror of anticipation. Or they may point to possible miscarriages of justice, stressing the finality of capital punishment as compared with imprisonment. For some, this objection is met if the number of innocent people put to death is still less than the number of innocent people who are saved as a result of the deterrent and preventive effects of capital punishment. This is hardly a sound moral argument, however, since the state has a duty to behave morally whatever individuals do. It matters in a different way, then, if the state takes an innocent life from the way it matters if an individual does so. On the other hand, the risk of error does not necessarily settle the matter, for it is possible to accept the imperfection of institutions, as long as they are operated in good faith. This, after all, was the dilemma that confronted Socrates, when he rejected the possibility of escaping the death penalty imposed on him by the Athenian court. He argued that, although he himself would pay the price, he ought to abide by laws which had benefited him in the past, and which he had implicitly accepted.[8]

Civil Disobedience

But what if the laws themselves are unjust? There are those who think that in that case it would be right simply to refuse to obey them. The contemporary period has provided many examples of civil disobedience used as a tool to change laws or political policy: the campaign of non-violent civil disobedience led by Gandhi against British rule in India; the civil rights campaign in America led by Martin Luther King; resistance to conscription for the Vietnam war; the nuclear disarmament movement; and more recently still, environmental and animal rights protests. Such non-violent campaigns may take a variety of forms, including marches, fasting, strikes and sit-ins. Their distinguishing mark is that, though they involve law-breaking, they are prompted by conscience, and they aim to bring about a change in the law.

It might seem that political activism of this sort is unnecessary and hence unjustified in an open society, but it can be argued that there is a place for civil disobedience in a liberal democracy under certain conditions. First, it is clearly easier to defend disobedience to a law that is, or that is believed to be, unjust – for example, discriminatory race laws – than it is to defend disobedience in the case of a law that is ethically sound and which has been democratically established. Secondly, it makes sense to insist that those who engage in civil disobedience should have some chance of achieving their goals. As Rawls put it: ' [T]he exercise of the right to civil disobedience should . . . be rationally framed to advance one's ends or the ends of those one wishes to assist."[9] Finally, it is often argued that it is a mark of a civil disobedience campaign, as opposed to more militant strategies, that the law-breakers must be ready to accept the legal penalty for their actions. This assumption, however, can be challenged. For, as Ronald Dworkin asks: 'Can it be right to prosecute men for doing what their conscience requires, when we acknowledge their right to follow their conscience?'[10] His answer is that there can often be sufficient vagueness or uncertainty about a law for there to be a case for *not* punishing those who oppose it on principle.

Patriotism or Pacifism?

But while these subtleties of law and punishment may be debated *within* nations, relations *between* nations are at an earlier ethical stage. Despite a succession of efforts to create something resembling a world government in the form of bodies like the League of Nations and its successor, the United Nations, and despite international agreements on universal human rights, nations remain closer to what Hobbes called 'a state of nature'. It would seem, then, that since they cannot confidently rely on a world police-force, they are entitled to take action on their own behalf. Diplomacy and negotiation may be the option of choice, but when these have failed, the only alternative may be to resort to force of arms. So what is the individual's duty under these circumstances? Or, as Socrates – and, later, Hobbes – asked, what if the state orders you out to war to kill and risk being killed?

One way to answer this is by appeal to the patriotic principle that demands both love and sacrifice of those who belong to a particular country – a principle summed up in a famous line of Latin poetry, *dulce et decorum est pro patria mori* (to die for one's country is a pleasant and proper thing). But many today adopt a rather more cynical approach than this to the duty of patriotism – some because they deny the premiss of nationhood on which patriotism depends; others because they take the pacifist view that all killing is wrong.

As for the first objection, while nationalism is often rejected by liberals as being a matter of irrational attachment to a particular place or group, these sentiments are not necessarily arbitrary. Particular attachments and national loyalties can resemble in some ways family attachments. Indeed, the origin of the word 'nation' is instructive. It comes from the Latin word *nasci* – to be born – and so is linked to the idea of family, tribe and ethnic group.[11] While, in modern times, worldwide migration and exchanges of population mean that the idea of a 'blood' link has dwindling importance, it is nevertheless implicit in any view that sees a nation as having a common history and a sense of a common future. The American experience as a nation of immigrants, however, has given added weight to the idea of nationhood by choice and by voluntary commitment to shared ethical and political ideals, rather than by lineage or descent.[12] It is an ideal that has much in common with the definition of nationhood put forward by J. S. Mill:

> A portion of mankind may be said to constitute a Nationality if they are united among themselves by common sympathies which do not exist between them and any others – which make them co-operate with each other more willingly than with other people, desire to be under the same government, and desire that it should be government by themselves or a portion of themselves exclusively.[13]

Nevertheless, when Mill describes the *causes* of such national sentiment, he finds them in factors that belong more naturally with the old rather than the new conception: a common language, or a shared religious faith; constricting geographical factors, or significant political antecedents which constitute a cohesive national history.[14] Contemporary analysts, too, see at least some of these factors as significant. The Oxford philosopher David Miller defines nationhood as 'a community constituted by mutual belief, extended in history, active in character, connected to a particular territory, and thought to be marked off from other communities by its members' distinctive traits'.[15] Miller argues:

1   that nationality is part of one's identity;
2   that it generates special obligations to fellow nationals; and
3   that politically a national community has a claim to self-determination.

Miller's willingness to take seriously, and treat sympathetically, the idea of nationhood – together with his view that a sense of nationhood is needed to undergird community – is unusual in that it is combined with a political position usually unsympathetic to nationalism in any form. Liberals, and later socialists, have traditionally embraced a form of internationalism based on solidarity across national frontiers. Only some such dimming of nationalism, they thought, could bring the long world history of wars to a close. The liberal dream, shared by Bentham and the *philosophes* of eighteenth-century France, was that war would die away as the people's will asserted itself over the machinations of rulers and as the competition of commerce replaced the competition of arms.[16] In the nineteenth century, the Marxist critique of society saw the remedy in class solidarity more narrowly construed, and the causes of war were attributed to the inherent contradictions of capitalism. For Marx, it was the bourgeoisie, not the aristocracy, that fomented war, while later still, for Lenin and his followers, it was the combination of capitalist exploitation and imperialism. It seems, however, that in the twentieth century, ethnicity has proved stronger than class, and stronger, too, than economic forces. As the American political commentator and former statesman David Patrick Moynihan writes: 'Fascism – Italian, then German – was much about "blood." The Second World War was as much pogrom as anything else, and far the greatest incidence of violence since has been ethnic in nature and in origin.'[17]

The continuation of violence in the world, then, leaves intact the dilemma of pacifism versus patriotism. The problem for the pacifist may be put in these terms: if it can be right to kill or injure someone in self-defence and right to kill or injure someone in defence of another person, can it be right in the same way to kill in defence of a community or nation? The absolute pacifist will, of course, reject the premiss, and pacifism has been a position adopted by a number of prominent philosophers, including Bertrand Russell, who, as a young man, was imprisoned as a conscientious objector during the First World War, and in his old age committed himself to the campaign for nuclear disarmament.

Nevertheless, when a situation is spelled out in sufficient detail, a position of absolute pacifism may be difficult to maintain. For the 'details' in question are likely to be the lives of people who may be close to the pacifist, and whose willingness to protect them may be critical for their safety and well-being. This is an *ad hominem* argument, but it relates closely to an argument of a more abstract and logical nature: that a pacifist position is essentially self-contradictory – or, as the American philosopher Jan Narveson argues, if there is a right not to be subject to violence, then there must be a right to use violence to defend that right.[18] Finally, too, it is difficult to avoid a feeling, whether rational or irrational, that to sit by and witness genocide or other atrocities is to incur some of the guilt for those crimes.

Nevertheless, despite these counter-arguments, pacifism has an immediate and direct appeal when compared with the horrors of war. For example, it is understandable that, in the light of the experience of their predecessors of a generation before, the members of the Oxford Union Debating Society, just before the Second World War, should have chosen to vote for a motion declaring that 'This house would refuse under any circumstances to fight for King and Country'. It is equally understandable, however, that many of those who had voted for that motion did in fact fight in what they later came to see as a just, or necessary, war. This might suggest that some qualification is needed to the pacifist position. Could there be, then, a form of *contingent* pacifism, which expresses itself in a willingness to discriminate between particular wars – to fight for certain causes and not others? This was indeed the position of many of those in the USA who resisted the Vietnam draft. Their objection was not to fighting, but to fighting in a war they believed was wrong. In practice, however, countries can ill afford the luxury of accommodating individual judgement to this extent, and hence the lot of the conscientious objector is not made easy; for practical reasons, too, the contingent pacifism of the critic of government policy is less readily accepted than the absolutism of the Quaker, who rejects a fighting role in *any* war.

Linked to the view that wars can be fought for just cause, both pacifists and non-pacifists may make a further claim: that if a war *is* to be fought, there can be a right and wrong way of going about it – that there can be crime in war, as there is in peace. Nevertheless, states in general do not extend to soldiers an ongoing right to personal moral judgement in the ordinary course of war; once someone has accepted the role of soldier, the right to question is withdrawn. Nevertheless, the Nuremberg trials which followed the ending of the Second World War established the important principle that in the case of orders being given to commit certain crimes – gross violations of human rights – it would be morally permissible, and indeed obligatory, for a soldier to disobey those orders.

These considerations and arguments are not new, for the idea that there may be just and unjust wars, and just and unjust ways of waging them, has been a subject for reflection since the world emerged from the fractious and lawless period known as the Dark Ages.

War and International Conflict

One of the earliest thinkers to raise such questions was St Thomas Aquinas (1225–74) who, considering the question of whether it is always wrong to wage war, answered the question by saying that there were three conditions that would need to be met.[19] The war must be ordered by a legitimate authority; it must be waged for a just cause – that is, those attacked must deserve their fate because of some fault they have committed; and the intention of those who wage war should be to do good and avert evil – something which might, for example, be demonstrated by not taking advantage of winning but agreeing a settlement which leaves the defeated enemy in a state to recover its own self-respect. Aquinas distinguished the question – described as *jus ad bellum* – of what is necessary to provide a justification for going to war from the question of what conditions are necessary for the moral conduct of a war, which is described as *jus in bello*. In contrast, the humanist thinker Erasmus (1466–1536) was probably the first person to express without qualification the view that war is such a bad thing that it could even be better to be conquered by an unjust enemy. His friend and contemporary Sir Thomas More (1478–1535) wrote of an ideal state – a Utopia – whose inhabitants 'hate and detest war as a thing manifestly brutal'.[20] However, the abolition of war was never an option, and the theory of the *just* war became an important theme in the writings of legal philosophers over the next two centuries. Hugo Grotius (1583–1645) deplored the lack of restraint in the conduct of war which characterized the Christian world of his day. He objected both to the fact that people resorted to war on the least provocation, or even on no provocation at all, and also that, once war was under way, they ignored the need to observe any kind of laws and discipline at all. For Grotius, a just cause had to be weighty enough to justify the killing and suffering that would ensue, but just causes could include restoring rights, protecting the innocent or imposing order.[21]

While *jus ad bellum* offered reasons for going to war in the first place, *jus in bello* sets out the conditions to be observed in the conduct of war. These fall under two broad headings: discrimination and proportionality. Discrimination involves distinguishing between combatants and non-combatants and respecting rules for the treatment of prisoners of war. Proportionality requires that the parties avoid using extreme or excessive means to achieve their ends. This includes outlawing altogether certain methods of waging war – in the present day, for example, the use of gas and chemical or biological weapons. It also means not continuing to fight when you have no chance of winning, unless the issue is one of self-defence or survival.

Contemporary writers and politicians have added a requirement that war must be a last resort – that negotiation and diplomacy are better than war. Today, indeed, many commentators would say that the *only* acceptable justification for engaging in war is self-defence; although others would maintain that aggressive action can be justified in certain circumstances.[22]

The just war doctrine is closely linked to natural law theory and rejects expediency as a justification for action, even in the extreme circumstances of war. But the view that, in politics, the end justifies the means also had an early exponent in the Italian political philosopher Machiavelli, whose book of guidance for successful government recommended ruthlessness in both peace and war.[23] More recently, the German philosopher Friedrich Nietzsche was another influential advocate of the use of power without moral restraint in pursuit of victory and conquest.

Whatever the intention of the adversaries, however, modern warfare makes a 'just war' difficult. It may be difficult, first of all, to wait to go to war until attacked – the line between defence and aggression is blurred by the existence of weapons whose sheer speed may justify a pre-emptive strike in some circumstances. Notoriously, during the Cold War, when the weapons of the Soviet Union confronted those of the USA and the free world, this led, in the area of nuclear technology, to the doomsday scenario of Mutually Assured Destruction (MAD) – a guarantee on both sides of a savage posthumous revenge.[24]

It is also much more difficult today to draw a line between combatants and non-combatants, since modern weapons have wide and indiscriminate impact. This issue was already a matter of concern at the time of the Second World War, when aerial bombing was, for the first time, directed on a massive scale at civilian populations of cities rather than at explicitly military targets. And even if it were possible to discriminate between the targets of modern warfare, separating the 'guilty' from the 'innocent', and avoiding altogether what is sometimes euphemistically called 'collateral damage', the question of who is innocent is itself a matter of dispute. The standard view of an innocent is of someone who has done no wrong; it may also mean one who poses no threat; or it may mean simply a non-combatant. But those not actively engaged in fighting may be contributing to the war-effort in other ways; even the elderly, and the families of soldiers, can be seen as aiding the armed forces by giving them moral support; a child, too, may be discounted as an innocent on the basis that he or she is a potential *future* enemy or combatant.

Even if it could be agreed that some people are indeed innocents, however, this does not put an end to all dispute. For some philosophers would consider that the principle of double effect applies in this case.[25] In other words, they would hold that no blame is incurred for the death or injury of innocent people if it is an unavoidable consequence of necessary military action. So, for example, if a party of foreign dignitaries, perhaps accompanied by children and family members, is riding on a train which must be blown up to prevent the delivery of crucial armament components, the principle of double effect means that their death is no crime since, although it is foreseen, it is not in fact an *intended* consequence of the action. Nevertheless, this moral concession still leaves many people feeling uneasy, even if they accept it in principle; for when unscrupulous leaders deliberately place innocents or hostages in proximity to war installations, democratic leaders who continue to want to respect the combatant–non-combatant distinction wherever possible find themselves confronting a difficult dilemma.

Many of these dilemmas apply to set-piece wars between nations. These, however, play a diminishing role in the modern world. They have been replaced by civil wars, breakaway movements and secessionist campaigns which reproduce some of the same ethical problems as conventional warfare but have added complexities of their own.

Secession

Freedom is a key moral concept, and it finds its political expression in the doctrines of popular sovereignty and self-determination. But the ideal of every religious and ethnic group having its own state is impossible to achieve in practice, so that inevitably the aspirations of minority groups must frequently be met within a multicultural, multi-ethnic framework. However, not all groups are prepared to accept this. Many have preferred to postpone peace until they have achieved self-determination or indeed have made nationhood a condition of peace. It becomes a matter of moral judgement, then, whether claims for national self-determination are exigent enough to justify violent action. There may be an ethical presumption against violence, but it is, after all, a fact that most successful anti-colonial movements in recent times have passed through a terrorist phase. If violence could only rightly be used to protect an already legitimated state, then no independence movement could ever be justified, unless conducted on Gandhian principles.

But it is not only methods that are questionable. There is a prior question about the moral legitimacy of the goal. So when is secession morally justified? And when is it right to seek to prevent secession? If a group of people wishes to switch its allegiance to a different regime, or else to obtain independent government for itself, is it morally entitled to do so? One way to justify secessionist aspirations would be to appeal to historical factors; another would be to make a case based on ethnic or cultural similarities; while a different type of justification altogether might be advanced when a group is subjected to injustice, persecution or oppression. The 'voluntarists', that is, those who believe in a basic right of choice in these matters, may derive a direct right to secede from the Lockean right to freedom of association.[26] An appeal could also be made to the Kantian principle that people should be subject only to their own self-imposed laws. The model here is provided by the pilgrims who set sail in the *Mayflower* to settle the regions of North America. John Stuart Mill was a voluntarist in this sense, although he acknowledged some qualifications to the principle of self-determination.[27] He writes: 'Where the sentiment of nationality exists in any force, there is a prima facie case for uniting all the members of the nationality under the same government, and a government to themselves apart.'[28]

While the English philosopher Henry Sidgwick (1838–1900) had a conception of nationhood not far removed from that of Mill – he wrote of 'a community of patriotic sentiment' – he was more sceptical of separatist tendences and was far-sighted enough to note that the ethical position might be different if secession were to involve the removal of natural resources or the alteration of natural boundaries.[29] A further condition, noted by Rawls, is that there can be no right to secession at the expense of the subjugation of another people – for example, if the object of the secessionists is to maintain an institution like slavery.[30]

Even where there is a right to secede, however, there might well be a further question as to whether that right should be exercised. The argument that featured in relation to civil disobedience can be put more strongly here: that if it is possible to make changes by democratic means, then violent challenge to the state must be unjustifiable. However, it seems that certain things never *could* be settled democratically, that is, by majority vote. For example, if the boundaries of a state are in dispute, it will also be a matter of dispute as to what the voting constituency should be, and the anwer to *this* question could entirely determine the outcome of any vote. Some will claim, therefore, a right of revolution – a right to wage a revolutionary war.

Terrorism

Those who embark on such acts may be called by a variety of names: freedom fighters, revolutionaries, guerrillas, irregular soldiers or terrorists – terms which obviously reflect the point of view of the speaker more than the character of the activists. So what is terrorism? The very use of the term is controversial. It is often pointed out that the state itself may be violent; indeed, the original meaning of the term 'terrorism' came from examples of violence on the part of the state – in particular, the Jacobin Reign of Terror following the French Revolution, and the Russian experience under Stalin. Neverthless, its focus has now shifted to mean unofficial violence, usually *against* the state.

Most would distinguish it from political assassination, and also from guerrilla warfare. But there are those who would include under the heading of terrorism such things as sabotage and hooliganism, violent trade-union protests and animal rights protests involving violence. One way to proceed in the face of such diverse opinions is to say that acts may be rightly described as terrorist if they are carried out by some recognized terrorist group. But, of course, a group is only recognized as a terrorist organization by the nature of the acts it carries out. So is it best to start by listing deeds? Or by listing acknowledged terrorist groups? It would seem that any definition of this sort is bound to be circular. Most writers on the subject, however, avoid the difficulty by offering an analysis of terrorism in terms of certain defining features. These may include:

- violence (or the threat of violence) with a political (or sometimes moral, religious or economic) motive;
- violence of a random nature, which strikes at its victims on an arbitrary basis;
- violence directed at victims who cannot themselves alter or affect the situation that provides the terrorists' grievance – for example, international passengers in an airport terminal or aeroplane;
- violence where there is an intention to wage war.[31]

Many of those who seek to define terrorism regard it as in principle wrong. Where violent actions are regarded as justified, they tend to be given another more neutral or even favourable description. But this exposes the root of the difficulty. Terrorism, under whatever name, fails to meet the conditions required for justice in war – since it is not ordered by a legitimate authority, it fails the *jus ad bellum* requirements, and, since it is typically indiscriminate in its targets, it does not meet the *jus in bello* requirements. In general, the underlying difficulty is the problem of *moral consistency*: can there be universalizable principles that legitimate certain acts of violence whilst justifying condemnation of others? The absence of such principles may be felt as a kind of moral schizophrenia. For many people, unless they are pacifist, look for universalizable principles to legitimate their own country's military position, inevitably involving physical violence or its threat, while wanting to condemn terrorist bombings or killings. The same people may condemn the use and effects of landmines and also defend their manufacture and sale to friendly governments.

It might seem that the problem can be solved by resort to ethical consequentialism. But both sides can make use of consequentialist arguments. It is a powerful justificatory weapon in the hands of those who wage terrorist campaigns as well as of those who are legitimate users of force within a territory. On the one hand, the principle that the end justifies the means is of great importance in justifying in their own eyes those who plant bombs or attack tourists and other civilian targets. On the other, the same type of reasoning also allows the legitimate user of force to take each case on its causal merits. For example, when there was an attempt, through the Hague Convention, to outlaw particularly horrific means of waging war – especially the use of gas or chemical weapons – the addition of a modest clause allowing exceptions for 'military necessity' provided in effect a sufficient justification for the later deployment of even nuclear or atomic weapons against civilian populations.

If a conflict between practical necessity and principle can arise in this way in the case of ordinary warfare, it is not surprising that it should be invoked again in connection with contemporary terrorism, which provides a classic test-case for the confrontation of utilitarianism with a morality based on absolute principles.

The situation is no simpler if the issue is seen in other moral terms, as a matter of rights. Terrorist campaigns are themselves very often waged on behalf of claimed rights, but at the same time they conspicuously violate the rights of others. Most typically, the lives that are taken are unrelated to the wrong that is claimed, and typically, too, their loss is unlikely to contribute directly to its redress. Because of this lack of symmetry, it is not possible to justify the rights violation by appeal to the principle that two wrongs may cancel each other out – a typical response when the issue is one of a life for a life.

There is another class of cases, however, which avoids the lack of symmetry involved in protecting one's own rights by attacking someone else's. This happens when those attacked are strictly and only those who are responsible for the rights violation in question. This is a defence that could be mounted by some of those campaigning against painful experiments on animals, or seeking to prevent irreversible ecological or environmental damage. It is also the defence most likely to be offered by those who mount attacks on abortion clinics and their personnel. The form of terrorism involved in these cases could be called defensive terrorism and its justification is not directly consequentialist – doing harm that good may come – but it has the positive aims of, first, intervening to prevent current and ongoing wrong by attacking those responsible for it, or, secondly, seeking to forestall some future wrong: for instance, to prevent planetary damage which may violate the rights of future people.

This defence is to be distinguished from the claim that *social* wrongs of various kinds are themselves a type of structural violence, so that violence in opposition to it has no case to answer, for this view depends upon a tricky and basically dishonest distortion of the meaning of the word 'violence'.[32] Nor is it the same as the utilitarian claim that the issue is to be decided on the basis of a balance of benefits. In contrast to either of these positions, defensive terrorism is designed to bring an end to (physical) suffering or rights deprivation either that already exists and will continue if there is no intervention from outside, or that is certain to come about in the future. In these cases it might be argued that, since some rights will be violated anyway, it is not inconsistent to violate some people's rights (the rights of those responsible) in an attempt to protect the rights of others. Where many kinds of political terrorism operate on the anti-Kantian principle of using some people as means rather than as ends in themselves, the defensive terrorist can offer a justification analogous to the standard justification of self-defence.

But although this provides a potential defence of terrorism on the basis of individual interests or claims, there are other moral considerations which need to be taken into account. One of these may well be the intuitive response of moral abhorrence which most terrorist acts – typically bombings, mutilation and murder – provoke. Whatever type of terrorism is in question, whether political or moral, and whether based on pure or impure motives, some weight should undoubtedly be given to that natural initial response of moral abhorrence. Indeed, this response may be deeply rooted in human nature and serve the long-term interests of human beings. In other words, as the British philosopher Stuart Hampshire has observed, it could be 'that the repugnance and horror surrounding some moral prohibitions are sentiments that have both a biological and a social function.'[33]

For a more reasoned response, however, it is necessary to turn to fundamental questions about civil order and disorder. Indeed, it may be necessary to go back to Aristotle, who contrasted all forms of government based on arbitrary power – whether of a single individual, or of a group or section of the population, or of the masses – with those same forms subject to the rule of law. Terrorism represents the extreme antithesis of commitment to the rule of law; thus there is something inherently paradoxical about endorsing private violence to bring about legal or constitutional change.

Private violence is inseparable from anarchy, whether its setting is national or international, and returns a society to an earlier Hobbesian state of 'war of every man against every man'. Terrorists claim a morality of their own, asserting their own infallibility and inverting the liberal principle of toleration. The argument about terrorism, then, cannot be settled by saying, 'It depends which side you're on.' Those who wish to support a moral point of view challenge the excesses of their own side and, difficult though it may be to achieve it, they will, after all, seek to work out a morally consistent position, for again, as Hampshire writes:

> A morality, with its ordering of virtues and its prohibitions, provides a particular ideal of humanity in an ideal way of life; and this moral ideal explains where and why killing is allowed and also for what purposes a man might reasonably give his life.[34]

Interlude

> Polemos had listened with politeness to what I had to say, but I realized that the distinction between war and terrorism, important though it was to me, was hardly relevant in his situation. For the Alloi closed their ranks against their enemies and, as had become clear when capital punishment for the non-political crime of murder had been touched upon, they saw no reason to tolerate attacks from within any more than attacks from without.
>
> The discussion had opened up wider issues and Polemos kept to his promise to introduce me to his colleague who had more interest in the causes of war than had Polemos himself. But as she arrived, I saw out of the corner of my eye that someone else was also waiting to talk to me.

Notes to Chapter 11

1 There is also the further consideration that the crimes most likely to arouse a desire for retribution are often those where the criminal is suffering from some recognizable psychological disorder and therefore thought not to be 'responsible' for the crime in a way which would justify retributive punishment.

2 Kant, *Metaphysical Elements of Justice*, p. 102.

3 Hegel, *Philosophy of Right*, p. 70.

4 See Bentham, *Principles of Morals and Legislation*.

5 Kant, *Metaphysical Elements of Justice*, p. 100.

6 Hart, 'Prolegomenon to the principles of punishment', p. 5.

7 Lewis, 'The humanitarian theory of punishment'.

8 The account of the discussion which took place in the prison where Socrates was held pending his execution is to be found in Plato's dialogue, the *Crito*.

9 Rawls, *A Theory of Justice*, p. 376.

10 Dworkin, *Taking Rights Seriously*, p. 188.

11 'As an ethnic or cultural group the nation, like the family, the clan, the tribe

and other ethnic and cultural groups, is primordial: the earliest extant texts in Hittite, Vedic Sanskrit and Mycenaean Greek all contain a word for it', Hinsley, cited by Moynihan, *Pandaemonium*, pp. 12–13.

12   Michael Ignatieff calls the first of these *ethnic* nationalism, the second, *civic* nationalism. See *Blood and Belonging: Journeys into the New Nationalism*.

13   Ibid., pp. 359–60.

14   He also offers the interesting suggestion that a nation is an entity that shares the same books and newspapers – a common media.

15   Miller, 'In defence of nationality', p. 21.

16   For an account of this liberal tradition, see Howard, *War and the Liberal Conscience*.

17   Moynihan, *Pandaemonium*, pp. 53–4.

18   Narveson, J., *Ethics* 75, 4, 1965.

19   Aquinas, *Summa Theologica*, part 2, second part.

20   More, *Complete Works*, p. 201. Cited by Michael Howard, *War and the Liberal Conscience*, p. 17.

21   See Grotius, *De Jure Belli ac Pacis*.

22   See, for example, Anscombe, 'War and murder'. Recent UN resolutions suggest that some members of that body believe in a right of intervention for humanitarian reasons.

23   Machiavelli, *The Prince*.

24   The possibilities were fictionally spelt out in the film *Dr Strangelove*.

25   This argument is put forward in Walzer, *Just and Unjust Wars*, p. 155.

26   The term 'voluntarist' is used by Paul Gilbert in his introduction to *Nations, Cultures and Markets*, Gilbert and Gregory, pp. 1–13. This volume also contains a number of useful discussions of these issues. See, for example, the article by George, 'The ethics of national self-determination', pp. 67–82 and Beran, 'The place of secession in liberal democratic theory', pp. 47–65.

27   He suggests it is to the advantage of an inferior nation to be absorbed in a superior one – he mentions the Basques, the Welsh, and the Scots! – and he also acknowledges that sometimes physical or geographical factors can constrain choice.

28   Mill, *Representative Government*, pp. 360–1.

29   Sidgwick, *The Elements of Politics*.

30   Rawls, 'The law of peoples', p. 47.

31   This is suggested by Paul Gilbert who holds that, particularly in the Irish case, it justifies treating a captured terrorist as a soldier rather than a criminal. See Gilbert, 'Terrorism: war or crime?'

32   A position taken by, for example, Honderich, that poverty, injustice and inequality are examples of violence.

33   Hampshire, 'Morality and pessimism', p. 20.

34   Ibid.

12

Temperance, Harmony and Environment

Twelfth Conversation

Physia: I came back because I wanted to speak to you about something particular – perhaps alone?

Traveller: I'll be glad to do that. Polemos is just leaving, but he has brought Sophrosyn to meet me, and I believe she has something she wants to discuss with me.

Physia: All right. My business will wait. I'll come back later.

Sophrosyn: Thank you. For my business, I fear, will not wait.

Traveller: That sounds ominous. May I ask what it was you wanted to discuss?

Sophrosyn: Well, perhaps I should first explain that I preside over a committee that looks after our community's affairs. We have been meeting from time to time ever since you arrived to hear reports from your visitors on what you had to tell them. You understood, I think, quite early on, that for us you represented an intriguing opportunity to explore an alien culture. To us you were, quite literally, a being from another world.

Traveller: Well, I hope I have told you what you wanted to know.

Sophrosyn: Up to a point, yes. At first we found what you had to tell us quite interesting – indeed we even found some of it amusing. But recently we have become rather troubled.

Traveller: Oh, why is that?

Sophrosyn: Well, I can explain. But first we have some questions about your world and way of life. Do you mind just supplying a few facts?

Traveller: By all means. As long as you appreciate, of course, that 'facts' are often in dispute!

Sophrosyn: All right. But first, is it true that in the world you come from,

very many people live in cities, and that some of these cities are of
enormous size?

Traveller: Yes, that's true.

Sophrosyn: Then how do they support themselves? Does everyone
have enough to eat?

Traveller: I must admit that there is a great deal of unevenness in the way
people live their lives – both unevenness *within* nations, and unevenness *between* nations. Some people and some nations are rich and
may squander their resources; some are poor, or even forced to live
at a level that cannot support them or their children into adult life.

Sophrosyn: I see. But can people trade with each other freely?

Traveller: I see the point of your question, for trade is often a way for
people to improve their position. So, yes, there is certainly trading
of goods on a world scale; indeed, we sometimes talk of the world
as a global village. But there is disagreement about how far this trade
should be conducted free of all restriction – not only because initial
resources may be very different, and bargains struck between
unequal partners may seem unfair, but also because this global trade
has created problems of a new and different sort.

Sophrosyn: For example?

Traveller: Well, there is a world-wide problem of disposing of the waste
generated by the world's industries – a problem the wealthy nations
sometimes try to solve at the expense of the poorer ones, by
exporting their waste-products to countries least equipped to
handle them. Rivers and seas are polluted by some of these wastes,
and there are problems, too, from other causes.

Sophrosyn: What sort of problems?

Traveller: Well, the cutting down of rain forests has produced soil
erosion and even global change in climate and temperature. Indeed,
some of our scientists believe that these and other developments
may have resulted in damage to the ozone layer that protects us
from the sun's harmful emissions. So hazards can no longer be kept
within the boundaries of any one country – they spill over into their
neighbour's, and even beyond. This means that accidents, too, can
take on a world scale. For example, a disaster at a nuclear power
station in Chernobyl affected plant and animal life in countries
across the globe.

Sophrosyn: But surely there must be some good things produced by
your knowledge and technology?

Traveller: Oh, yes. There have certainly been many gains. As far as food intake is concerned, the gap between rich and poor countries has narrowed – there have been huge improvements in grain harvests and farming production, some of it achieved in the laboratory by the genetic engineering of plants, making them more fruitful and more resistant to pests and blight. Many human diseases, too, have been brought under control – although admittedly that has been as much through measures of public health as through more dramatic advances, like the discovery of antibiotics and the host of new developments in medical science and technology.

Sophrosyn: Are you saying, then, that there is no cause for concern?

Traveller: Well, I would not want to mislead you, so I suppose I should add that new diseases and new viruses are appearing that seem to threaten us, and that some of the old diseases we thought we had conquered for ever – TB and cholera, for instance – are re-emerging as new strains resistant to our antibiotics.

Sophrosyn: Then we were right to be disturbed. And surely all this must be made much worse by that increase in numbers of people that you spoke about.

Traveller: Many people think so. But poverty and density of population do not always go hand-in-hand. After all, there are some sparsely populated countries that suffer extremes of poverty; and there are some densely-populated countries that are prosperous. But yes, certainly many people would say that the increasing number of the world's poor is one of the main obstacles to achieving justice in the world.

Sophrosyn: Well, we have real doubts about the way you use that word 'justice'. I could probably explain our doubts best in your own terms. Very early on, you told us about a philosopher of antiquity called Plato, who had explored the idea of justice.

Traveller: Yes, that's right.

Sophrosyn: Well, you said that he found it in a kind of analogy between the individual and the state – that justice in the individual is a matter of keeping all the parts of one's personality in the right sort of balance, so that one isn't governed, to one's cost, by unruly desires, or passions that get out of hand. And according to Plato, I think you said, a well-balanced personality is just like a well-ordered state in which you have the right people in charge and everyone attends efficiently and conscientiously to their own business.

Traveller: I would not want to quarrel with that account.

Sophrosyn: Well, then, I wonder why it hasn't occurred to you to apply that notion of justice more broadly – for example, to some of the ways in which you and the people in your part of the world deal with matters beyond your immediate locality? For I must say that the people I talk to are greatly disturbed by what you say about a world where numbers grow uncontrollably, and in which nature – which we regard as our friend – is enslaved and exploited in the way you have described. They are troubled, too, at hearing of weapons of mass destruction in the hands of irresponsible leaders, and of wars and massacres in distant places – and they are wondering whether, not only the future of *your* children, but also *our* way of life might not be threatened if, as we now realize, we share the globe – the earth we live in – with the dangerous tribes that you seem to represent.

Traveller: What do you mean?

Sophrosyn: I mean that when you look beyond the individual and beyond what you call the state, there is in *your* world nothing but imbalance – imbalance in what people and nations have; imbalance in the way you treat the non-human part of our world; imbalance in the way in which you seem to look after your *own* interests even at the cost of the future – your children and your descendants.

Traveller: I didn't intend to alarm you – only to answer your questions honestly. And certainly some people think that science itself can be relied upon to solve many of these problems in due course, especially if it is linked to the operations of a free market that places a realistic price on activities that pollute the environment or damage health. So you can be sure these are matters we take seriously, too, and there are many debates on all these issues. May I try to set out some of these arguments for you?

Sophrosyn: By all means. I'd certainly like to hear what you have to say on these matters, and indeed, perhaps you won't mind if some of the people you have already met come back to hear your answer, because these are matters that concern us all.

Traveller: That seems a good idea.

Poverty and Population

In the twentieth century, the pessimistic analysis of human expectations offered by Thomas Malthus two centuries earlier found new exponents.

Malthus had argued that population and territory needed to be in balance, and that if a population exceeded the carrying capacity of its land, nature would restore the balance through the unwelcome mechanisms of war, famine and disease. But the problem, according to Malthus, is that population grows exponentially (constantly doubling) while food supply increases at best only arithmetically (in a steady progression).[1] The neo-Malthusians of the twentieth century have a similar concern about the effects of population increase and, where personal and family decisions are unable to achieve the necessary limits, they recommend leaving poverty to take its toll of the lives of those nations or individuals who produce more progeny than they can support, and insist that the transfer of populations from poorer to richer countries is no solution. One writer, Garrett Hardin, has described the situation through the metaphor of a lifeboat:

> Metaphorically each rich nation can be seen as a lifeboat full of comparatively rich people. In the ocean outside each lifeboat swim the poor of the world, who would like to get in, or at least share some of the wealth. What should the lifeboat passengers do?[2]

His answer is that first they must recognize the limited capacity of the lifeboat and resist any temptation to help, for:

> The harsh ethics of the lifeboat become even harsher when we consider the reproductive differences between the rich nations and the poor nations. The people inside the lifeboats are doubling in number every eighty-seven years; those swimming outside are doubling, on the average, every thirty-five years, more than twice as fast as the rich. And since the world's resources are dwindling, the difference in prosperity between the rich and the poor can only increase.[3]

There can be no doubt about the accuracy of Hardin's reference to the rapidly growing world population, which rose from just 1 billion in 1800 to 5.5. billion in 1993. Nor is it surprising that awareness of this rate of population increase should have raised the spectre of global starvation. In 1968, the biologist, Paul Ehrlich, opened his book *The Population Bomb* with the warning: 'The battle to feed all of humanity is over.'[4] His thesis was that survival is a function of three things: the number of people or organisms in a locality; their level of consumption; and how they interact with their environment – the benignity or otherwise of their technology.

Ehrlich's prognosis was pessimistic in the extreme, but prophets of doom have often been wrong, and the period immediately following publication of Erlich's book was one of great improvement in agricultural yield. Nor have Malthus' estimates of population growth proved any more correct, for despite the growth of the world's population, it has not expanded at the rate he predicted. In particular, the populations of most of the countries of the developed world have not merely achieved the 'zero-growth' state recommended by those concerned with population increase; they are actually in decline. Indeed, as the role of women changes and child-bearing is deferred or rejected altogether by some individuals, European countries like France, Germany and Britain have fallen below replacement rate and face demographic change with the 'greying' of their populations.

They are also threatened by two of the dangers Malthus warned of – new and intractable diseases such as AIDS, and the silent menace of weaponry with enormous destructive potential in the hands of potential foes. And finally, there is a further unanticipated internal threat: the proliferation of recreational drugs which diminish, temporarily or permanently, their users' rationality – the only secure survival tool for creatures as physically limited and ineffective in their environment as human beings. While these dangers also threaten the poorer countries, it is neverthless they, on the whole, who face the problem of uncontrolled population growth. However, knowing that each inhabitant of the developed world consumes vastly more resources than their own citizens, they are often disposed to see the pressure from richer countries for population control as an imperialistic form of interference from quasi-genocidal motives.

It is in this difficult and confused setting that the further message that populations must live within the limits of their physical environment – that they must aim at only sustainable development – has been propagated. The philosophical and ethical content of this message is the desirability of down-scaling aspirations. Ivan Illich was one of the first to promote this idea, recommending both literally and metaphorically, dirt roads and modest trucks rather than four-lane highways and fast cars; simple medical care rather than high-tech hospitals; and universal primary education rather than universities for the rich and privileged.[5]

Illich's claim was that the world's resources would never permit the standard of living of the affluent 'North' to be extended to the poor 'South', and he argued for reducing the expectations of the rich at the same time as improving the lot of the poor, though never to the level of their current unfulfillable aspirations. The fact is, however, that the rich are on the whole unwilling to surrender very much of their accustomed standard of living, and the poor – or at least their leaders – are unwilling to abandon their aspirations to imitate that prosperity. Africa, India and China, for example, follow the lead of the USA and Europe in the profligate burning of fossil fuels. In addition, people in these countries want refrigerators, computers, automobiles and all the technological apparatus of the developed countries. In general, the less developed countries, because of their starker economic and political problems, have a more pressing need than the affluent ones to seek short-term material improvements even at the cost of long-term ecological damage.

The recommendation to scale down aspirations is based not only on sensitivity to the environment, but also on the premiss of limited resources. However, this premiss is disputed by some commentators on both sides of the political spectrum. As far as resources in general are concerned, there is an optimistic claim – which, necessarily, cannot be substantiated – that is made by those concerned to defend market pursuits from environmental controls that new resources are bound to be found to replace those that are used up. At the same time, other theorists, denying the thesis of shortage for quite different reasons, endorse an economic analysis which, as far as food resources are concerned, finds the principal cause of malnutrition not in droughts or the population explosion, but in socio-economic factors. The Canadian philosopher Kai Nielsen writes that 'hunger, malnutrition and famine are fundamentally questions of distribution of income and the entitlements to food.'[6] Nielsen argues, too, that strategies to improve the situation in poorer countries, such as the food aid programme that followed the Second World War, simply helped to turn self-sufficient agrarian countries into economically dependent ones, while cheap food from the USA encouraged the growth of urban populations in the Third World. The idea that misconceived aid is a purely temporary palliative that can devastate a fragile local economy, possibly contributing to further population growth, is now broadly accepted by world aid organizations and charities, and most prefer to follow the principle of providing opportunities for self-help, such as setting up irrigation schemes or agricultural projects, rather than shipping food or goods direct to places of need.

While Nielsen's solution is the radical one of seeking fundamental transformation of the economic system through the common ownership of the means of production, those on the other side of the political spectrum who share his pessimistic assessment of conventional policies of famine relief and assistance believe that the unhampered operations of the free market and the fresh winds of competition will themselves provide a remedy.

Helping the Poor

It would be facile, then, to construe these issues simply in terms of help – the disputes may well be more about economic facts and consequences than ethical principles. And as far as the latter are concerned, some would say that any ethical requirements based on justice are for non-interference only, rather than positive assistance – that justice provides only for a system of negative rights. As the political economist Adam Smith (1723–90) put it: 'Mere justice is . . . but a negative virtue and only hinders us from hurting our neighbour.'[7] Nevertheless, from a less restricted ethical point of view, this may seem too limited a view of neighbourly duties. Most religious perspectives, for instance, impose an obligation on those who have more to help those who have less. And it is not hard to agree that it is wrong, if human action can prevent it, that some people should be left at a level of existence which is entirely governed by the threat of disease, malnutrition and early mortality.

The obligation to help them, however, might well be limited to the minimal goal of supplying *basic* needs, for inequality as such is not objectionable, as long as those needs are met. Beyond the level of basic needs, too, the reasons for a situation become relevant, and considerations such as desert and effort come into the picture. There is also the further more practical consideration that a universal raising of standards to a level that could be described as comfort is a forever-retreating will-o'-the-wisp – an aspiration which it is in principle impossible to fulfil. This means, then, that there are both ethical and practical reasons for gearing help to the relief of absolute rather than relative poverty – to a conception of poverty, that is, that can be unambiguously expressed in terms of life expectancy and infant mortality rates.

But if there is an obligation to help, within whatever limitations may be agreed, the question remains, 'What sort of obligation is it?' Traditionally, the obligation to help other people has been considered a charitable duty, and hence a matter of compassion or benevolence rather than justice. This is a form of obligation that fits well with utilitarian theory, and it is not inconsistent with other ethical approaches. Whatever ethical perspective is adopted, however, the acceptance of an obligation to help opens up a further series of questions: to begin with, *who* should receive aid? Then, whose obligation it is to give? And how much they should give?

As to the first question, a well-established approach often favoured by world aid organizations is the principle of triage. This is a principle of allocating aid that involves seeing those who need help as falling into three categories: those who will survive anyway, albeit with difficulty; those who will survive if helped; and those who will go under whether helped or not. Aid is then directed to the second group rather than the first or third. Triage, however is a harsh strategy away from the field of battle where the principle was first formulated, for it involves ignoring the most needy or tragic cases and helping some who are better off. It is likely to be rejected, then, particularly when its consequences are brought, through the mass media, directly to the consciousness and conscience of people far from the events. But, for such reasons, if the answer to the first question is the broad one that all those in need of help should be regarded as potential subjects of help, the second question becomes more pressing: whose responsibility is it to provide this help?

One possible answer is the correspondingly broad one that it is the responsibility of everyone who is in a position to help or, as Peter Singer puts it: 'If we can prevent a great moral evil without sacrificing anything of comparable importance, we ought to do so'.[8] But to what extent does an individual really have responsibility for a starving stranger, or someone in another country dying from a treatable disease? Singer supports the idea of a universal personal duty to help through the further claim that acts and omissions are morally equivalent – that it is as bad to kill someone as merely to allow them to die. However, most people would see a clear divide between a murderer who sets out with a gun to kill, and a person who walks past someone collecting for charity, or who ignores a beggar in the street. So are the two cases really the same, or are there significant ethical differences between them?

This question is best answered by pointing to some features of the two cases which do indeed present a contrast. First, there is at least a difference in the degree of responsibility involved in the two cases. The stranger may indeed die, but it is not certain that he will; my failure to supply money leads to no identifiable victim, and in the case of the distant poor, it is undoubtedly a fact that, even if I am able to help one person, many other people will die from poverty whatever I do.

Secondly, it seems important from the point of view of moral culpability that the motives are ethically different in the case of murder and in the case of failing to help: while the first involves malevolence and a positive desire to bring about someone's death, the second is only a matter of indifference or carelessness. And thirdly, while a moral prohibition on murder is a limited and clearly defined rule which it is relatively easy to follow, to take on a responsibility to help everyone is so demanding a requirement as to lack credibility as a moral duty.

There are, then, significant differences between the two cases. But there is also a reason of a different kind for setting limits to duties to help people at a distance. It is often argued that people have special and much stronger duties to those who are close to them, particularly those for whom they have accepted personal responsibility. But if duties to close associates are placed on exactly the same footing as duties to everyone else, this may not just entail doing less for them; it may mean reducing them to a very meagre mode of existence – even, perhaps, to just above subsistence level. If this is correct, most people would not only deny that this is a moral duty; they would actually think it wrong. The practical point is often made, too, that direct aid to someone close is likely to be more effective, and less subject to misuse, than attempts to offer support at a distance in unknown situations. Some would argue, nevertheless, that showing a special preference for one's 'own' partner or children is selfish.[9] However, the view that attributes selfishness to the person who chooses to help a family member rather than a stranger is plausible only if 'own' is taken in a property sense; and in fact a person's own spouse or partner is no more that person's property than is their 'own' Member of Parliament, their employer or their local railway station.[10]

As for the third question – how much to give? – Singer recognizes the difficulty posed, particularly for utilitarians, by the unlimited implications of acknowledging a duty to help, and he proposes a remedy which consists of stipulating a lesser obligation, although it is one he admits to be fairly arbitrary. That is to say, accepting that people would not in fact respond to a moral argument which entailed that they must reduce their own and their family's standard of living to just above subsistence level, there is, Singer suggests, a utilitarian justification for asking only that they should give a more acceptable sum – perhaps one tenth of their disposable income. But, of course, most taxpayers in the affluent nations already contribute beyond this level, and so it is open to them to argue that they have no obligation to go further on a personal basis, and to prefer to interpret their responsibility to people in other parts of the world as the more indirect one of seeking to ensure that their government's policies and the share of national expenditure assigned to Third World causes, are effective and adequate.

Migration

Whatever figure is agreed upon, and whatever mechanisms of delivery are deemed appropriate, the image here is of rich and privileged people sending money or goods to people who remain at a distance. But what if they should turn up on the giver's own doorstep, as refugees, asylum seekers or economic migrants? It may be easier to give to people who remain at a distance than to admit them to a full share in a wealthy way of life.

It might seem that this, too, is an issue to be determined on largely utilitarian grounds. But the interests of those affected in this case may well conflict. As far as the residents of the poorer countries are concerned, their individual interests would often seem to justify migration. For, attachment to place of birth apart, why should people remain in a setting which holds out only a prospect of life-long poverty, if they can secure admission to one of the privileged locations of the world? As far as the receiving countries are concerned, however, the issue of the asymmetry of population growth within the sending countries remains the dominating factor. For this very reason, then, the chances of resolving this issue by utilitarian calculation are remote. For if the rate of population increase of receiving countries declines, and the population of sending countries increases, the steady state needed to make utilitarian calculations is missing.

At the same time, rights considerations are equally divisive. Those wishing to move may rightly claim that their life is threatened by their current living conditions and they have a right to seek to protect it; those wishing to refuse them entry, on the other hand, may claim a right to preserve their own culture, comfort and way of life, as well as pointing to the sheer impossibility of absorbing numbers on an unlimited basis.

Obligations to Future Generations

The problem of movement of populations is ethically and practically difficult, then, and is in many ways comparable to another, less immediate and less visible problem: the issue of our obligations to people who are distant by reason of time rather than current geographical situation. An appeal to rights in this case is unlikely to help, because it is not possible to assign rights to people who do not exist. However, there are problems for the utilitarian, too, in that, since it is impossible to know about the wishes or preferences of future people – or even if those people will in fact exist, and in what numbers – it will be impossible to do the calculations on which utilitarian ethical choice depends. Moreover, if we *were* able to know them, the infinity of future preferences would outweigh all present preferences.

Nevertheless, it is hard to accept that there are in fact no moral obligations to future people – that, as far as their interests are concerned, anything goes. But what might provide a basis for such obligations? There are several possibilities.

The fair share principle: It can be argued that for one generation to privilege itself, leaving nothing for future generations, is for it to take more than its fair share, and the principle that it is wrong to take more than one's fair share can be loosely derived from the familiar principle that it is wrong to make an exception of yourself. This notion fits closely with the requirement of universalizability which features so strongly in Kant's moral philosophy.

The gratitude principle: It is also possible to appeal to a principle of gratitude – another well-established moral requirement. In the case of the generations, however, it is unavoidably asymmetric; for any debt to past generations can only be repaid to future generations. This does not invalidate it, however, if we are able to accept the idea of what Edmund Burke described as 'a partnership between those who are living, those who are dead, and those who are to be born'.[11]

An obligation of gratitude in these terms may, of course, be rejected on the grounds that our ancestors were as morally mixed as ourselves; they did both good and evil. But our ancestors could do little *irreversible* damage; we, in contrast, have set in motion new chains of physical causation, unpredicted and possibly uncontrollable in their effects. It is not unreasonable to say that this creates a new ethical situation in which the question of our obligation to the future takes on starker dimensions.

The justice principle: This is a more straightforward 'justice' obligation than the first. It is the socio-economic principle, originally proposed by Rawls, that each generation ought to replace the stock of capital goods inherited on a 'just savings' principle.

The practical consequences of applying these principles could well be summed up in two more general principles:

1   Not closing down options for future generations by, for example, using up resources, making irreversible changes or eliminating important species.
2   Maximizing future choices by setting as a priority the protection of the most essential items for human existence: clean air, water and energy.

These principles can themselves be summed up as: conservation of options; conservation of quality; and conservation of access.

Some of these are familiar ethical considerations. There is another consideration, however, of a less obvious and more self-focused nature. Part at least of what it is for a human being to flourish is for there to be continuity in human existence. It could be said, then, that the well-being of our descendants is part of our *own* flourishing – a thought that echoes the saying of the wise Greek statesman Solon: 'Call no man happy till he is dead.' No doubt Solon was referring to the sum of a person's own life. But it is easy to extend the thought forward into the future. For would our own projects – cultural, political or personal – have any worth if they, as well as ourselves, had no future? As human beings, it seems, we inevitably want long-term human well-being.

Even this, however, may on reflection turn out to be too minimal or limited a desire, for humankind has achieved a dominant position amongst the myriad species on the planet – a situation which may be incompatible with its own future and long-term flourishing. In other words, human flourishing, including that of future generations, may well be bound up with a still broader conception of well-being – one that extends beyond the human species.

Humans and Other Animals

That human beings are and should be dominant on the planet is an old idea, for which people in European cultures historically claimed the authority of the Bible. The Bible – in particular the account of creation given in the Book of Genesis – certainly lays on human beings a duty to care, not only for non-human animals but also for the rest of nature. But this is better seen as an obligation of stewardship rather than a licence to exploit, and it leaves open the question of whether the object of that obligation is the interests of animals or the interests of humans. Kant put what has become the liberal (humanistic) view that human beings have no direct duties to animals, but that 'our duties towards animals . . . are merely indirect duties towards mankind . . . Animals are not self-conscious and are there merely as a means to an end. The end is man.'[12] Others, however, including both religious and non-religious theorists, claim that if we have duties to animals, or if such duties were laid on human beings by divine ordinance, it is because animals matter for their own sake and in their own right. Today's animal rights theorists, such as the American philosopher, Tom Regan, regard animals as having inherent value simply in virtue of being 'the subject-of-a-life'. More broadly, Regan holds that life has inherent value and that anything having life has rights.

But does it make sense to say that animals have rights, even if this is interpreted minimally, as the claim that the higher animals at least are deserving of moral consideration for their own sake? A number of philosophers believe that the answer to this question turns on the issue of how far, if at all, animals can be regarded as persons – as part of the moral community to which human beings themselves belong.[13]

The idea that animals share many of the same feelings and impulses as ourselves has been familiar since antiquity. The Pythagoreans around the fifth century BC, and later philosophers such as Plutarch (*c*.46–120) and Porphyry (*c*.232–305) were aware of the sensibilities of animals and it led them to advocate vegetarianism. The most influential philosophical voice, however, at the start of the modern period of philosophy, was Descartes, who held that animals were mere automata – animal machines. He gave as a reason for this belief the fact that 'they are unable to speak as we do, that is, so as to show that they understand what they say.'[14]

Although Descartes went on to say that the absence of speech did not mean the absence of feeling, and although sceptical doubts about animal feelings could be exactly parallelled in sceptical but nevertheless ultimately unconvincing doubts about human beings, Descartes' view was taken as justifying vivisection – a significant consequence at a time when new discoveries about the function of the heart and the circulation of blood made it convenient to give public demonstrations of those discoveries on conscious, living animals. The French philosopher Voltaire protested in the strongest terms:

> Barbarians seize this dog which in friendship surpasses man so prodigiously; they nail it on a table, and they dissect it alive in order to show the mesenteric veins. You discover in it all the same organs of feeling that are in yourself. Answer me, machinist, has nature arranged all the means of feeling in this animal, so that it may not feel?[15]

However, the practice of vivisection continued to go hand in hand with scientific enquiry, and the apparent pain responses of animals were taken as reflexes involving no real sensations of pain or distress, while protests from objectors were dismissed as sentimental foolishness.[16] In more recent times, while many experimenters still take a view of this sort, other prominent scientists – including the founder of evolutionary theory, Charles Darwin (1809–82), and the medical missionary and theologian, Albert Schweitzer (1875–1965) – while accepting the necessity of research on animals, have nevertheless also accepted the reality of animal suffering and urged stringent limits and controls. Schweitzer, who recommended a principle of 'reverence for life' wrote: 'Wherever any animal is forced into the service of man, the sufferings which it has to bear on that account are the concern of every one of us.'[17]

The 'personhood' of animals is not only an important claim for those who defend animal rights, however. Utilitarians, too, take the issue as central. They do so, in the main, by rejecting speech and reason as criteria of personhood, and by putting a different question, originally succinctly expressed by Bentham, who said of animals that the issue was not, 'Can they *reason*? nor, Can they *talk*? but, Can they *suffer*?'[18] To deny that this common capacity to suffer also creates an obligation in common is, according to Bentham's present-day successors, 'speciesism'. This is a term devised to parallel the terms 'racism' and sexism' and to suggest that a species, like a race or a sex, is being wrongly and unreasonably privileged or disadvantaged.

Nevertheless, persuasive though this may be, the argument that animals are moral persons in the same way as humans seems to be too strong for its purpose. Few, for example, would hesitate to sacrifice a dog or a snake that was attacking a child. There are, however, more moderate anti-speciesist claims to be made such as, for example, that, while it might be justifiable to cause modest discomfort to an animal for a major human good, it would be wrong to inflict agony on an animal for trivial human advantage. In other words, even if the claim to absolute equality is rejected, that is no reason to count non-human animals as negligible.

While the question of whether it is right to subject animals to painful and distressing experiments is clearly a matter of moral concern, the use of animals for food also raises ethical considerations. The issues involved include aspects of farming and husbandry practices in which animals are described as 'agricultural products' and treated accordingly; this often means using production-line techniques which ignore nature and animals' natural instincts in the interests of uncritical cost-saving. Practical considerations are involved here, too, for it is these practices that have generated new threats of disease, as every animal residue is utilized and fed to animals who have been tricked into cannibalism in a grotesque imitation of the closed cycles of ecology.

Outside the area of farming practices and the use of animals for food, there are other uses and abuses of species, including genetic alteration, not for species improvement, but for purposes such as that of proneness to disease – for example, the 'onco-mouse', which has been bred to be genetically susceptible to cancer and is therefore as a suitable subject for cancer research. Finally, the pursuit of cloning as a means of producing livestock represents the ultimate separation of an animal from nature, by bypassing altogether the cycle of sexual reproduction.

It is possible to criticize such practices without insisting that human beings should turn to a totally vegetarian diet, including rejection of fish and fowl as food resources. And indeed some conservationists favour human use and consumption of animals and fish as part of the general pattern of nature, in which species feeds upon species. The American conservationist Aldo Leopold (1887–1949) recommended a form of conservationism based on the ideal of 'harmony with nature', and took for granted the hunting, fishing and eating of animals.

One further feature of the thesis of the 'personhood' of animals is that it seems to lie outside the framework of standard ethical theories. The judgement that animals matter – that they are in our moral universe, or moral community – cannot itself be made on utilitarian grounds, for the utilitarian requirement of equal consideration of interests starts from an assumed basis of agreement about who is able to make this claim. It cannot itself be used to determine this. Both the utilitarian and the rights theorist therefore must fall back on the negative argument that there is no morally relevant difference between humans and animals.

There is, however, another and more plausible way to put this point. Instead of arguing that animals are persons, it may be better to emphasize the indisputable fact that human persons are animals. This in itself would be sufficient to lead to a shift from a purely anthropocentric view to a recognition that an earth that contained only humans and their artifacts would eventually become a dead world. It is also to recognize the interconnection of species – the 'Great Chain of Being' that ties human interests firmly in with those of the rest of the planet.

The Environmental Debate

Here, then, is the heart of the environmental debate. Metaphysically, it is concerned with the recognition of the holistic system which binds together the various aspects of nature. Politically, it involves recognition that a combination of individual free choices, each innocuous in itself, can produce environmental disaster. This is the modern 'tragedy of the commons'.

The contemporary debate includes a variety of positions, represented by terms such as ecofeminism, ecoanarchism and ecofascism. The ecofeminist sees a parallel between men exploiting women and humans exploiting nature. The ecoanarchist aims at small-scale decision-making and the rejection of centralized planning, together with its usual goal of economic growth. But ecoanarchism may well be a contradictory notion. For the root of the notion of ecology is one of planetary interconnectedness, while anarchy, in contrast, suggests the idea of units or atoms taking their own path without relation to each other.

'Ecofascism', in contrast, is a term coined not by its supporters but by its opponents to describe those who press for compulsory measures of environmental protection and international control. Critics see such moves as a new form of dictatorship and a constraint on the freedom of individuals, particularly the freedom of entrepreneurs and business people.[19] However, if the concern is to defend individual rights, then the fact is that many environmental issues are about the power that some individuals or groups may have to impose dangerous risks on others, and about the rights of other individuals to protect themselves and their children from physical harm coming to them through environmental deterioration. And so, unlike environmental annoyances such as noise or visual pollution, for which negotiation and compensation are appropriate remedies, there is a valid libertarian reason for accepting controls designed to prevent *irreversible* changes in the situation of present and future human beings. For such developments violate individual rights by pre-empting future choice.

As far as future choice and individual freedom is concerned, too, it is worth reflecting that the longest civilization of mankind – that of Egypt – lasted only 5,500 years, while wastes have been created in the last few decades that will retain their toxicity for more than 20,000 years. Their mere existence, then, binds the descendants of the present generation to strong forms of political control, and to risks, tasks and political and military arrangements that can hardly at present be envisaged. To leave such problems to future people is to constrain their freedom in ways no previous generation has been constrained, and in the light of this consideration, the words of Tom Paine take on a special and unintended significance:

> There never did, nor never can exist a parliament, or any description of men, or any generation of men, in any country, possessed of the right or the power of binding or controlling posterity 'to the end of time' . . . The vanity and presumption of governing beyond the grave is the most ridiculous and insolent of all tyrannies.[20]

Of course, it is foolish to seek to arrest change, and ecology is governed by its own dynamism and movement. But if an unchanging equilibrium is an impossibility, there is still reason to seek to preserve balance and harmony, even through change. There is value, too, in recognizing the virtues of temperance and control – of avoiding excess – and in promoting the flourishing of the planet and its rich variety of life, including human life, in its myriad forms.

Interlude

I had in this conversation given more information about the way of life in the world from which I came than in any of my previous conversations, and I began to wonder if this had been wise. Despite those closing remarks that I had been careful to make, I saw the faces around me becoming grim and solemn, and some of my listeners had begun whispering amongst themselves. So I was not sorry when Physia came up to me and led me away for the private conversation she had asked for earlier.

Notes to Chapter 12

1 See Malthus, *An Essay on the Principle of Population.*
2 Hardin, 'Lifeboat ethics: the case against helping the poor', p. 280.
3 Ibid., p. 281.
4 Erlich, *The Population Bomb.*
5 See in particular, Illich, *De-schooling Society* and *Limits to Medicine.*
6 Nielsen, 'Global justice, capitalism and the Third World'.
7 Smith, *Theory of Moral Sentiments* II ii 1.
8 Singer discusses the issue comprehensively in *Practical Ethics*, ch. 8.
9 For a defence of this point of view, see Belsey, 'World poverty, justice and equality'.
10 See also the discussion of this issue in relation to utilitarian theory in chapter 3, pp. 43–7.
11 Burke, *Reflections on the Revolution in France.*
12 From Kant, 'Duties to animals and spirits' in *Lectures on Ethics*, p. 239–41.
13 See in particular Singer, *Practical Ethics*, ch. 5.
14 Descartes, *Discourse on Method*, p. 45.
15 From Voltaire, *Philosophical Dictionary.*
16 See Rupke, *Vivisection in Historical Perspective.*
17 From Schweitzer, *Philosophy of Religion.*
18 Bentham, *Introduction to the Principles of Morals and Legislation*, ch. XVII sec. 1.
19 For the arguments supporting this point of view, see the special issue of the journal *Economic Affairs*, 'International Trade and the Environment', vol. 16, no. 5, 1996.
20 Paine, *Rights of Man*, p. 6.

Postscript: The Traveller's Return

Last Conversation

Traveller: So why have you come? You wanted to speak to me alone?

Physia: I came to warn you. You don't seem to understand your position. My people really are disturbed by the things you have told us. At first, we treated you just as a specimen – we are scientists; you were an oddity, a unique discovery for we had never encountered a civilized, reasoning being like you before. The enemies we know in these forests are primitive people; we do not even try to converse with them; we just try to make them fear us and see to it that they don't threaten or annoy us. But you were *interesting* to us. It was a challenge to learn your language and to hold these conversations. Our scientists wanted to construct a picture of the world you come from and the principles and ideas your people live by. And at the end, as perhaps you began to suspect, when we had drained you dry, learned everything we wanted to learn, we would have either kept you for our amusement and entertainment, or killed you, because we would have no further use for you.

But now people have become very angry. It seems you and your world are a threat to us. *Our* world, *our* sky, *our* water, is at risk, whether we meet your people or not – but who knows when our hidden private world will be invaded? So it is still intended that you die, but not only that – now there is an intention that you suffer as well. People want you to pay the penalty for the wrong-doing of your world.

Traveller: But that's not right. It's not fair. Can't I be allowed to plead my own cause? Perhaps the very people in my world who caused the trouble can put it right. We have scientists working on all the problems that you mention, and we have economists and politicians who are trying to set a new and fairer framework. And as for your world, perhaps no one else will ever find this place. You can take my word for it that *I* would never reveal its location if I ever managed to get back to my own home.

Physia: We would expect those protestations from you. But I'm not sure my people will believe you.

Traveller: Then let me put my case differently: even if everything were as bad as people here think, why should *I* pay the penalty? I want to return to my own country and my own people. Surely I have a right to do that? Surely I have a right not to be killed for something I didn't do?

Physia: That's why I came. You remember I differ from some of my people. I share the view you have just expressed. And so – it's risky for me, I have to tell you – I have come to give you a chance to escape. There is a path that very few people know about that leads across the great ravine. And although that has no way of entry from your world other than the long fall that brought you to us, there may be a way of escape. It is a long narrow rock chimney I found myself as a child, and which I have never told anyone else about. I can't guarantee it can be negotiated. I did not dare to try to tackle it myself, so yours will be a first attempt. You will have to find your way up it yourself, and the most I am sure of is that it won't be easy. I ask only that after you have climbed, you tip boulders and soil into the channel so that it can never be used again. That at least I owe my people. That is where I will have to leave you, for it is indeed a journey of no return.

*   *   *

Traveller: Since I am here to tell this tale, my readers will know that Physia's plan worked – I need hardly go into details – and once on the other side of the great divide, after a few days travel, I was sighted by a helicopter chartered by some friends of mine three years to the day from my disappearance.

But I have reflected a great deal on my experiences, and especially on those conversations. I had, to begin with, named the people amongst whom I had lived as a prisoner, the Alloi – the others. There were two reasons for this: one was my suspicion and distrust of people I saw as strangers; the other was my sense that many of their beliefs and ideas were odd and unfamiliar. But when I found myself, against all my expectations, safely home again, I began to reflect once more on my view of the people I had met. I remembered in particular an ancient tale which will, I think, bear retelling here.

It concerns another traveller who was on his way from one place to another when he met a stranger on the road. 'Tell me,' said the traveller, 'what are the people like in the town to which I am heading?' The stranger looked at him and replied, 'What are the people like in the town you have just left?' 'Ah,' said the traveller, 'they are a nasty, mean and unpleasant lot on the whole. I'll be glad to be free of them.' 'Well, that is how you will find the ones in Newtown, too,' said the stranger. A second traveller happened to come along just then, and he put the same question to the stranger, who once again replied with the same question. The second traveller answered: 'I've always found the people in Oldtown friendly, helpful, and trustworthy. I'll certainly miss them.' 'Well,' said the stranger, 'that is how you will find the ones in Newtown, too.'

Learning from the moral of this tale, I came in the end to realize that the Alloi were not strangers after all. Hometown was no different. The people I had encountered existed there too, as did these opinions. And just as I had found a mixture, in the end, of good and bad, even amongst people who regarded me as an enemy, the same applied to the people I had left when setting out on my travels.

For the best and the right ideas to have a place and to be heard – this, I concluded, is as much as it is possible to hope. As amongst the Alloi, the enemies of the true and the good may well outnumber their defenders, just as false and evil ideas necessarily crowd out the single simple line of truth – there can be many lies, but only one truth; many ways of getting things wrong, but not so many ways, on the whole, of getting them right. And if my exploration of ethics has come to an end with a logical rather than an ethical truth, how can I complain?

Key to the Characters

Name	Philosophical position or theme	Greek word	Meaning
Ananke	determinism	*ananke*	necessity
Egoge	egoism	*ego*	I
Panhedon	utilitarianism	*pan + hedone*	all + pleasure
Polydox	relativism	*poly + doxa*	much/many + opinion
Nomia	social convention/ contractarianism	*Nomos*	law
Physia	[natural] rights	*physis*	nature
Deon	Kantian deontology	*dei*	ought
Gignos	intuitionism	*gignosco*	I know
Arete	virtue theory	*arete*	virtue
An	} human relationships	*aner*	man
Gyna		*gyne*	woman
Jatros	bioethics	*iatros*	doctor
Isos	egalitarianism	*isos*	equal
Polemos	conflict theory	*polemos*	war
Sophrosyn	harmony	*sophrosune*	temperance, moderation, self-control
Alloi	tribe's name	*alloi*	others

Note on pronunciation: Since the Traveller in this tale made up these names, there is no 'correct' pronunciation. Feel free to pronounce them just as you wish!

Reading Guides and Bibliographies

Reading Guide for Chapter 1

The problem of free will has been the subject of debate in philosophy from ancient times. The arguments and implications were discussed by philosophers in ancient Greece, and the problem later became an important subject of controversy for Christian theologians who were concerned with the theological aspects. For a brief historical survey and illuminating discussion, see Isaiah Berlin's essay. 'From hope and fear set free'. D. J. O'Connor also provides a clear account of the issues in his book *Free Will*, while there is a useful selection of readings in the volume edited by Gary Watson, *Free Will*.

The difficulties in positing free will are well set out in Ayer's lecture 'Man as a subject for science', which is published in his book *Metaphysics and Commonsense*. Daniel Dennett defends a compatibilist view in *Elbow Room: The Varieties of Free Will worth Wanting*. The deterministic thesis is presented by B. F. Skinner from the viewpoint of behavioural psychology in *Beyond Freedom and Dignity*. See also his science-fiction novel *Walden Two*. Charles Taylor discusses behaviourist assumptions in the social sciences in *Explanation of Behaviour*. See also his later book *Sources of the Self*.

For a defence of the importance for morality of a conception of individual freedom, see Ilham Dilham's *Mind, Brain and Behaviour*, and for a political extension of the argument, see *Awakening from Nihilism: Why Truth Matters* by Michael Novak, which was published by the London-based IEA (Institute for Economic Affairs).

In contrast, there is one philosopher who has propounded an ethical theory developed on a wholly deterministic basis. For this, see Spinoza's *Ethics*.

Bibliography for Chapter 1

Ayer, A. J., 'Man as a subject for science' in *Metaphysics and Commonsense*, London, Macmillan, 1967.

——, 'Can offect preçede its cause?' in *Philosophical Esays*, London, Macmillan, 1954.

——, 'Freedom and necessity' in *Philosophical Essays*, London, Macmillan, 1954.

Berlin, I., 'From hope and fear set free', *Proceedings of the Aristotelian Society*, 1963, reprinted in his *Concepts and Categories*, London, Hogarth, 1978.

Brown, J. A. C., *Freud and the Post-Freudians*, Harmondsworth, Penguin, 1964.

Chomsky, N., 'A review of B. F. Skinner's "Verbal behavior" ' in Fodor and Katz, 1964.

Dennett, D., *Elbow Room: The Varieties of Free Will Worth Wanting*, Oxford, Clarendon Press, 1984.

Dilham, I., *Mind, Brain and Behaviour*, London, Routledge, 1988.

Dummett, M., 'Bringing about the past' in Gale, 1968.

Durkheim, E., *The Rules of Sociological Method*, New York, The Free Press, 1938.

Fodor, J. and Katz, J., *The Structure of Language*, Englewood Cliffs, NJ, Prentice-Hall, 1964.

Frisby, D., *The Positivist Dispute in German Sociology*, Frisby, D. (ed.), London, Heinemann, 1977.

Gale, R. M. (ed.), *The Philosophy of Time*, London, Macmillan, 1968.

Kant, I., *Groundwork of the Metaphysic of Morals*, translated as *The Moral Law*, Paton, H. (ed.), London, Hutchinson, 1948.

——, *Critique of Pure Reason*, Smith, N. K. (trans.), London, Macmillan, 1963. First published 1781; 2nd edn 1787.

MacIntyre, A., *Whose Justice? Which Rationality?*, London, Duckworth, 1988.

Marx, K., *The German Ideology*, vol. 1 part 1, Moscow, Progress Publications, 1976.

Midgley, M., *The Ethical Primate*, London, Routledge, 1994.

Novak, M., *Awakening from Nihilism: Why Truth Matters*, London, Institute for Economic Affairs, 1995.

O'Connor, D. J., *Free Will*, Garden City, New York, Doubleday, 1971.

Plato, *The Last Days of Socrates*, Tredennick, H. (ed.), Harmondsworth, Penguin, 1968.

Popper, K., *The Poverty of Historicism*, London, Routledge, 1957 and later editions.

Sartre, J.-P., *L'être et le néant: essai d'ontologie phénoménologique*, 1943, translated as *Being and Nothingness*, Barnes, H. (trans.), London, Methuen, 1957.

Skinner, B., *Beyond Freedom and Dignity*, Harmondsworth, Penguin, rev. edn 1973.

——, *Walden Two*, New York, Macmillan, 1976.

Spinoza, B., *The Collected Works of Spinoza*, vol. 1, Curley, E. (trans.), Princeton, NJ, Princeton University Press, 1985. First published 1677.

Taylor, C., *Explanation of Behaviour*, Atlantic Highlands, NJ, Humanities Press, 1964.

——, *Sources of the Self*, Cambridge, Cambridge University Press, 1989.

Watson, G. (ed.), *Free Will*, Oxford, Oxford University Press, 1982.

Weber, M., 'Letter to Mommsen' in Frisby, 1976.

Reading Guide for Chapter 2

Many philosophers, including both Plato and Aristotle, have assumed that if a course of action is to be recommended as right or just it is necessary to show that it is for a person's own good, or at least that it is not in conflict with it. Plato and Aristotle, however, did not interpret individual good in narrow materialist terms. When it *is* interpreted in these terms, as in the theory known as psychological hedonism, it leaves no room for altruistic action, or for action from a purely moral motive. Hobbes is often interpreted as offering a theory of this sort, and of making it the basis of his political theory and an argument for ceding control to a powerful sovereign. Other political philosophers, including Rousseau and Hume, have acknowledged the existence of altruism, or concern for others, as a motive for human conduct. Rousseau's theory is set out in his essay, *The Social Contract*.

The narrower form of psychological hedonism became one of the pillars of Bentham's utilitarian theory, expressed in the claim that human beings are motivated solely by the desire to avoid pain and seek pleasure. In *An Introduction to the Principles of Morals and Legislation*, he seeks to base a rational strategy for society on this assumption.

Bishop Butler also recommended rational egoism in his *Sermons*, although not as a first option, and it was accompanied by a refutation of psychological hedonism. Adam Smith offered a famous economic and moral defence of pursuing self-interest – that is, individual profit – in *The Wealth of Nations*. Ethical egoism was strongly advocated by Nietzsche in his writing. See in particular *Beyond Good and Evil* and *On the Genealogy of Morals*.

The argument from sociobiology, presented in Dawkins' book *The Selfish Gene* and in Wilson's *Sociobiology: The New Synthesis*, is attacked by Mary Midgley in her article, 'Gene-juggling'. See also her book *Beast and Man*. In another book, *Wickedness*, she argues that it is only by recognizing the human capacity for wickedness, as opposed to explaining it away under such labels as social conditioning or mental illness, that a realistic approach to morality can be developed. See also Peter Singer's discussion of sociobiology in *The Expanding Circle*.

Bibliography for Chapter 2

Aristotle, *Ethics*, Thomson, J. A. K. (trans.), revised by Tredennick, H., Harmondsworth, Penguin, 1976.

Bentham, J., *An Introduction to the Principles of Morals and Legislation*, London, Athlone Press, 1970. First published 1789.

Butler, J., *Fifteen Sermons*, in *The Works of Joseph Butler*, vol. 1, Bernard, J. H. (ed.), London, Macmillan, 1990. First published 1726.

Campbell, R. and Sowden, L. (eds), *Paradoxes of Rationality and Cooperation – Prisoner's Dilemma and Newcomb's Problem*, Vancouver, University of British Columbia, 1985.

Dawkins, R., *The Selfish Gene*, London, Paladin, 1978.

Hobbes, T., *Leviathan*, MacPherson, C. B. (ed.), Harmondsworth, Penguin, 1981. First published 1651.

Hume, D., *Enquiries concerning Human Understanding and concerning the Principles of Morals*, 3rd edn, Selby-Bigge, L. A. (ed.), revised Nidditch, P., Oxford,

Clarendon Press, 1975. First published 1751.

——, *A Treatise of Human Nature*, Selby-Bigge, L. A. (ed.), revised by Nidditch, P., Oxford, Oxford University Press, 1978. First published 1739–40.

Machiavelli, N., *The Prince*, Bondanella, P. (ed.), Oxford, Oxford University Press, 1984. First published 1513.

Midgley, M., 'Gene-juggling', *Philosophy* 54, 1979, pp. 439–58.

——, *Beast and Man: The Roots of Human Nature*, Hassocks, Harvester Press, 1979.

——, *Wickedness: A Philosophical Essay*, London, Routledge and Kegan Paul, 1984.

Nietzsche, F., *Beyond Good and Evil*, Hollingdale, R. J. (trans.), Harmondsworth, Penguin, 1971.

——, *On the Genealogy of Morals*, Smith, D. (trans.), Oxford, Oxford University Press, 1997.

Plato, *The Last Days of Socrates*, Tredennick, H. (trans.), Harmondsworth, Penguin, 1968.

——, *Republic*, 2nd edn, Lee, D. (trans.), Harmondsworth, Penguin, 1974. Also translated by Waterfield, R., Oxford, Oxford University Press, 1993.

Rousseau, J.-J., *The Social Contract*, Cranston, M. (trans.), Harmondsworth, Penguin, 1984.

Sidgwick, H., *The Methods of Ethics*, 7th edn, London, Macmillan, 1911. First published 1874.

Singer, P., *The Expanding Circle: Ethics and Sociobiology, The New Synthesis*, Cambridge, Mass., Harvard University Press, 1985.

Smith, A., *A Theory of Moral Sentiments*, Oxford, Oxford University Press, 1976. First published 1759.

——, *An Inquiry into the Nature and Causes of the Wealth of Nations*, Sutherland, K. (ed.), Oxford, Oxford University Press, 1993. First published 1776.

Wilson, E. O., *Sociobiology: The New Synthesis*, Cambridge, Mass., Harvard University Press, 1975.

Reading Guide for Chapter 3

While there are elements of utilitarianism in earlier philosophers, Bentham offered a fully developed theory in his *An Introduction to the Principles of Morals and Legislation*. A more subtle and less materialistic development of the theory was provided by J. S. Mill in his essay, *Utilitarianism*. G. E. Moore's attack on naturalistic theories of ethics was damaging to utilitarianism in its classical form but, in *Principia Ethica* and in *Ethics*, Moore offered a non-naturalist version of the theory, sometimes described as Ideal Utilitarianism. While it was consequentialist in the same way as other utilitarian theories, it interpreted the good that is to be maximized as an indefinable moral quality.

Contemporary writings that either reflect upon or present a utilitarian perspective include R. B. Brandt's *A Theory of the Good and the Right*, James Griffin's *Well-Being* and R. M. Hare's *Moral Thinking: Its Levels, Methods and Point*. Hare's ethical theory, known as universal prescriptivism, combines utilitarianism, with elements of Kantianism. David Lyons, in *Forms and Limits of Utilitarianism*, argues that there is in effect no essential distinction between act and rule utilitarianism.

In *The Poverty of Historicism* and elsewhere, Karl Popper recommends a negative version of utilitarianism – that in the political sphere the goal of reducing misery is to be preferred to utopian and potentially totalitarian strategies intended to maximize some over-arching conception of the good.

Peter Singer, in *Practical Ethics*, applies a utilitarian moral stance to practical ethical issues, including animal welfare, the relief of poverty, environmental issues, abortion, infanticide and euthanasia.

Useful collections of articles offering critical discussion of utilitarian theory include *Utilitarianism and its Critics* edited by Jonathan Glover, *Consequentialism and its Critics*, edited by S. Scheffler, and *Utilitarianism and Beyond*, edited by Amartya Sen and Bernard Williams. G. E. M. Anscombe has been a particularly influential critic of utilitarianism through the wide impact of her 1958 article 'Modern moral philosophy' and, in 'Moral saints', Susan Wolf argues that utilitarianism is too stringent to be either feasible or attractive.

In *Utilitarianism: For and Against*, J. J. C. Smart argues the case for utilitarianism and Bernard Williams offers some counter-considerations based on developing the notion of personal integrity.

Bibliography for Chapter 3

Anscombe, G. E. M., 'Modern moral philosophy', *Philosophy* 33, 1958, pp. 1–19. Reprinted in Anscombe, G. E. M., *Collected Philosphical Papers*, vol. 3, *Ethics, Religion and Politics*, Oxford, Blackwell, 1981.

Bentham, J., *An Introduction to the Principles of Morals and Legislation*, London, Athlone Press, 1970. First published 1789.

Brandt, R. B., *A Theory of the Good and the Right*, Oxford, Clarendon Press, 1979.

Glover, J. (ed.), *Utilitarianism and its Critics*, New York, Macmillan, 1990.

Griffin, J., *Well-Being*, Oxford, Clarendon Press, 1986.

Hare, R. M., *Moral Thinking: Its Levels, Methods and Point*, Oxford, Clarendon Press, 1981.

Koestler, A., 'The dilemma of our times – noble ends and ignoble means', *Commentry* 1, 1946, pp. 1–3.

Lyons, D., *Forms and Limits of Utilitarianism*, Oxford, Clarendon Press, 1985.

Mill, J. S., *Utilitarianism*, London, Dent, 1977. First published 1861.

Moore, G. E., *Principia Ethica*, Cambridge, Cambridge University Press, 1903, revised by Baldwin, T., 1993.

——, *Ethics*, Oxford, Oxford University Press, 1947.

Nozick, R., *Anarchy, State and Utopia*, Oxford, Blackwell, 1974.

Popper, K., *The Poverty of Historicism*, London, Routledge, 1957.

Rosenbaum, S. P. (ed.), *The Bloomsbury Reader*, Oxford, Blackwell, 1993.

Scheffler, S. (ed.), *Consequentialism and its Critics*, Oxford, Oxford University Press, 1988.

Sen, A. and Williams, B. (eds), *Utilitarianism and Beyond*, Cambridge, Cambridge University Press, 1982.
Singer, P., *Practical Ethics*, 2nd edn, Cambridge, Cambridge University Press, 1993.
—— (ed.), *Ethics*, Oxford, Oxford University Press, 1994.
Smart, J. J. C. and Williams, B., *Utilitarianism: For and Against*, Cambridge, Cambridge University Press, 1973.
Wolf, S., 'Moral saints', *Journal of Philosophy* 79, 1982, pp. 419–39, reprinted in Singer, 1994.

Reading Guide for Chapter 4

Relativism is a dominant theme in contemporary philosophy, but its roots are deep, and relativist views feature in several of Plato's dialogues through the mouths of spokesmen such as Protagoras and Thrasymachus. It is addressed critically by Hilary Putnam in *Reason, Truth and History* and sympathetically by Richard Rorty in *Contingency, Irony and Solidarity*. The theme is also discussed by Thomas Nagel in *The View from Nowhere*. The current mode of relativism is postmodernism – the rejection of ideals of reason and rationality. For a feminist perspective on this issue, see the collection edited by Linda Nicholson, *Feminism and Postmodernism*.

David Wong has discussed ethical relativism in his book *Moral Relativity*. Useful selections of articles on the subject are to be found in *Ethical Relativism* edited by John Ladd and in *Relativism, Cognitive and Moral*, edited by Michael Krausz and Jack W. Meiland. Contemporary ethical writers who endorse a broadly relativist position are J. L. Mackie, in *Ethics: Inventing Right and Wrong*, and Gilbert Harman in his essay 'Moral relativism defended' and in *The Nature of Morality*.

In a discussion of Wittgenstein's 'Lecture on ethics' Rhees attributes to Wittgenstein a relativist viewpoint, linked to discussion of a moral dilemma. Moral dilemmas are also discussed by Judith Wagner de Cew in relation to relativism in 'Moral conflicts and ethical relativism'. There are two useful collections of articles, both with the title *Moral Dilemmas*, one edited by W. Sinnott-Armstrong, the other by G. W. Gowans.

For a brief presentation of the emotive theory of ethics, see A. J. Ayer's *Language, Truth and Logic*. Another version of the theory was presented in Stevenson's *Ethics and Language*.

The classic text on toleration is J. S. Mill's *On Liberty*. H. Kamen provides a useful account of the history and origins of the idea in *The Rise of Toleration*.

Bibliography for Chapter 4

Almond, B., *Moral Concerns*, Atlantic Highlands, NJ, The Humanities Press, 1987.
Ayer, A. J., *Language, Truth and Logic*, 2nd edn, London, Gollancz, 1946.
Bordo, S., 'Feminism, postmodernism and gender scepticism' in Nicholson, 1991, pp. 136–7.
Bury, J. B., *History of Greece*, London, Macmillan, 1959.

De Cew, J. W., 'Moral conflicts and ethical relativism', *Ethics* 111, 1990.

Devlin, P., *The Enforcement of Morals*, Oxford, Oxford University Press, 1978.

Foot, P., 'Moral arguments', *Mind* 67, 1958. Reprinted in her *Virtues and Vices*, Oxford, Blackwell, 1978.

Gowans, G. W. (ed.), *Moral Dilemmas*, Oxford, Oxford University Press, 1987.

Harman, G., *The Nature of Morality*, Oxford, Oxford University Press, 1977.

——, 'Moral relativism defended', *Philosophical Review* 84, 1975, pp. 3–22.

Hare, R. M., *The Language of Morals*, Oxford, Oxford University Press, 1952.

——, *Freedom and Reason*, Oxford, Oxford University Press, 1963.

——, *Moral Thinking*, Oxford, Oxford University Press, 1981.

Hart, H. L. A., *Law, Liberty and Morality*, London, Oxford University Press, 1971.

Hume, D., *A Treatise of Human Nature*, Selby-Bigge, L. A. (ed.), revised Nidditch, P., Oxford, Clarendon Press, 1978. First published 1739–40.

Kamen, H., *The Rise of Toleration*, London, Weidenfeld & Nicolson, 1967.

Kluckhohn, G., 'Ethical relativity – sic or non?' *Journal of Philosophy* 52, 1955, pp. 663–77.

Krausz, M. and Meiland, J. W., *Relativism, Cognitive and Moral*, Notre Dame, Ind., University of Notre Dame Press, 1982.

Ladd, J. (ed.), *Ethical Relativism*, Belmont, Calif., Wadsworth, 1973.

Mackie, J., *Ethics: Inventing Right and Wrong*, Harmondsworth, Penguin, 1977.

Mill, J. S., *On Liberty*, London, Dent, 1910 and subsequent reprints. First published 1859.

Nagel, T., *The View from Nowhere*, New York, Oxford University Press, 1986.

Nicholson, L. (ed.), *Feminism and Postmodernism*, London, Routledge, 1991.

Phillips Griffiths, A. P., 'Knowledge and belief', London, Oxford University Press, 1967.

Plato, *Republic*, 2nd edn, Lee, D. (trans.), Harmondsworth, Penguin, 1974. Also translated by Waterfield, R., Oxford, Oxford University Press, 1993.

Putnam, H., *Reason, Truth and History*, Cambridge, Cambridge University Press, 1981.

Rhees, R., 'Some developments in Wittgenstein's view of ethics', *Philosophical Review* 74, 1965, pp. 17–26.

Rorty, R., *Contingency, Irony and Solidarity*, Cambridge, Cambridge University Press, 1989.

Ross, W. D., *The Right and the Good*, Oxford, Clarendon Press, 1930.

Sinnott-Armstrong, W. (ed.), *Moral Dilemmas*, Oxford, Blackwell, 1988.

Stevenson, C. L., *Ethics and Language*, New Haven, Conn., Yale University Press, 1944.

Taylor, P. 'Social science and ethical relativism', *Journal of Philosophy* 55, 1958, pp. 32–4.

Wittgenstein, L., 'A lecture on ethics', *Philosophical Review* 74, 1968, pp. 4–14.

Wong, D., *Moral Relativity*, Berkeley, Calif., 1984.

Reading Guide for Chapter 5

The idea of contract was basic to the political theories of Hobbes, Locke and Rousseau. See Hobbes's *Leviathan*, Locke's *Second Treatise on Civil Government*, and Rousseau's *The Social Contract*. A present-day development of contract theory is Rawls's *A Theory of Justice*. Rawls also develops the theory on an international level in a later book, *Political Liberalism*. For discussion of Rawls's earlier work, see Brian Barry's *Theories of Justice*. There are also a number of collections of critical essays on Rawls, including *Reading Rawls*, edited by N. Daniels. Another contemporary presentation of contract theory is David Gauthier's *Morals by Agreement*.

For a comprehensive account of rights and their origin in the theory of natural law, see *Natural Law and Natural Rights* by John Finnis, who writes from a Thomist point of view. Maurice Cranston offers a clear presentation of the nature and history of the idea of human rights in *What are Human Rights?* An excellent collection of articles on the subject is *Theories of Rights* edited by J. Waldron. See also, by the same author, *Nonsense upon Stilts: Bentham, Burke and Marx on the Rights of Man*. For a contemporary discussion of rights with a specifically ethical focus, see *The Moral Basis of Rights* by L. Sumner. *Rights* by Alan White discusses the topic from a conceptual and analytic perspective.

Bibliography for Chapter 5

Aristotle, *Ethics*, Thomson, J. A. K. (trans.), revised by Tredennick, H., Harmondsworth, Penguin, 1976.

Barry, B., *Theories of Justice*, Berkeley, Calif., University of California Press, 1989.

Bentham, J., *An Introduction to the Principles of Morals and Legislation*, London, Athlone Press, 1970. First published 1789.

Braithwaite, R. B., *Theory of Games as a Tool for the Moral Philosopher*, Cambridge, Cambridge University Press, 1955.

Brandt, R. B., *A Theory of the Good and the Right*, Oxford, Clarendon Press, 1979.

Cranston, M., *What are Human Rights?* London, Bodley Head, 1973.

Daniels, N. (ed.), *Reading Rawls*, New York, Basic Books, 1975.

D'Entrèves, A. P., *Natural Law*, London, Hutchinson, 1970. First published 1951.

Dworkin, R., *Taking Rights Seriously*, London, Duckworth, 1978.

Finnis, J., *Natural Law and Natural Rights*, Oxford, Clarendon Press, 1989.

Gewirth, A., *Human Rights: Essays on Justification and Applications*, Chicago, University of Chicago Press, 1983.

Gauthier, D., *Morals by Agreement*, Oxford, Oxford University Press, 1981.

Hayek, F. A., *The Constitution of Liberty*, London, Routledge & Kegan Paul, 1960.

Hobbes, T., *Leviathan*, Macpherson C. B. (ed.), Harmondsworth, Penguin, 1968. First published 1651.

Hohfeld, W. N., *Fundamental Legal Conceptions*, London and New Haven, Conn., Greenwood Press, 1964. First published 1919.

Hollis, M., *The Cunning of Reason*, Cambridge, Cambridge University Press, 1987.

Locke, J., *Two Treatises of Government,* Laslett, P. (ed.), Cambridge, Cambridge University Press, 1988. First published 1690.

Neumann, J. von and Morgenstern, O., *Theory of Games and Economic Behavior,* Princeton, NJ, Princeton University Press, 1947.

Macdonald, M., 'Natural Rights' in Waldron 1984.

MacIntyre, A., *After Virtue,* London, Duckworth, 1981, 2nd edn 1984.

——, *Whose Justice? Which Rationality?* London, Duckworth, 1988.

Mill, J. S., *Utilitarianism,* London, Dent, 1977.

Nozick, R., *Anarchy, State and Utopia,* Oxford, Blackwell, 1974.

Rawls, J., *A Theory of Justice,* Cambridge, Mass., Harvard University Press, 1971.

——, *Political Liberalism,* New York, Columbia University Press, 1993.

Rousseau, J.-J., *The Social Contract,* Cranston, M. (trans.), Harmondsworth, Penguin, 1984. First published 1762.

Sumner, L., *The Moral Basis of Rights,* Oxford, Clarendon Press, 1987.

Waldron, J. (ed.), *Theories of Rights,* Oxford, Oxford University Press, 1984.

——, *Nonsense upon Stilts: Bentham, Burke and Marx on the Rights of Man,* London, Methuen, 1987.

White, A. R., *Rights,* Oxford, Oxford University Press, 1984.

Reading Guide for Chapter 6

Kant's short but influential *Groundwork of the Metaphysic of Morals* is best studied in the edition edited by Paton under the title *The Moral Law.* This provides helpful summaries of the chapters and arguments. It is well worth reading also Kant's brief essay 'On a supposed right to tell lies from benevolent motives', if only to disagree with the argument! For a recent discussion of Kant's ethical theory, see *Constructions of Reason: Explorations of Kant's Practical Philosophy* by O. O'Neill.

The intuitionist point of view is succinctly presented in Prichard's 1912 article 'Does moral philosophy rest on a mistake?' which is reprinted in his book *Moral Obligation.* W. D. Ross set out a modified intuitionist position, including the theory of *prima facie* duties, in his book *The Right and the Good.* Butler's moral views were presented in his *Sermons.*

G. E. Moore formulated a different type of intuitionist approach in *Principia Ethica,* based on an intuitive knowledge of good, rather than on obligation or duty. This is set out in the book's preface. Note, however, that Moore is also classified as an ideal utilitarian (see chapter 3).

For a contemporary defence of moral realism, see J. Dancy, *Moral Reasons.* There is also a collection of contemporary writings on the subject: *Essays on Moral Realism,* edited by G. Sayre-McCord.

Bibliography for Chapter 6

Abbott, T. K., *Kant's Critique of Practical Reason and other Works on the Theory of Ethics,* 3rd edn, London, Longmans, 1883.

Butler, J., *Fifteen Sermons*, in *The Works of Joseph Butler*, vol. 1, Bernard, J. H. (ed.), London, Macmillan, 1990. First published 1726.

Dancy, J., *Moral Reasons*, Oxford, Blackwell, 1993.

Hare, R. M., *Moral Thinking: Its Levels, Methods and Point*, Oxford, Clarendon Press, 1981.

Hume, D., *A Treatise of Human Nature*, Selby-Bigge, L. A. (ed.), revised by Nidditch, P., Oxford, Clarendon Press, 1978. First published 1739–40.

Kant, I., *Groundwork of the Metaphysic of Morals*, translated as *The Moral Law*, Paton, H. (ed.), London, Hutchinson, 1948.

——, 'On a supposed right to tell lies from benevolent motives', in Abbott, 1883, pp. 361–5. Also reprinted in Singer, 1994, pp. 280–1.

Mackie, J., *Ethics: Inventing Right and Wrong*, Harmondsworth, Penguin, 1977.

Moore, G. E., *Principia Ethica*, Cambridge, Cambridge University Press, 1903.

O'Neill, O., *Constructions of Reason: Explorations of Kant's Practical Philosophy*, Cambridge, Cambridge University Press, 1989.

Paton, H., *The Categorical Imperative*, London, Hutchinson, 1947.

Prichard, H. A., *Moral Obligation*, Oxford, Clarendon Press, 1949.

——, 'Does moral philosophy rest on a mistake?' *Mind*, 1912, reprinted in Prichard, *Moral Obligation*, 1949, pp. 1–17.

Ross, W. D., *The Right and the Good*, Oxford, Clarendon Press, 1930.

Sayre-McCord, G. (ed.), *Essays on Moral Realism*, Ithaca, NY, Cornell University Press, 1988.

Singer, P. (ed.), *Ethics*, Oxford, Oxford University Press, 1994.

Reading Guide for Chapter 7

Aristotle's discussion of the virtues is to be found in his *Ethics*. For Aquinas's ethical theory, see the edition of *Summa Theologiae* translated and edited, along with other writings, by P. Sigmund under the title *St Thomas Aquinas on Politics and Ethics*. An ethical approach which follows Aristotle in focusing on character and the virtues is associated with Alastair MacIntyre's *After Virtue*, itself taking some of its inspiration from Anscombe's 1958 article, 'Modern moral philosophy'. See also Phillipa Foot, *Virtues and Vices* and Martha Nussbaum, *The Fragility of Goodness*. Iris Murdoch's *The Sovereignty of Good* and Bernard Williams's *Ethics and the Limits of Philosophy* are also seen as associated with this direction in ethics. For a politically oriented discussion of virtue ethics, see Gertrude Himmelfarb, *The De-moralization of Society: from Victorian Virtues to Modern Values*. Greg Pence provides a valuable summary of virtue theory in his chapter under that title in *A Companion to Ethics*, edited by P. Singer. See also Michael Slote, *Goods and Virtues*. Relevant collections of articles include *The Virtues: Contemporary Essays on Moral Character* edited by R. Kruschwitz and R. Roberts, *Essays on Aristotle's Ethics* edited by Amélie Rorty, and *How Should One Live? Essays on the Virtues*, edited by Roger Crisp.

Piaget's theory of moral development appeared in *The Moral Judgement of the*

Child, while Kohlberg's research is described in his *Essays on Moral Development, Vol. 1: The Philosophy of Moral Development*. For a critical discussion of the theory of moral education with an account of its philosophical history from Plato and Aristotle to MacIntyre and Nussbaum, see Paul Crittenden's *Learning to be Moral*.

The research by Carol Gilligan which led to the idea of a female ethic is presented in her book *In a Different Voice*. A philosophical approach which builds on this research is Nell Noddings's *Caring: A Feminine Approach to Ethics and Moral Education*. A helpful article on the issue is L. A. Blum's 'Gilligan and Kohlberg: implications for moral theory'. See also the discussion on this subject in Crittenden.

Bibliography for Chapter 7

Anscombe, G., 'Modern moral philosophy', *Philosophy* 33, 1958, pp. 1–19. Reprinted in Anscombe, G. E. M., *Collected Philosophical Papers*, vol. 3, *Ethics, Religion and Politics*, Oxford, Blackwell, 1981.

Aquinas, T., *Summa Theologia* in Sigmund, 1988.

Aristotle, *Ethics*, Thomson, J. A. K. (trans.), revised by Tredennick, H., Harmondsworth, Penguin, 1976.

Blum, L. A., 'Gilligan and Kohlberg: implications for moral theory', *Ethics* 98, 1988, pp. 472–91.

Crisp, R. (ed.), *How Should One Live? Essays on the Virtues*, Oxford, Oxford University Press, 1997.

Crittenden, P., *Learning to be Moral: Philosophical Thoughts about Moral Development*, Atlantic Highlands, NJ, The Humanities Press, 1980.

Foot, P., *Virtues and Vices*, Berkeley, Calif., University of California Press, 1978.

Gilligan, C., 'In a different voice: women's conception of self and morality', *Harvard Education Review* 47, pp. 481–517.

——, *In a Different Voice: Psychological Theory and Women's Development*, Cambridge, Mass., Harvard University Press, 1982, 2nd revised edn 1993.

Himmelfarb, G., *The De-Moralization of Society: from Victorian Virtues to Modern Values*, London, Institute of Economic Affairs, 1995.

Kohlberg, L., *Essays on Moral Development*, vol. 1: *The Philosophy of Moral Development*, San Francisco, Harper & Row, 1981.

Kruschwitz, R. and Roberts, R. (eds), *The Virtues: Contemporary Essays on Moral Character*, Belmont, Calif., Wadsworth, 1987.

MacIntyre, A., *After Virtue*, London, Duckworth, 1981, 2nd edn 1984.

McDowell, J., 'Virtue and reason', *Monist* 62, 1979, pp. 331–50.

Murdoch, I., *The Sovereignty of Good*, London, Routledge & Kegan Paul, 1970.

Noddings, N., *Caring: A Feminine Approach to Ethics and Moral Education*, Berkeley and Los Angeles, Calif., University of California Press, 1984.

Nussbaum, M., *The Fragility of Goodness: Luck and Ethics in Greek Tragedy and Philosophy*, Cambridge, Cambridge University Press, 1986.

Piaget, J., *The Moral Judgement of the Child*, Gabain, M. (trans.), London, Routledge & Kegan Paul, 1960. First published in England 1932.

Pence, G., 'Virtue theory' in Singer, pp. 249–58.

Rorty, A. (ed.), *Essays on Aristotle's Ethics*, Berkeley, Calif., University of California Press, 1980.

Sigmund, P. E. (trans. and ed.), *St Thomas Aquinas on Politics and Ethics: a New Translation, Backgrounds, Interpretations*, New York, Norton, 1988.

Singer, P. (ed.), *A Companion to Ethics*, Oxford, Blackwell, 1991.

Slote, M., *Goods and Virtues*, Oxford, Oxford University Press, 1983.

——, *From Morality to Virtue*, New York, Oxford University Press, 1992.

Smart, J. J. C. and Williams, B., *Utilitarianism: For and Against*, Cambridge, Cambridge University Press, 1973.

Williams, B., *Ethics and the Limits of Philosophy*, Cambridge, Mass., Harvard University Press, 1985.

Reading Guide for Chapter 8

Plato's dialogue the *Symposium* is the classic discussion of love, but the role of the desires is also discussed in other dialogues, in particular the *Phaedrus*.

The issue of human relationships is discussed by Paul Gilbert in *Human Relationships* and the philosophical aspects of love are also discussed by Ilham Dilman in *Love and Human Separateness*. See also the article 'Human bonds' by B. Almond. Brian Trainor presents the views on marriage of major historical philosophers, including Hobbes, Locke and Rousseau, in his article 'The state, marriage and divorce'. J. S. Mill, personally rejecting the legal implications of marriage that prevailed in his day, which gave husbands full authority over their wives, criticized that tradition and women's subordinate role in *On the Subjection of Women*. For feminist approaches to the issues, see *The Sexual Contract* by Carole Pateman and Alison Jaggar's *Feminist Politics and Human Nature*. Bertrand Russell wrote on marriage in *Marriage and Morals*, and the contemporary philosopher Roger Scruton provides an extensive and wide-ranging discussion of these issues in his book *Sexual Desire*. Homosexuality is discussed by Michael Ruse in *Homosexuality: A Philosophical Inquiry* and is treated critically by Michael Levin in 'Why homosexuality is abnormal'. Alan H. Goldman's article 'Plain sex' seeks to detach sex from connection with personal relations. It is included in *Philosophy and Sex*, a collection edited by Baker and Elliston. Another useful collection of articles on these subjects is *The Philosophy of Sex: Contemporary Readings*, edited by Alan Soble.

The family is often discussed from a factual and sociological point of view, but philosophical discussions are rarer. It is the subject, however, of J. Blustein's *Parents and Children: The Ethics of the Family*. See also the collection edited by Onora O'Neill and William Ruddick, *Having Children: Philosophical and Legal Reflections on Parenthood*. The family is attacked from a Marxist perspective by Engels in *The Origin of the Family, Private Property and the State* and, at least in its present form, from a contemporary feminist perspective by Susan Okin in *Justice, Gender and the Family*.

Bibliography for Chapter 8

Almond, B., 'Human bonds', *Journal of Applied Philosophy* 5, 1989. Reprinted in Almond and Hill, 1991.

Almond, B. and Hill, D. (eds.), *Applied Philosophy: Morals and Metaphysics in Contemporary Debate*, London, Routledge, 1991.

Baker, R. and Elliston, F. (eds), *Philosophy and Sex*, Buffalo, NY, Prometheus, 1984.

Blustein, J., *Parents and Children: The Ethics of the Family*, Oxford, Oxford University Press, 1982.

Beauvoir, S. de, *The Second Sex*, Parshley, H. M. (trans. and ed.), Harmondsworth, Penguin, 1972. First published (in French) 1949.

——, *The Prime of Life*, Harmondsworth, Penguin, 1965. First published (in French) 1960.

Dennis, N. and Erdos, G., *Families without Fatherhood*, London, Institute for Economic Affairs, 1993.

Dennis, N., *Rising Crime and the Dismembered Family: How Confident Intellectuals have Campaigned Against Common Sense*, London, Institute for Economic Affairs, 1993.

Dilman, I., *Love and Human Separateness*, Oxford, Blackwell, 1987.

Engels, F., *The Origin of the Family, Private Property and the State*, London, Lawrence & Wishart, 1972. First published 1884.

Epictetus, *The Discourses*, Gill, C. and Hard, R. (eds), London, Dent, 1996.

Gilbert, P., *Human Relationships*, Oxford, Blackwell, 1991.

Godwin, W., *An Enquiry concerning Political Justice*, Harmondsworth, Penguin, 1976. First published 1793. Penguin text based on third edn of 1798.

Goldman, A., 'Plain sex', *Philosophy and Public Affairs* 6, 1977, pp. 158–67. Reprinted in Baker and Elliston, 1984.

Hegel, G. W. F., *Elements of the Philosophy of Right*, Cambridge, Cambridge University Press, 1991. First published 1821.

Jaggar, A., *Feminist Politics and Human Nature*, Brighton, Harvester Press, 1983.

Levin, M., 'Why homosexuality is abnormal', *Monist* 67, 1984.

Locke, D., *A Fantasy of Reason*, London, Routledge, 1980.

Mill, J. S., *On the Subjection of Women*, in Rossi, 1970.

Okin, S., *Justice, Gender and the Family*, New York, Basic Books, 1989.

O'Neill, O. and Ruddick, W. (eds), *Having Children: Philosophical and Legal Reflections on Parenthood*, Oxford, Oxford University Press, 1979.

Pateman, C., *The Sexual Contract*, Cambridge, Polity Press, 1988.

Plato, *Symposium* and *Phaedrus* in *The Collected Dialogues*, Hamilton, E. and Cairns, H. (eds), Princeton, NJ, Princeton University Press, 1961.

Rossi, A. S. (ed.), *Essays on Sex Equality*, Chicago, University of Chicago Press, 1970.

Ruse, M., *Homosexuality: A Philosophical Inquiry*, Cambridge, Mass., Blackwell, 1990.

Russell, B., *Marriage and Morals*, London, Allen & Unwin, 1961 and subsequent reprints. First published 1929.

Scruton, R., *Sexual Desire*, London, Weidenfeld & Nicholson, 1986.

Shelley, P. B., 'Against legal marriage' in *Shelley on Love*, Holmes, R. (ed.), London, Anvil Press, 1980.

Singer, P., *Practical Ethics*, 2nd edn, Cambridge, Cambridge University Press, 1993.

Soble, A. (ed.), *The Philosophy of Sex: Contemporary Readings*, Savage Place, Md., Rowman & Littlefield, 1991.

Trainor, B., 'The state, marriage and divorce', *Journal of Applied Philosophy* 9, 1992, pp. 135–48.

Wasserstrom, R., 'Is adultery immoral?' in *Today's Moral Problems*, Wasserstrom, R. (ed.), New York, Macmillan, 1979.

Wollstonecraft, M., *A Vindication of the Rights of Woman*, Harmondsworth, Penguin, 1978. First published 1792.

Reading Guide for Chapter 9

Max Charlesworth provides a clear and readable introduction to topics treated in this chapter in *Bioethics in a Liberal Society*. A widely used and substantial textbook introduction is Beauchamp and Childress's *Principles of Biomedical Ethics*. Peter Singer has treated a number of issues in *Practical Ethics* as has John Harris in *The Value of Life* and subsequent publications. David Lamb deals with some common arguments in the medical area in *Down the Slippery Slope*, and with issues relating to death and dying in *Death, Brain Death and Ethics*. In *A Question of Life*, the philosopher Mary Warnock makes recommendations on the way the law should respond to the new technologies of reproduction, while the social anthropologist Marilyn Strathern considers the issues from the point of view of culture and society in *Reproducing the Future: Anthropology, Kinship and the New Reproductive Technologies*. The effects of the new technologies on conceptions of personal identity, and on family relationships, are also dealt with in several articles in *The Family in the Age of Biotechnology* edited by Carole Ulanowsky. Christine Overall presents a feminist viewpoint in *Human Reproduction: Principles, Practices, Policies*.

On several aspects of new genetic discoveries, see the essays in *Genetics, Reproduction and Control* edited by Ruth Chadwick. See also her essay 'The gene revolution' in *Introducing Applied Ethics* edited by B. Almond.

Rosalind Hursthouse provides an excellent discussion from an Aristotelian perspective of the arguments concerning abortion, while the subject is treated from a utilitarian viewpoint by a number of philosophers including Singer in *Practical Ethics* and Michael Tooley in *Abortion and Infanticide*. See, too, L. W. Sumner, *Abortion and Moral Theory*. There are a number of edited collections of articles on abortion, including *The Problem of Abortion*, edited by Joel Feinberg.

Ronald Dworkin discusses both abortion and euthanasia in *Life's Dominion*, as does Jonathan Glover in *Causing Death and Saving Lives*. Also on euthanasia, see *The End of Life: Euthanasia and Morality* by James Rachels and *Ending Lives* by R. Gbit

Campbell and Diane Collinson. Derek Humphry and Ann Wickett provide a historical and campaigning perspective in *The Right to Die: Understanding Euthanasia*. Some key texts on these topics are reprinted in *Applied Ethics* edited by Peter Singer, while Raanan Gillon has edited a very comprehensive and wide-ranging collection of articles in *Principles of Health Care Ethics*. See also *Matters of Life and Death*, edited by Tom Regan.

Bibliography for Chapter 9

Almond, B. (ed.), *Introducing Applied Ethics*, Oxford, Blackwell, 1995.

Beauchamp, T. L. and Childress, J. F. (eds), *Principles of Biomedical Ethics*, 3rd edn, 1989.

Campbell, R. and Collinson, D., *Ending Lives*, Oxford, Blackwell, 1988.

Chadwick, R. (ed.), *Ethics, Reproduction and Genetic Control*, London, Routledge, 1986.

——, 'The gene revolution', in Almond, 1995, pp. 118–29.

Charlesworth, M., *Bioethics in a Liberal Society*, Cambridge, Cambridge University Press, 1993.

Douglass, F., *Narrative of the Life of Frederick Douglass, an American Slave*, Harmondsworth, Penguin, 1982.

Dworkin, R., *Life's Dominion: An Argument about Abortion and Euthanasia*, London, HarperCollins, 1995.

Feinberg, J. (ed.), *The Problem of Abortion*, 2nd edn, Belmont, Calif., Wadsworth, 1984.

Gillon, R. (ed.), *Principles of Health Care Ethics*, Chichester, Wiley, 1994.

Glover, J., *Causing Death and Saving Lives*, Harmondsworth, Penguin, 1977.

Glover, J. *et al. Fertility and the Family: The Glover Report on Reproductive Technologies to the European Commission*, London, Fourth Estate, 1989.

Gunning, J. and English, V., *Human In Vitro Fertilization*, Aldershot, Dartmouth, 1993.

Harris, J., *The Value of Life*, London, Routledge, 1985.

Holland, A., 'A fortnight of my life is missing', *Journal of Applied Philosophy* 7, 1990, pp. 25–37.

Humphry, D. and Wickett, A., *The Right to Die: Understanding Euthanasia*, New York, Harper & Row, 1986.

Hursthouse, R., *Begining Lives*, Oxford, Blackwell, 1987.

Kass, L., 'Making babies revisited' in *Moral Problems in Medicine*, 2nd edn, Gorowitz, S. *et al.* (eds), Englewood Cliffs, NJ, Prentice-Hall, pp. 344–55.

Kumar, D., 'Should one be free to choose the sex of one's child?' *Journal of Applied Philosophy* 2, 1985. Reprinted in Chadwick, 1986.

Lamb, D., *Down the Slippery Slope*, London, Croom Helm, 1988.

——, *Death, Brain Death and Ethics*, London, Croom Helm, 1985.

Marquis, Don, 'Why abortion is immoral', *Journal of Philosophy* 86, 1989, pp. 183–202. Reprinted in White, 1994, pp. 118–26

Moore, G. E., 'A defence of common sense' in *Contemporary British Philosophy*, Muirhead, J. H. (ed.), 2nd series, 1925. Reprinted in Moore, *Philosophical Papers*, London, Allen & Unwin, 1959.

Murayama, T. C., 'A comparison of the hospice movement in the West and Japan', Ph.D. thesis, Swansea, 1995.

Overall, C., *Human Reproduction: Principles, Practices, Policies*, Oxford, Oxford University Press, 1993.

Rachels, J., *The End of Life: Euthanasia and Morality*, Oxford, Oxford University Press, 1986.

Regan T. (ed.), *Matters of Life and Death*, 3rd edn, New York, McGraw-Hill, 1993.

Singer, P., *Practical Ethics*, 2nd edn, Cambridge, Cambridge University Press, 1993.

——, 'A German attack on applied ethics: a statement by Peter Singer', *Journal of Applied Philosophy*, 9, 1992.

—— (ed.), *Applied Ethics*, Oxford, Oxford University Press, 1986.

Singer, P. and Kuhse, H., *Should the Baby Live?* Oxford, Oxford University Press, 1985.

Strathern, M., *Reproducing the Future: Anthropology, Kinship and the New Reproductive Technologies*, Manchester, Manchester University Press, 1992.

Sumner, L. W., *Abortion and Moral Theory*, Princeton, NJ, Princeton University Press, 1981.

Thomson, J. J., 'A defense of abortion', *Philosophy and Public Affairs*, 1, 1971. Reprinted in Singer, 1986.

Tooley, M., *Abortion and Infanticide*, Oxford, Oxford University Press, 1983.

Ulanowsky, C., *The Family in the Age of Biotechnology*, Aldershot, Avebury, 1995.

Warnock, M., 'Do human cells have rights?' *Bioethics*, 1, 1987, pp. 1–14.

——, *A Question of Life: The Warnock Report on Human Fertilisation and Embryology*, Oxford, Blackwell, 1985.

Warren, Mary Anne, *Gendercide*, Roman & Allen-Held, 1985.

White, J. E. (ed.), *Contemporary Moral Problems*, 4th edn, St Paul, Minn., West Publishing, 1994.

Reading Guide for Chapter 10

John Rawls's *A Theory of Justice* treats the issue of equality as fundamental to the theory of justice. See also *Liberal Equality* by Amy Gutmann and *Spheres of Justice: A Defence of Pluralism and Equality* by Michael Walzer. Equality in relation to the specific issue discrimination is discussed in Singer's *Practical Ethics*, and there are several articles on discrimination in relation to sex and race in part 1 of *Moral Problems* edited by James Rachels. The collection edited by M. Cohen, T. Nagel and T. Scanlon, *Equality and Preferential Treatment* includes a variety of relevant articles. See also *Justice and Reverse Discrimination* by A. H. Goldman.

On the broad topic of multiculturalism, see the various contributions to Charles Taylor, *Multiculturalism: Examining the Politics of Recognition*, edited by Amy Gutmann. See also *Multicultural Citizenship: A Liberal Theory of Minority Rights* by Will Kymlicka.

The debate on communitarianism and liberalism is described by S. Mulhall and A. Swift in *Liberals and Communitarians*, and there are useful readings in *Communitarianism and Individualism* edited by S. Avineri and A. De Shalit. See also *Liberalism, Community and Culture* by W. Kymlicka and *Market, State and Community* by David Miller.

Bibliography for Chapter 10

Appiah, K. A., 'Identity, authenticity, survival: multicultural societies and social reproduction' in Taylor, 1994.

Avineri, A. and De Shalit, A. (eds), *Communitarianism and Individualism*, Oxford, Oxford University Press, 1992.

Beauvoir, S. de, *The Second Sex*, Parshley, H. M. (trans. and ed.), Harmondsworth, Penguin, 1972. First published in French 1949.

Beiner, R., *What's the Matter with Liberalism?* Berkeley, Calif., University of California Press, 1990.

Cohen, M., Nagel, T. and Scanlon, T., *Equality and Preferential Treatment*, Princeton, NJ, Princeton University Press, 1978.

Eliot, T. S., *Notes toward the Definition of Culture*, London, Faber and Faber, 1948.

Feinberg, J., *Social Philosophy*, Englewood Cliffs, NJ, Prentice-Hall, 1973.

Flew, A., 'Three concepts of racism', *Encounter*, 73, September 1990.

——, *The Politics of Procrustes: Contradictions of Enforced Equality*, London, Temple Smith, 1981.

Goldman, A. H., *Justice and Reverse Discrimination*, Princeton, NJ, Princeton University Press, 1979.

Gutmann, A., *Liberal Equality*, Cambridge, Cambridge University Press, 1980.

Hare, R. M., *Freedom and Reason*, Oxford, Oxford University Press, 1963.

Kymlicka, W., *Multicultural Citizenship: A Liberal Theory of Minority Rights*, Oxford, Clarendon Press, 1995.

——, *Liberalism, Community and Culture*, Oxford, Clarendon Press, 1991.

Locke, J., *Two Treatises of Government*, Laslett, P. (ed.), Cambridge, Cambridge University Press, 1988. First published 1690.

Mill, J. S., *On Liberty*, London, Dent, 1910, and many subsequent reprints. First published 1859.

Miller, D., *Market, State and Community: Theoretical Foundations of Market Socialism*, Oxford, Clarendon Press, 1989.

Moynihan, D. P., *Pandaemonium*, Oxford, Oxford University Press, 1993.

Mulhall, S. and Swift, A., *Liberals and Communitarians*, Oxford, Oxford University Press, 1992.

PNL Policy Statement on Equal Opportunities, London, The Equal Opportunities Unit, Polytechnic of North London, 1988.

Popper, K., *The Open Society and its Enemies*, London, Routledge, 1945, 5th revised edn 1966.

Rachels, J., *Moral Problems*, 3rd edn, New York, Harper & Row, 1979.

Rawls, J., *A Theory of Justice*, Cambridge, Mass., Harvard University Press, 1971.

Raz, J., *The Morality of Freedom*, Oxford, Oxford University Press, 1986.

Singer, P., *Practical Ethics*, 2nd edn, Cambridge, Cambridge University Press, 1993.

Skillen, A., 'Racism: Flew's three concepts of racism', *Journal of Applied Philosophy* 10, 1993.

Talmon, J. L., *The Origins of Totalitarian Democracy*, London, Mercury Books, 1961.

Taylor, C., *Multiculturalism: Examining the Politics of Recognition*, Princeton, NJ, Princeton University Press, 1994.

Wals, E., 'Hate in the United States and Europe: a legal analysis of laws that increase punishment for crimes motivated by hate,' MA dissertation, University of Amsterdam, 1994.

Walzer, M., *Spheres of Justice: A Defence of Pluralism and Equality*, Oxford, Blackwell, 1985.

Reading Guide for Chapter 11

Kant's retributivist view of punishment is to be found in *The Metaphysical Elements of Justice*, part I of the *Metaphysic of Morals*. For Bentham's detailed utilitarian theory of punishment, see his *Principles of Morals and Legislation*. Igor Primoratz gives a thorough account of philosophical theories of punishment in his *Justifying Legal Punishment*. See also *Crime, Guilt and Punishment* by C. L. Ten and *Trials and Punishments* by R. A. Duff. Glover discusses the taking of life particularly in relation to capital punishment in chapter 4 of *Causing Death and Saving Lives*. It is also the subject of E. Pincoffs's *The Rationale of Legal Punishment*. The issue of responsibility for wrongdoing is discussed in *Punishment and Responsibility: Essays in the Philosophy of Law* by H. L. A. Hart. See also Flew, *Crime or Disease?*

The earliest discussion of civil disobedience is to be found in Plato's *Crito*. The issue was discussed in the nineteenth century by Thoreau in 'Civil disobedience' and in the twentieth century in *Non-violent Resistance* by Gandhi, who made practical use of the strategy in campaigning against British rule in India. Contemporary writings on the subject include Vinit Haksar's *Civil Disobedience, Threats, and Offers: Gandhi and Rawls*, and *Taking Rights Seriously* by R. Dworkin. A useful collection of readings is *Civil Disobedience in Focus* edited by Hugo Bedau, which includes extracts from the writings of Martin Luther King, the black American civil rights leader.

War and the Liberal Conscience by Michael Howard offers a clear and readable account of historical and contemporary arguments about the morality of war. Contemporary authors engaging in the debate include Michael Walzer in *Just and Unjust Wars* and Richard Norman in *Ethics, Killing and War*. See also *On War and Morality* by R. L. Holmes and *Pacifism and the Just War: A Study in Applied Philosophy* by Jenny Teichman. The theory of the just war is also discussed in Douglas Lackey's *The Ethics of Peace and War*. A useful collection of articles is edited by M. Cohen, T. Nagel and T. Scanlon under the title *War and Moral Responsibility*. For a specific perspective on terrorism, see *Terrorism and the Liberal State* by Paul Wilkinson and *Terrorism and Collective Responsibility* by B. T. Wilkins

The issue of nationality is addressed by David Miller in his book *On Nationalism* and by Ernest Gellner in *Nations and Nationalism*. Yael Tamir defends a view sympathetic to nationalism in *Liberal Nationalism*. The topic of secession is treated by A. Buchanan in *Secession* and a number of papers relevant to these topics are included in *Nations, Cultures and Markets* edited by Paul Gilbert and Paul Gregory.

Bibliography for Chapter 11

Anscombe, G. E. M., 'War and murder' in Wasserstrom, 1970.

Aquinas, St Thomas, *Summa Theologiae*, Gilby, T. (ed.), London, Eyre & Spottiswoode, 1963–75.

Bedau, H. (ed.), *Civil Disobedience in Focus*, London, Routledge, 1991.

Bentham, J., *An Introduction to the Principles of Morals and Legislation*, London, Athlone Press, 1970. First published 1789.

Buchanan, A., *Secession*, Boulder, Colo., Westview Press, 1991.

Cohen, M., Nagel, T. and Scanlon T., *War and Moral Responsibility*, Princeton, NJ, Princeton University Press, 1974.

Duff, R. A., *Trials and Punishments*, Cambridge, Cambridge University Press, 1986.

Dworkin, R. M., *Taking Rights Seriously*, London, Duckworth, 1978.

Flew, A., *Crime or Disease?* New York, Barnes & Noble, 1973.

Gandhi, M., *Non-violent Resistance*, New York, Schocken Books, 1961.

Gellner, E., *Nations and Nationalism*, Oxford, Blackwell, 1993.

Gilbert, P., 'Terrorism: war or crime?', *Cogito* 3, 1989.

Gilbert, P. and Gregory, P., *Nations, Cultures and Markets*, Aldershot, Avebury, 1994.

Glover, J., *Causing Death and Saving Lives*, Harmondsworth, Penguin, 1977.

Grotius, H., *De Iure Belli ac Pacis*, Kelsey, F. W. (trans.), Oxford, Clarendon Press, 1925. First published 1625.

Haksar, V., *Civil Disobedience, Threats and Offers: Gandhi and Rawls*, Delhi, Oxford, Oxford University Press, 1986.

Hampshire, S., 'Morality and pessimism' in *Public and Private Morality*, Cambridge, Cambridge University Press, 1978.

Hart, H. L. A., 'Prolegomenon to the principles of punishment', Presidential Address to the Aristotelian Society, *Proceedings of the Aristotelian Society*, 1959–60.

——, *Punishment and Responsibility: Essays in the Philosophy of Law*, Oxford, Oxford University Press, 1968.

Hegel, G. W., *Philosophy of Right*, Knox, T. (trans.), Oxford, Clarendon Press, 1942.

Holmes, R. L., *On War and Morality*, Princeton, NJ, Princeton University Press, 1989.

Honderich, T., *Punishment: The Supposed Justifications*, Hardmondsworth, Penguin, 1971.

Howard, M., *War and the Liberal Conscience*, Oxford, Oxford University Press, 1978.

Ignatieff, M., *Blood and Belonging: Journeys into the New Nationalism*, Harmondsworth, Penguin, 1993.

Kant, I., *The Metaphysical Elements of Justice*, Ladd, J. (trans.), Indianapolis, Ind., Liberal Arts, 1979. First published 1796.

Lackey, D. P., *The Ethics of War and Peace*, Englewood Cliffs, NJ, Prentice-Hall, 1989.

Lewis, C. S., 'The humanitarian theory of punishment', *Twentieth Century*, 1949.

Machiavelli, N., *The Prince*, Bondanella, P. (ed.), Oxford, Oxford University Press, 1984. First published 1513.

Mill, J. S., *Utilitarianism, On Liberty* and *Considerations on Representative Government*, London, Dent, 1977.

Miller, D., 'In defence of nationality' in Gilbert and Gregory, 1994, pp. 15–32.

——, *On Nationality*, Oxford, Clarendon Press, 1995.

More, St T., *Complete Works*, Surtz, E. and Hexter, J. H. (eds), New Haven, Conn., Yale University Press, 1965.

Moynihan, D. P., *Pandaemonium: Ethnicity in International Politics*, Oxford, Oxford University Press, 1993.

Norman, R., *Ethics, Killing and War*, Cambridge, Cambridge University Press, 1995.

Pincoffs, E. L., *The Rationale of Legal Punishment*, Atlantic Highlands, NJ, Humanities Press, 1966.

Plato, *Crito* in *The Collected Dialogues*, Hamilton, E. and Cairns, H. (eds), Princeton, NJ, Princeton University Press, 1961.

Primoratz, I., *Justifying Legal Punishment*, Atlantic Highlands, NJ, Humanities Press, 1989.

Rawls, J., 'The law of peoples', *Critical Enquiry* 20, 1993.

Raz, J., *The Authority of Law*, Oxford, Oxford University Press, 1979.

Sidgwick, H., *The Elements of Politics*, 4th edn, London, Macmillan, 1919. First published 1891.

Tamir, Y., *Liberal Nationalism*, Princeton, NJ, Princeton University Press, 1993.

Ten, C. L., *Crime, Guilt and Punishment: A Philosophical Introduction*, Oxford, Clarendon Press, 1987.

Teichman, J., *Pacificism and the Just War: A Study in Applied Philosophy*, Oxford, Blackwell, 1986.

Thoreau, H. D., 'Civil disobedience', 1849, reprinted in Bedau, 1991, pp. 27–48.

Walzer, M., *Just and Unjust Wars*, Harmondsworth, Penguin, 1987; 2nd edn, New York, Basic Books, 1992.

Wasserstrom, R. (ed.), *War and Morality*, Belmont, Calif., Wadsworth, 1970.

Wilkins, B. T., *Terrorism and Collective Responsibility*, London, Routledge, 1992.

Wilkinson, P., *Terrorism and the Liberal State*, 2nd edn, London, Macmillan, 1986.

Reading Guide for Chapter 12

The question of international obligations, particularly of the richer nations to the poorer ones, is discussed from a Kantian perspective by Onora O'Neill in *Faces of Hunger*. See also *Poverty and Famines: An Essay on Entitlement and Deprivation* by Amartya Sen and, more broadly Robert Goodin's *Protecting the Vulnerable: A Reanalysis of our Social Responsibilities*. Garrett Hardin's essay 'Lifeboat ethics: the case against helping the poor' argues against international aid on grounds comparable to those put forward by Malthus in *An Essay on the Principle of Population*. Useful collections of articles on the theme of international obligation are *World Hunger and Moral Obligation*, edited by William Aiken and Hugh La Follette, *Lifeboat Ethics: The Moral Dilemmas of World Hunger* edited by George T. Lucas and Thomas Ogletree, and *International Justice and the Third World* edited by Robin Attfield and Barry Wilkins.

Peter Singer's *Animal Liberation* was an early stimulus to the current debate on the ethics of human–animal relations, closely followed by Stephen Clark's philosophical treatment of the issue in *The Moral Status of Animals*. See also Tom Regan's *The Case for Animal Rights* and *Animals and why they Matter* by Mary Midgley. For views less sympathetic to the cause of animals, see Michael Leahy's *Against Liberation*, and *Interests and Rights: The Case Against Animals* by Raymond Frey. A useful collection of articles on the subject is *Animal Rights and Human Obligations* edited by Tom Regan and Peter Singer. This includes extracts from Descartes, Kant and Bentham as well as the work of recent and contemporary writers. An account of the influence of Descartes' views on animals is provided by L. C. Rosenfeld in *From Beast-machine to Man-machine*, and B. Rollin provides a history of twentieth-century thought on animal consciousness in *The Unheeded Cry*.

John Passmore's *Man's Responsibility for Nature* offers an account of human responsibilities in respect of the environment from the viewpoint of a liberal and humanistic ethic, as does *Ecological Ethics and Politics* by H. J. McCloskey. Conservationists and philosophers offering a biocentred rather than a human-centred perspective include Aldo Leopold, whose *A Sand County Almanac* is a classic of environmental philosophy, Warwick Fox, who sets out the deep ecologist position in *Toward a Transpersonal Ecology*, J. Baird Callicott, whose views are to be found in his *In Defense of the Land Ethic: Essays in Environmental Philosophy* and Holmes Rolston III, author of *Environmental Ethics: Duties to and Values in the natural world*. James Lovelock offers a scientist's view of the interdependence of life-forms in *Gaia: A New Look at Life on Earth*. Useful collections include *Environmental Ethics* edited by R. Elliott, *Ethics and the Environment* edited by D. Scherer and T. Attig, *Environmental Philosophy* edited by M. E. Zimmerman, and *Earthbound: New Introductory Essays in Environmental Ethics*, edited by T. Regan. See also Robin Attfield, *The Ethics of Environmental Concern*.

All the themes of this chapter are discussed by Singer in *Practical Ethics*, who considers them from a utilitarian perspective, and there is an excellent selection of key texts in *Ethics in Practice* edited by Hugh La Follette.

Bibliography for Chapter 12

Aiken, W. and La Follette, H., *World Hunger and Moral Obligation*, Englewood Cliffs, NJ, Prentice-Hall, 1977.

Attfield, R., *The Ethics of Environmental Concern*, 2nd edn, Athens, GA, and London, University of Georgia Press, 1991.

Attfield, R. and Wilkins, B. (eds), *International Justice and the Third World*, London, Routledge, 1992.

Belsey, A., 'World poverty, justice and equality' in Attfield and Wilkins, 1992, pp. 35–49.

Bentham, J., *An Introduction to the Principles of Morals and Legislation*, London, Athlone Press, 1970. First published 1789.

Burke, E., *Reflections on the Revolution in France*, Harmondsworth, Penguin, 1981.

Callicott, J. B., *In Defense of the Land Ethics: Essays in Environmental Philosophy*, Albany, NY, State University of New York Press, 1989.

Clark, S., *The Moral Status of Animals*, Oxford, Clarendon Press, 1977.

Descartes, R., *Discourse on Method*, Veitch, J. (trans.), London, Dent, Everyman, 1912 and later reprints. First published 1637.

Elliott, R. (ed.), *Environmental Ethics*, Oxford, Oxford University Press, 1993.

Ehrlich, P., *The Population Bomb*, New York, Ballantine Books, 1968; revised edn New York, Rivercity Books, 1975.

Fox, W., *Toward a Transpersonal Ecology: Developing New Foundations for Environmentalism*, Devon, Resurgence Books, 1995.

Frey, R., *Rights, Killing and Suffering*, Oxford, Blackwell, 1983.

——, *Interests and Rights: The Case Against Animals*, Oxford, Clarendon Press, 1980.

Goodin, R., *Protecting the Vulnerable: A Re-analysis of our Social Responsibilities*, Chicago, University of Chicago Press, 1985.

Hardin, G., 'Lifeboat ethics: the case against helping the poor', *Psychology Today* 8, 1974, pp. 38–43, 123–6. Reprinted in Rachels, 1979, pp. 279–91 and in Aiken and La Follette, pp. 11–21.

Illich, I., *De-schooling Society*, London, Calder & Boyars, 1971.

——, *Limits to Medicine*, London, Calder & Boyars, 1976.

International Trade and the Environment, *Economic Affairs*, vol. 16, no. 5, London, 1996.

Kant, I., *Lectures on Ethics*, Infield, L. (trans.), New York, Harper & Row, 1963.

La Follette, H. (ed.), *Ethics in Practice*, Oxford, Blackwell, 1997.

Leahy, M., *Against Liberation*, London, Routledge, 1991.

Leopold, A., *A Sand County Almanac*, Oxford, Oxford University Press, 1993. First published 1949.

Lovelock, J., *Gaia: A New Look at Life on Earth*, Oxford, Oxford University Press, 1979.

Lucas, G. T. and Ogletree, T. (eds), *Lifeboat Ethics: The Moral Dilemmas of World Hunger*, New York, Harper & Row, 1976.

Malthus, T. R., *An Essay on the Principle of Population*, Winch, D. (ed.), Cambridge, Cambridge University Press, 1992. First published 1798.

McCloskey, H. J., *Ecological Ethics and Politics*, Totowa, NJ, Rowman & Littlefield, 1983.

Midgley, M., *Animals and Why They Matter*, Harmondsworth, Penguin, 1984.

Nielsen, K., 'Global justice, capitalism and the Third World', *Journal of Applied Philosophy* 1, 1984, pp. 175–86. Reprinted in Attfield and Wilkins, 1992, pp. 17–34.

O'Neill, O., *Faces of Hunger*, London, Allen & Unwin, 1986.

Paine, T., *The Rights of Man*, Benn, T. (ed.), London, Dent, Everyman, 1993.

Passmore, J., *Man's Responsibility for Nature*, 2nd edn, London, Duckworth, 1980.

Rachels, J. (ed.), *Moral Problems*, 3rd edn, New York, Harper & Row, 1979.

Regan, T., *The Case for Animal Rights*, London, Routledge, 1983.

—— (ed.), *Earthbound: New Introductory Essays in Environmental Ethics*, New York, 1984.

Regan, T. and Singer, P. (eds), *Animal Rights and Human Obligations*, 2nd edn, Englewood Cliffs, NJ, Prentice-Hall, 1989.

Rollin, B., *The Unheeded Cry*, New York, Oxford University Press, 1989.

Rolston, H., *Environmental Ethics: Duties to and Values in the Natural World*, Philadelphia, Pa., Temple University Press, 1988.

Rosenfeld, L. C., *From Beast-machine to Man-machine*, New York, Octagon Books, 1968.

Rupke, N. A. (ed.), *Vivisection in Historical Perspective*, London, Routledge, 1990.

Scherer, D. and Attig, T. (eds), *Ethics and the Environment*, Englewood Cliffs, NJ, Prentice-Hall, 1983.

Schweitzer, A., *The Philosophy of Civilization*, Amherst, NY, Prometheus Books, 1988.

Sen, A. K., *Poverty and Famines: An Essay on Entitlement and Deprivation*, Oxford, Clarendon Press, 1981.

Singer, P., *Animal Liberation*, 2nd edn, New York, Random House, 1990.

——, *Practical Ethics*, 2nd edn, Cambridge, Cambridge University Press, 1993.

Smith, A., *Theory of Moral Sentiments*, Oxford, Oxford University Press, 1976. First published 1759.

Voltaire, *Philosophical Dictionary*, Harmondsworth, Penguin, 1984.

Zimmerman, M. E. (ed.), *Environmental Philosophy*, Englewood Cliffs, NJ, Prentice-Hall, 1993.

Index